REA's Test Prep Boc

(a sample of the <u>hundreds of letters</u> REA receives each year)

" I did well because of your wonderful prep books... I just wanted to thank you for helping me prepare for these tests. "

Student, San Diego, CA

" My students report your chapters of review as the most valuable single resource they used for review and preparation. "

Teacher, American Fork, UT

" Your book was such a better value and was so much more complete than anything your competition has produced (and I have them all!). "

Teacher, Virginia Beach, VA

" Compared to the other books that my fellow students had, your book was the most useful in helping me get a great score. "

Student, North Hollywood, CA

" Your book was responsible for my success on the exam, which helped me get into the college of my choice... I will look for REA the next time I need help. "

Student, Chesterfield, MO

" Just a short note to say thanks for the great support your book gave me in helping me pass the test... I'm on my way to a B.S. degree because of you! "

Student, Orlando, FL

(more on next page)

(continued from front page)

" I just wanted to thank you for helping me get a great score
on the AP U.S. History exam... Thank you for making great test preps! "
Student, Los Angeles, CA

" Your Fundamentals of Engineering Exam book was the absolute best
preparation I could have had for the exam, and it is one of the major
reasons I did so well and passed the FE on my first try. "
Student, Sweetwater, TN

" I used your book to prepare for the test and found that the advice and the
sample tests were highly relevant... Without using any other material, I earned
very high scores and will be going to the graduate school of my choice. "
Student, New Orleans, LA

" What I found in your book was a wealth of information sufficient to shore up
my basic skills in math and verbal... The section on analytical ability was
excellent. The practice tests were challenging and the answer explanations most
helpful. It certainly is the Best Test Prep for the GRE! "
Student, Pullman, WA

" I really appreciate the help from your excellent book. Please keep up
the great work. "
Student, Albuquerque, NM

" I am writing to thank you for your test preparation... your book helped me
immeasurably and I have nothing but praise for your GRE preparation."
Student, Benton Harbor, MI

(more on back page)

The Best Test Preparation for the

FTCE

Florida Teacher Certification Examination—Professional Education Test

---

Julienne H. Empric, Ph.D.
Professor of Literature
Eckerd College
St. Petersburg, FL

Erin Spanier-Evers, M.A.
Language Arts Coordinator
Staten Island, NY

Christine Hudak, M.A.
Kindergarten Teacher
School 4 Annex
Linden, NJ

Paul Linnehan, Ph.D.
Associate Professor of English
University of Tampa
Tampa, FL

Judy Downs-Lombardi, Ph.D.
Educational Consultant
Temple Terrace, FL

Donald E. Orlosky, Ed.D.
Professor Emeritus
University of South Florida
Tampa, FL

Gail M. Platt, Ph.D.
Director, Learning Center
South Plains College
Levelland, TX

Gail Rae, M.A.
Department of English
McKee Technical High School
Staten Island, NY

Sally Stevens, M.A.
Pre-Kindergarten Teacher
School 4 Annex
Linden, NJ

Christine Zardecki
Research Associate
Rutgers University
Piscataway, NJ

Research & Education Association
61 Ethel Road West
Piscataway, New Jersey 08854

The Best Test Preparation for the FTCE:
Florida Teacher Certification Examination
Professional Education Test

Year 2001 Printing

Printed in the United States of America

Library of Congress Control Number 99-74677

International Standard Book Number 0-87891-091-3

Research & Education Association
61 Ethel Road West
Piscataway, New Jersey 08854

REA supports the effort to conserve and
protect environmental resources by
printing on recycled papers.

ABOUT RESEARCH & EDUCATION ASSOCIATION

Research & Education Association (REA) is an organization of educators, scientists, and engineers specializing in various academic fields. Founded in 1959 with the purpose of disseminating the most recently developed scientific information to groups in industry, government, high schools, and universities, REA has since become a successful and highly respected publisher of study aids, test preps, handbooks, and reference works.

REA's Test Preparation series includes study guides for all academic levels in almost all disciplines. Research & Education Association publishes test preps for students who have not yet completed high school, as well as high school students preparing to enter college. Students from countries around the world seeking to attend college in the United States will find the assistance they need in REA's publications. For college students seeking advanced degrees, REA publishes test preps for many major graduate school admission examinations in a wide variety of disciplines, including engineering, law, and medicine. Students at every level, in every field, with every ambition can find what they are looking for among REA's publications.

While most test preparation books present practice tests that bear little resemblance to the actual exams, REA's series presents tests that accurately depict the official exams in both degree of difficulty and types of questions. REA's practice tests are always based upon the most recently administered exams, and include every type of question that can be expected on the actual exams.

REA's publications and educational materials are highly regarded and continually receive an unprecedented amount of praise from professionals, instructors, librarians, parents, and students. Our authors are as diverse as the fields represented in the books we publish. They are well-known in their respective disciplines and serve on the faculties of prestigious high schools, colleges, and universities throughout the United States and Canada.

ACKNOWLEDGMENTS

In addition to our authors, we would like to thank Dr. Max Fogiel, President, for his overall guidance, which brought this book to completion; Nicole Mimnaugh, Manager of New Book Development, for her guidance and management of the editorial staff through every phase of the project; Cara V. Lemantovich, Project Manager, for coordinating the development of the book; Johanna Claps, Kristin Massaro, James Nobel, Craig Pelz, and Sharon Tucker for their editorial contributions; and Paula Musselman for typesetting the book.

CONTENTS

Chapter 1
PASSING THE FTCE 1
    About this Book 3
    About the Test 3
    How to Use this Book 5
    Format of the FTCE 5
    About the Review Sections 6
    Scoring the FTCE 6
    Studying for the FTCE 7
    Test-Taking Tips 7
    The Day of the Test 8
    FTCE Study Schedule 10

Chapter 2
COMPETENCY 1 11
    Definition of Competency 13
    Student Development and Maturation 13
    Theories of Cognitive Development 15
    Identity Achievement and Diffusion 17
    Environmental Factors 19
    Maslow's Hierarchy of Needs 20
    Effective Instruction 21
    Metacognition 23
    Motivation 25
    Jointly Constructed Meaning 26
    Learning About the Community 31
    Stabilizing Strengths of the Community 32
    Coping with Problems in the Community 34

Chapter 3
COMPETENCY 2 37
    Definition of Competency 39
    Nature and Nurture 39
    Diversity 42

Chapter 4
COMPETENCY 3 .... **49**
   Definition of Competency 51
   Physical Environment 51
   Social and Emotional Climate 52
   Academic Learning Time 53

Chapter 5
COMPETENCY 4 .... **55**
   Definition of Competency 57
   Classroom Behavior 57
   Behavior Patterns 59

Chapter 6
COMPETENCY 5 .... **61**
   Definition of Competency 63
   Behaviors That Indicate a Tendency Toward
      Substance Abuse 64
   Physical and Behavioral Characteristics of Students
      Under the Influence of Drugs 66
   The Use of Referrals 67
   Teaching About the Dangers of Substance Abuse 68

Chapter 7
COMPETENCY 6 .... **71**
   Definition of Competency 73
   Symptoms of Abuse 73
   Visible Signs of Abuse 75
   How to Report Suspicions of Abuse 75

Chapter 8
COMPETENCY 7 .... **77**
   Definition of Competency 79
   Cognitive Development and Moral Decision Making 80
   Learning Styles and Personality Types 82
   Standards for Classroom Behavior 83
   Rules and the Student's Role in Decision Making 85
   The Teacher's Role 86
   Rules and School Safety Issues 90

Chapter 9
COMPETENCY 8..**95**
    Definition of Competency....................................... 97
    "With It"-Ness in the Classroom 97
    Parent-Teacher Communication 99

Chapter 10
COMPETENCY 9..**101**
    Definition of Competency..................................... 103
    Purposes of Assessment 103
    Teacher-Made Tests 103
    Authentic Assessments 104
    Standardized Testing 107
    Performance-Based Assessment 109

Chapter 11
COMPETENCY 10 ....**111**
    Definition of Competency..................................... 113

Chapter 12
COMPETENCY 11 ....**117**
    Definition of Competency..................................... 119
    Identifies Knowledge, Skills, and Attitudes 119
    Constructs or Adapts Short-Range Objectives 120
    Organizes and Sequences Short-Range Objectives.... 120

Chapter 13
COMPETENCY 12 ....**123**
    Definition of Competency..................................... 125
    Educational Resources 125
    Visual Materials 127
    Human Resources 128

Chapter 14
COMPETENCY 13 ....**131**
    Definition of Competency..................................... 133
    Procedures for Learning Success............................ 133
    Organizing Activities 134
    Outcome-Oriented Learning................................. 135

Chapter 15
COMPETENCY 14 ....**137**
Definition of Competency.. 139
Planning and Performance of the Classroom Teacher 139
Beginning Classwork Promptly 140
Student Activity 140
Transitions 141
Summary 143

Chapter 16
COMPETENCY 15 ....**145**
Definition of Competency.. 147
Principles of Verbal Communication.............................. 147
Voice 148
Nonverbal Communication 148
Eye Contact 149
Body Language 149
Media Communication 150
Summary 150

Chapter 17
COMPETENCY 16 ....**151**
Definition of Competency.. 153
Planning Processes 153
Self-Directed Learning 155

Chapter 18
COMPETENCY 17 ....**157**
Definition of Competency.. 159
Deductive Strategies 159
Inductive Strategies 160
Cooperative Strategies 163
Discussion Strategies 163
Comparison/Contrast 164

Chapter 19
COMPETENCY 18 ....**165**
   Definition of Competency 167
   Teaching Styles 167
   Directions 169
   Objectives 170
   Performance Standards 170
   Supplies 171
   Classroom Assessment 172

Chapter 20
COMPETENCY 19 ....**175**
   Definition of Competency 177
   Questioning 177
   The Six Levels of Taxonomy 178

Chapter 21
COMPETENCY 20 ....**181**
   Definition of Competency 183
   Vary Practice Activities 184
   Reinforce Retention of Specific Information 185
   Provide a Variety of Activities to Promote Retention 186
   Assist Students During Seatwork 187
   Practice Activities Promote Long-Term Retention 188

Chapter 22
COMPETENCY 21 ....**189**
   Definition of Competency 191
   Effective Use of Language 191
   Relationships Between Teachers and Students 191
   Feedback 192
   Digressions 193
   Connected Discourse 194
   Marker Expressions 194
   Task Attraction and Challenge 194
   Scrambled Discourse, Vagueness, and Question Overload 195
   Summary 195

Chapter 23
COMPETENCY 22 ....**197**
    Definition of Competency.. 199
    Provide Clear Feedback to Students 199
    Make Specific Statements About Students' Responses 202
    Methods of Correcting Students' Errors....................... 204

Chapter 24
COMPETENCY 23 ....**209**
    Definition of Competency.. 211
    Recapping Significant Points 212
    Thesis, Antithesis, and Synthesis................................. 213
    Recapping Discussion and Reviewing Subject Matter.............. 214
    End of the Lesson Recap 215
    Journal Writing.. 215
    Cooperative Learning 215
    Weekly and Monthly Reviews 217
    Summary 218

Chapter 25
COMPETENCY 24 ....**221**
    Definition of Competency.. 223
    Classroom Tests... 223
    Principles of Test Construction 224
    Test Blueprints 224
    Test Items 226
    Constructing Test Questions....................................... 228
    Scoring the Test 231
    Evaluating and Revising Tests 232
    Conclusion 235

Chapter 26
COMPETENCY 25 ....**237**
    Definition of Competency.. 239
    Preparation for Testing... 239
    Test Administration 241
    Formative Feedback 242
    Summary 243

Chapter 27
COMPETENCY 26 ....**245**
    Definition of Competency.. 247
    Recording Student and Class Progress 247
    Reporting Student and Class Progress.. 250
    Maintaining Permanent Student Records 251
    Understanding the Responsibilities of Student Records 252

Chapter 28
COMPETENCY 27 ....**253**
    Definition of Competency.. 255
    Educational Technology in the Primary Classroom 255
    Educational Technology in the Secondary Classroom 257
    Copyright Laws for Computer Programs 260

Practice Test 1 ....**263**
    Answer Key 297
    Detailed Explanations of Answers 298

Practice Test 2 ....**317**
    Answer Key 364
    Detailed Explanations of Answers 365

Answer Sheets **387**

FTCE

Florida Teacher Certification Exam—
Professional Education Test

Chapter 1
Passing the FTCE

Chapter 1

PASSING THE FTCE

ABOUT THIS BOOK

This book will provide you with an accurate and complete representation of the Florida Teacher Certification Examination (FTCE) Professional Education test. Inside you will find reviews that are designed to provide you with the information and strategies needed to pass the exam. Two practice tests are provided which are based on the most recently administered FTCE. You are allowed two and one-half hours to complete the actual test and this is the same amount of time allotted to take each of our practice tests. The practice tests contain every type of question that you may expect to appear on the FTCE. Following each test, you will find an answer key with detailed explanations designed to help you more completely understand the test material.

ABOUT THE TEST

Who takes the test and what is it used for?

The FTCE is taken by individuals seeking initial teacher certification in Florida. Educators must pass the Professional Education test as one of the requirements for their first five-year Florida Professional Certificate. If you meet any one of the following criteria, you are eligible to take the test:

- are currently enrolled in a college or university teacher-preparation program;
- are a teacher with provisional certification;
- are a teacher making a career change to public school teaching;

If you do not do well on the FTCE, do not panic! The test can be taken again, so you can work on improving your score in preparation for your next FTCE. A score on the FTCE that does not match your expectations does not mean you should change your plans about teaching.

Who administers the test?

The FTCE is developed and administered by the Florida Department of Education. A test development process was designed and is implemented to ensure that the content and difficulty level of the test are appropriate.

When should the FTCE be taken?

The test should be taken just before or right after graduation for those seeking certification right out of school. The FTCE is a requirement to teach in Florida, so if you are planning on being an educator, you must take and pass this test. However, you may be issued a two-year temporary certificate while testing and completing your teaching requirements.

When and where is the test given?

The FTCE is usually administered four times a year in several locations throughout Florida. The usual testing day is Saturday but the test may be taken on an alternate day if a conflict such as religious obligation exists. Special accommodations can also be made for applicants who are visually impaired, hearing impaired, physically disabled, or specific learning disabled.

To receive information on upcoming administrations of the FTCE, consult the FTCE Registration Bulletin, which can be obtained by contacting:

FTCE Inquiries
Florida Department of Education
325 West Gaines Street, Suite 414
Tallahassee, Florida 32399-0400
Phone (850) 488-8198

The FTCE Registration Bulletin also includes information regarding test retakes and score reports.

Is there a registration fee?

To take the FTCE, you must pay a registration fee. You may pay by personal check, money order, cashier's check, or VISA or MASTERCARD. Cash will not be accepted.

HOW TO USE THIS BOOK

What do I study first?

Read over the reviews and the suggestions for test-taking. Studying the reviews thoroughly will reinforce the basic skills you will need to do well on the exam. Make sure to take the practice tests to become familiar with the format and procedures involved with taking the actual FTCE.

To best utilize your study time, follow our FTCE Independent Study Schedule located in the front of this book. The schedule is based on a seven-week program, but can be condensed to four weeks if necessary.

When should I start studying?

It is never too early to start studying for the FTCE. The earlier you begin, the more time you will have to sharpen your skills. Do not procrastinate! Cramming is *not* an effective way to study, since it does not allow you the time needed to learn the test material.

FORMAT OF THE FTCE

The Professional Education test contains 140 questions designed to assess your knowledge of the information described in the competencies included in our review sections. Both versions of the exam test the same material.

The test covers the 27 generic teaching competencies identified by the Florida Department of Education. These competencies are the minimum teaching skills required by those who wish to teach in Florida. The content included in each of the competencies will be tested by one or more items on the examination. Individual test items require different thinking levels, ranging from simple recall to evaluation and problem solving.

The competencies are broad statements written in a way that reflect the information an entry-level educator needs in order to be a truly effective teacher. Within the reviews, the competency should be broken down into the competency statement and a description of what the competency covers. The competencies will not be discussed in the actual FTCE test.

All the questions on the FTCE are in multiple-choice format. Each question will have four options, lettered A through D, from which to choose. You should have plenty of time in which to complete the FTCE, but be aware of the amount of time you are spending on each question so that you allow yourself time to complete the test. Although speed is not very important, a steady pace should be maintained when answering the questions. Using the practice tests will help you prepare for this task.

ABOUT THE REVIEW SECTIONS

The reviews in this book are designed to help you sharpen the basic skills needed to approach the FTCE, as well as provide strategies for attacking the questions. By using the reviews in conjunction with the practice tests, you will better prepare yourself for the actual test.

Each competency is covered in a separate chapter. The 27 competencies are extensively discussed and the review sections should give you a better understanding of what the FTCE tests.

Most of what you need to answer the questions on the test, you have learned through your schooling. The education classes you took should have provided you with the know how to make important decisions about situations you will face as a teacher. Our review is designed to help you fit the information you have acquired into its specific competency. Reviewing your class notes and textbooks along with studying our competency reviews will give you an excellent start towards passing the FTCE.

SCORING THE FTCE

How do I score my practice test?

There are 140 total questions on the FTCE Professional Education Test. A score of 200 or higher, which is equivalent to 56% correct, is needed to pass. In other words, you need to answer approximately 78 questions correctly to achieve a passing score.

If you do not achieve a passing score, review the detailed explanations for the questions you answered incorrectly. Note which types of questions you answered wrong, and re-examine the corresponding review. After further review, you may want to retake the practice tests.

When will I receive my score report and what will it look like?

Approximately one month after you take the test, your score report will be mailed to you. You will receive two original score reports and are responsible for sending one to the Bureau of Teacher Certification. A copy of your score report is provided to one Florida college or university and one Florida school district. You should have requested this information on your registration application.

When you receive your score report and have passed with a 200 or higher, the word **PASS** is only reported. If you did not pass, you will receive a numeric score and will have to retake the test.

STUDYING FOR THE FTCE

It is very important for you to choose the time and place for studying that works best for you. Some individuals may set aside a certain number of hours every morning to study, while others may choose to study at night before going to sleep. Other people may study during the day, while waiting on line, or even while eating lunch. Only you can determine when and where your study time will be most effective. But, be consistent and use your time wisely. Work out a study routine and stick to it.

When you take the practice tests, try to make your testing conditions as much like the actual test as possible. Turn your television and radio off, and sit down at a quiet table free from distraction.

As you complete each practice test, score your test and thoroughly review the explanations to the questions you answered incorrectly; however, do not review too much at any one time. Concentrate on one problem area at a time by reviewing the question and explanation, and by studying our review until you are confident that you completely understand the material.

Keep track of your scores. By doing so, you will be able to gauge your progress and discover general weaknesses in particular sections. You should carefully study the reviews that cover your areas of difficulty, as this will build your skills in those areas.

TEST-TAKING TIPS

Although you may not be familiar with tests such as the FTCE, this book will help acquaint you with this type of examination and help alleviate your test-taking anxieties. Listed below are ways to help you become accustomed to the FTCE, some of which may be applied to other tests as well.

Become comfortable with the format of the FTCE. When you are practicing, simulate the conditions under which you will be taking the actual test. Stay calm and pace yourself. After simulating the test only once, you will boost your chances of doing well, and you will be able to sit down for the actual FTCE with much more confidence.

Read all of the possible answers. Just because you think you have found the correct response, do not automatically assume that it is the best answer. Read through each choice to be sure that you are not making a mistake by jumping to conclusions.

Use the process of elimination. Go through each answer to a question and eliminate as many of the answer choices as possible. By eliminating two answer choices, you have given yourself a better chance of getting the item correct since there will only be two choices left from which to make your guess. Do not leave an answer blank; it is better to guess than to not answer a question on the FTCE test.

Work quickly and steadily. You will have two and one-half hours to complete the test, so work quickly and steadily to avoid focusing on any one problem too long. Taking the practice tests in this book will help you learn to budget your precious time.

Learn the directions and format of the test. Familiarizing yourself with the directions and format of the test will not only save time, but will also help you avoid nervousness (and the mistakes caused by getting nervous).

Be sure that the answer circle you are marking corresponds to the number of the question in the test booklet. Since the test is multiple-choice, it is graded by machine, and marking one wrong answer can throw off your answer key and your score. Be extremely careful.

THE DAY OF THE TEST

Before the Test

On the day of the test, make sure to dress comfortably, so that you are not distracted by being too hot or too cold while taking the test. Plan to arrive at the test center early. This will allow you to collect your thoughts and relax before the test, and will also spare you the anguish that comes with being late. You should check your FTCE Registration Bulletin to find out what time to arrive at the testing center.

Before you leave for the test center, make sure that you have your admission ticket and two forms of identification, one of which must contain a recent photograph, your name, and signature (i.e., driver's license). You will not be admitted to the test center if you do not have proper identification.

YOU MUST BRING SEVERAL SHARPENED NO. 2 PENCILS WITH ERASERS, AS NONE WILL BE PROVIDED AT THE TEST CENTER.

If you would like, you may wear a watch to the test center. However, you may not wear one that makes noise, because it may disturb the other test takers. No dictionaries, textbooks, notebooks, calculators, briefcases, or packages will be permitted. Drinking, smoking, and eating are prohibited.

During the Test

The FTCE is administered in one sitting with no breaks. Procedures will be followed to maintain test security.

Once you enter the test center, follow all of the rules and instructions given by the test supervisor. If you do not, you risk being dismissed from the test and having your scores cancelled.

When all of the materials have been distributed, the test instructor will give you directions for filling out your answer sheet. Fill out this sheet carefully since this information will be printed on your score report.

During the test, be sure to mark only one answer per question, erase unwanted answers and marks completely, and fill in answers darkly and neatly.

After the Test

When you finish your test, hand in your materials and you will be dismissed. Then, go home and relax—you deserve it!

FTCE STUDY SCHEDULE

The following study course schedule allows for thorough preparation to pass the FTCE Professional Education Test. This is a suggested seven-week course of study. However, this schedule can be condensed if you have less time available to study, or expanded if you have more time. But be sure to keep a structured schedule by setting aside ample time each day to study. Depending on your schedule you may find it easier to study throughout the weekend. No matter which schedule works best for you, the more time you devote to studying for the FTCE, the more prepared and confident you will be on the day of the actual test.

Week	Activity
1	Take the first exam as a diagnostic exam. Your score will be an indication of your strengths and weaknesses. Make sure to take the test under simulated exam conditions. Review the explanations for the questions you answered incorrectly.
2	Study REA's FTCE Review. Highlight key terms and information. Take notes on the reviews as you work through them, as writing will aid in your retention of information.
3 and 4	Review your references and sources. The Florida Department of Education's *Domains: Knowledge Base of The Florida Performance Measurement System* may be helpful in this area. Use any other supplementary material which your counselor or the Florida Department of Education suggests.
5	Condense your notes and findings. You should develop a structured outline detailing specific facts. You may want to use index cards to aid you in memorizing important facts and concepts.
6	Test yourself using the index cards. You may want to have a friend or colleague quiz you on key facts and items. Then, take the second full-length exam. Review the explanations for the questions you answered incorrectly.
7	Study any areas you consider to be your weaknesses by using your study materials, references, and notes. You may want to retake the tests using the extra answer sheets provided in the back of the book.

FTCE

Florida Teacher Certification Exam—
Professional Education Test

Chapter 2
Competency 1

Chapter 2

COMPETENCY 1

DEFINITION OF COMPETENCY

The teacher employs a knowledge of physical, academic, and social developmental patterns and of individual differences to satisfy the instructional needs of all students in the classroom and to counsel students about those needs.

This competency relates to the importance of teachers having a basic understanding of the principles of human development in its many dimensions: physically, mentally, emotionally, and socially. It is also important that teachers appreciate a dynamic and interactive view of human development. This approach to understanding human development is one which recognizes that human beings do not develop in a vacuum. People exist in an environment which, friendly or unfriendly, supportive or non-supportive, evokes and provokes reactions from individuals; moreover, it is not a one-way street with the environment doing all the driving. People also act in certain ways to shape and form their environment. There is a constant interaction or interplay between people and their environments. Thus, effective teachers must be sensitive to and knowledgeable of both personal characteristics of students and characteristics of their environment.

STUDENT DEVELOPMENT AND MATURATION

A teacher does not have to be an expert in anatomy and physiology to see the physical changes that accompany students' growth and maturity. The preschool child has trouble grasping pencils or crayons in a manner to facilitate handwriting; however, even most two-year olds can grasp crayons sufficiently to make marks on papers and, thus, enjoy the creative excitement of art.

Physiological changes play a significant role in the development of children as they increase their control of bodily movements and functions and refine their motor skills. Their ability to engage in simple to complex classroom and playground activities increases as they develop. Classroom and playground activities must be adjusted and adapted in order to be developmentally appropriate for the skill levels of the children.

As students enter junior high or begin their secondary education, they again experience important physiological changes with the onset of puberty. With puberty comes changes in primary sexual characteristics and the emergence of secondary sexual characteristics. In addition to bodily characteristics, there is a change in bodily feelings, and there is an increase in sex drive.

Girls, on average, reach maturational milestones before boys. Physical changes may cause embarrassment to both females and males when they draw unwelcome attention; moreover, these changes almost always create some discomfort as adolescents find the body they were familiar and comfortable with to be quite different, sometimes seemingly overnight.

David Elkind has noted two developmental characteristics of adolescence which share a relationship to the physiological changes accompanying maturation. These two characteristics are the *imaginary audience* and the *personal fable*. First, adolescents, preoccupied with their own physiological changes, often assume that others are equally intrigued by these changes in appearance and behavior; they may feel that others are staring at them, watching their every move, scrutinizing their behavior for one misstep or their appearance for any flaws. If everyone is watching, then it is imperative to be, to act, and to look just right. In today's culture, that means wearing the right clothes and having all the right brand names and status symbols. Because of adolescents' sensitivity to attention (especially the wrong kind of attention, that is, not fitting in, not being "right"), it is especially important that teachers of this age group be aware of the *imaginary audience* phenomenon and be sensitive to social interactions in the classroom. It, indeed, is important that teachers not contribute to creating unwanted attention or to stigmatizing or stereotyping students.

Personal fable refers to the belief that "My life is different from everyone else's; therefore, no one can understand how I feel or what I think. No one has ever felt or thought what I feel and think." This out-of-focus view tends to support both a feeling of isolation (which may be precipitated by the changing sensations from a body that is undergoing biological changes) and a willingness to engage in risky behaviors (thinking that only others have car accidents when they drive dangerously).

In sum, these two characteristics of adolescence are examples of how physical changes accompany, and perhaps even evoke, emotional and cognitive changes as individuals grow and mature. Both phenomena of imaginary audience and personal fable have emotional features (fear of rejection, fear of isolation, fear of difference, shame, guilt from increased sexual feelings, frustration, and so forth) and both describe a feature of adolescent cognitive ability: the ability to think about one's self as an object of one's own and of others' thoughts. The developmental epistemologist, Jean Piaget, explained that this way of thinking represents the cognitive stage of formal operations.

Cognition is a term commonly used to refer to all the processes whereby knowledge is acquired; the term can be used to cover very basic perceptual processes, such as smell, touch, sound, and so forth, to very advanced operations, such as analysis, synthesis, and critical thinking.

THEORIES OF COGNITIVE DEVELOPMENT

Until his death in 1980, Jean Piaget was a predominant figure in the field of cognitive psychology. It is safe to postulate that perhaps no other single individual has had greater influence on educational practices than Piaget. Basically, his theory of cognitive development is based on the notion that cognitive abilities (or one's ability to think) are developed as individuals mature physiologically, and they have opportunities to interact with their environment. Piaget described these interactions as the *equilibration* of *accommodation* and *assimilation* cycles or processes. In other words, when individuals (who, according to Piaget, are innately endowed with certain cognitive predispositions and capabilities) encounter a new or novel stimulus, they are brought into a state of *disequilibrium.*

That is a way of saying that they are thrown off balance; they do not know or understand that which is new or unfamiliar. However, through the complementary processes of *accommodation* (adjusting prior knowledge gained through former experiences and interactions) and *assimilation* (fitting together the new information with what has been previously known or understood), individuals come to know or understand that which is new. Once again, individuals are returned to a state of *equilibrium* where they remain until the next encounter with something unfamiliar. For Piaget, this is how learners learn.

Piaget also predicted that certain behaviors and ways of thinking characterize individuals at different ages. For this reason, his theory is considered a *stage* theory. *Stage* theories share the common tenet that certain characteristics will occur in predictable sequences and at certain times in the life of the individual.

According to Piaget, there are four stages of cognitive development, beginning with the *sensorimotor stage* describing individuals from birth to around the age of two. The second stage, *preoperational* (describing cognitive behavior between the ages of two and seven), is characterized by egocentrism, rigidity of thought, semilogical reasoning, and limited social cognition; some cognitive psychologists have observed that this stage seems to describe how individuals think more in terms of what they can't do than what they can do. This stage describes the way that children in preschool and kindergarten go about problem-solving; also, many children in the primary grades may be at this stage in their cognitive development.

The next two stages, however, may be most important for elementary and secondary school teachers since they describe cognitive development during the times that most students are in school. The third stage, *concrete operations,* is the beginning of operational thinking and describes the thinking of children between the ages of 7 and 11. Learners at this age begin to decenter. They are able to take into consideration viewpoints other than their own. They can perform transformations, meaning that they can understand reversibility, inversion, reciprocity, and conservation. They can group items into categories. They can make inferences about reality and engage in inductive reasoning; they increase their quantitative skills, and they can manipulate symbols if they are given concrete examples with which to work. This stage of cognitive development is the threshold to higher-level learning for students.

Finally, *formal operations* is the last stage of cognitive development and opens wide the door for higher-ordered, critical thinking. This stage describes the way of thinking for learners between the ages of 11 and 15 and, for Piaget, constitutes the ultimate stage of cognitive development (thus also describing adult thinking). Learners at this stage of cognitive development can engage in logical, abstract, and hypothetical thought; they can use the scientific method, meaning they can formulate hypotheses, isolate influences, and identify cause-and-effect relationships. They can plan and anticipate verbal cues. They can engage in both deductive and inductive reasoning, and they can operate on verbal statements exclusive of concrete experiences or examples. These cognitive abilities characterize the highest levels of thought.

Another theoretical approach to understanding human development is offered by Erik Erikson, another important stage theorist, who described psychosocial development. For each of eight stages, he identified a developmental task explained in terms of two polarities. For the purposes of this discussion, only those stages describing school-aged individuals will be included.

According to Erikson, preschoolers and primary-school aged children must be able to function in the outside world independently of parents; when children are able to do this, they achieve a sense of *initiative;* when children are not able to move away from total parental attachment and control, they experience a sense of *guilt.* Thus, this stage of psychosocial development is the stage of *initiative versus guilt.* The child's first venture away from home and into the world of school has considerable significance when viewed in light of this theory; it is imperative that teachers assist students in their first experiences on their own, away from parental control.

Erikson's next stage of development is one involving a tension between *industry* and *inferiority.* For example, if the child who enters school (thus achieving initiative) acquires the skills (including academic skills such as reading, writing, and computation, as well as social skills in playing with others, communicating with others, forming friendships, and so forth) which enable him or her to be successful in school, then the child achieves a sense of *industry;* failure to achieve these skills leads to a sense of *inferiority.*

IDENTITY ACHIEVEMENT AND DIFFUSION

Around the time students enter junior high, they begin the developmental task of achieving *identity.* According to Erikson, the struggle to achieve identity is one of the most important developmental tasks and one which creates serious psychosocial problems for adolescents. For example, even the individual who has successfully achieved all the important developmental milestones (such as initiative and industry) now finds him- or herself in a state of flux—everything (body, feelings, thoughts) is changing. The adolescent starts to question, "Who am I?" Erikson believed that if adolescents find out what they believe in, what their goals, ideas, and values are, then they attain identity achievement; failure to discover these things leads to identity diffusion.

By the time many students reach high school, they are entering a stage of young adulthood—for Erikson, a psychosocial stage characterized by the polarities of *intimacy* and *isolation*. Individuals at this stage of development begin to think about forming lasting friendships, even marital unions. Erikson would argue that many psychosocial problems experienced by young adults have their origin in the individual's failure to achieve identity during the preceding stage; the young man or woman who does not know who he or she really is cannot achieve true intimacy.

For the classroom teacher, knowledge of psychosocial stages of human development can result in greater effectiveness. For example, the effective teacher realizes the importance of helping students achieve the skills necessary to accomplish crucial developmental tasks. According to Erikson's theory, teachers of elementary school-aged learners would do well to focus on teaching academic and social skills, helping students to gain proficiency in skills that will enable learners to be productive members of society. On the other hand, secondary school teachers would do well to keep in mind, as they engage students in higher-ordered thinking activities appropriate to their stage of cognitive development, that students have pressing psychological and social needs in their struggle to achieve identity and to attain intimacy.

By understanding key principles of human development in its multiple dimensions, effective teachers provide students with both age-appropriate and developmentally-appropriate instruction. This, in sum, is the best instruction. It is instruction that addresses all the needs of students—physical, emotional, and social—as well as cognitive (or intellectual) needs.

Sample

Rueben Stein is a middle-school teacher who wants to teach his class about the classification system in the animal kingdom. He decides to introduce this unit to his class by having the students engage in general classification activities. He brings to class a paper bag filled with 30 household items. He dumps the contents of the bag onto a table and then asks the students, in groups of three or four, to put like items into piles and then to justify or explain why they placed certain items into a particular pile.

By assigning this task to his students, Mr. Stein is providing his students with a developmentally-appropriate task because

(A) middle-school students like to work in groups.

(B) the items in the bag are household items with which most students will be familiar.

(C) the assignment gives students the opportunity to practice their skills at categorizing.

(D) the assignment will give students a task to perform while the teacher finishes grading papers.

The correct response is **(C)**; According to Piaget's theory of cognitive development, students in middle school would be at the stage of concrete operational thought.

Students at this stage of cognitive development would be able to categorize items. Choices (A), (B), and (D) are inappropriate for the following reasons. Choice (A) is a false statement. Although some students will like to work in groups, some students will prefer to work alone—at this and at any age group or cognitive stage. Preferring to learn in groups (or socially) or to learn alone (or independently) is a characteristic of learning style or preference, not a characteristic of cognitive or affective development. Choice (B) is irrelevant to the teacher's intent in assigning the task. Students could just as easily work with unfamiliar items, grouping them by observable features independent of their use or function. Choice (D) is not a good choice under any circumstances. Teachers should assiduously avoid giving students assignments merely to keep them busy while the teacher does something else. All assignments should have an instructional purpose.

ENVIRONMENTAL FACTORS

The teacher considers environmental factors that may affect learning in designing a supportive and responsive classroom community that promotes all students' learning and self-esteem. This competency addresses the need that teachers have to be able to recognize and identify both external and internal factors which affect student learning. The preceding discussion on human development emphasized primarily the characteristics of learners or what may be considered internal factors. Internal factors, beyond the general characteristics that humans share as they grow and mature, also include factors such as students' personality characteristics, their self-concept and sense of self-esteem, their self-discipline and self-control, their ability to cope with stress, and their general outlook on life.

External factors are those things outside the student personally, but which impact on the student. They include the home environment and family relationships, peer relationships, community situations, and the school environment. In other words, external factors constitute the context in which the student lives and learns.

MASLOW'S HIERARCHY OF NEEDS

Abraham Maslow's hierarchy of human needs is a model applicable to many diverse fields, including education, business and industry, health and medical professions, and more. Maslow identified different levels of individuals' needs in a hierarchical sequence, meaning that lower-level needs must be satisfied before individuals can ascend to higher levels of achievement. He identified the fulfillment of basic physiological needs as fundamental to individuals' sense of well-being and their ability to engage in any meaningful activity. Simply stated, students' physiological needs (to have hunger and thirst satisfied, to have sleep needs met, to be adequately warm, and so forth) must be met before students can perform school tasks. Today's schools provide students with breakfast and lunch when needed, and great effort and expense is often directed toward heating and cooling school buildings.

Maslow's second level of need concerns safety. Again, students must feel safe from harm and danger before they are ready to learn. Today, schools are often equipped with metal detectors to increase students' sense of safety. In some schools, guards and security officers patrol the halls.

The third level of need, according to Maslow's theory, is the need for affiliation or the need to belong and to be accepted by others. Although this need may, at first glance, seem less related to the student's environment, it does, indeed, refer to the student's social environment. Students need the opportunity to develop social relationships and to establish friendships among their peers. In essence, Maslow, through his theory, determined that environmental factors are important in education.

Another significant principle of human development arises from a long debate between experts who believe that innate characteristics (those the individual is born with) play the most important role in determining who the individual will become and what he or she will do versus those who believe that environmental characteristics are most important. This argument is referred to in the literature as the *nature versus nurture* debate.

EFFECTIVE INSTRUCTION

The teacher understands how learning occurs and can apply this understanding to design and implement effective instruction. It is one thing for teachers to have command of their subject matter. It is a given that English teachers will be able to write well, that math teachers will be able to compute and calculate, that science teachers will know and understand science, and so forth. However, it is something else—and something at least as important—that teachers know how to teach.

When teachers understand learners, that is, when teachers understand developmental processes common to all learners and how environmental features and learning styles, varied and diverse, affect learning, then teachers are better able to design and deliver effective instruction. Although there may be some intuitive aspects to teaching (and it seems that some people were born to teach), teaching skills can be acquired through processes of introspection, observation, direct instruction, self-evaluation, and experimentation.

How teachers teach should directly relate to how learners learn. Theories of cognitive development describe how learners learn new information and acquire new skills. There are many theories of cognitive development, two of which will be included in this review; they are (a) Piagetian (or Neo-Piagetian) theory, and (b) information processing theory.

Piagetian theory (including Neo-Piagetian theory) describes learning in discrete and predictable stages. Therefore, teachers who understand this theory can provide students with developmentally-appropriate instruction. This theory also describes learners moving from simpler ways of thinking to more complex ways of problem solving and thinking. For teachers, there are many important implications of this theoretical perspective. For example, teachers must create enriched environments that present learners with multiple opportunities to encounter new and unfamiliar stimuli— whether they are objects or ideas. Teachers must also provide learners with opportunities to engage in extended dialogue with adults. According to Piaget's theory, conversational interactions with adults are a key component in cognitive development, especially in the acquisition of formal operations (or higher-ordered thinking skills). Moreover, it is important that adults (and teachers in particular) model desired behaviors; teachers must reveal their own complex ways of thinking and solving problems to students.

On the other hand, information processing theories of human development take a different approach to describing and understanding how learners learn. Based on a computer metaphor and borrowing computer imagery to describe how people learn, information processing theories begin by determining the processing demands of a particular cognitive challenge (or problem to solve) necessitating a detailed task-analysis of how the human mind changes external objects or events into a useful form according to certain, precisely-specified rules or strategies, similar to the way a computer programmer programs a computer to perform a function. Thus, information processing theories focus on the process—how the learner arrives at a response or answer.

A brief analysis of one information processing theory will serve to illustrate this point. Sternberg's (1985) triarchic theory of intelligence is a theory taking into account three features of learning. Those three features are (a) the mechanics or components of intelligence (including both higher-ordered thinking processes, such as planning, decision making and problem solving, and lower-ordered processes, such as making inferences, mapping, selectively encoding information, retaining information in memory, transferring new information in memory, and so forth); (b) the learner's experiences; and (c) the learner's context (including the adaptation to and the shaping and selecting of environments).

According to Sternberg, learners' use of the mechanics of intelligence is influenced by learners' experiences. To illustrate, some cognitive processes (such as those required in reading) become automatized as a result of continued exposure to and practice of those skills. Learners who come from homes where parents read, and where there are lots of different reading materials, tend to be more proficient readers; certainly, learners who read a lot become more proficient readers. Those learners who are exposed to reading activities and who have ample opportunities to practice reading have greater skill and expertise in reading; and, in a cyclical manner, students who have skills in reading like to read. Conversely, those who lack reading skills don't like to read. Students who don't like to read, don't read; thus, their reading skills, lacking practice, fail to improve.

An information processing approach acknowledges that not only are individuals influenced by their environments and adapt to those environments, individuals also are active in shaping their own environments. In other words, a child who wants to read but who has no books at home may ask parents to buy books, or may go to the library to read, or check out books to read at home.

Information processing theory is of interest to educators because of its insistence on the idea that intelligent performance can be facilitated through instruction and direct training. In sum, intelligent thinking can be taught. Sternberg has urged teachers to identify the mental processes that academic tasks require and to teach learners those processes; he challenges teachers to teach students what processes to use, when and how to use them, and how to combine them into strategies for solving problems and accomplishing assignments.

Teachers who wish to follow Sternberg's advice might choose to begin teaching by identifying *instructional objectives,* that is, what students should be able to do as a result of instruction. Second, teachers would analyze the objectives in terms of identifying the *instructional outcomes,* those being the tasks or assignments that students can perform as a result of achieving the instructional objectives. Third, teachers would analyze instructional outcomes in terms of the *cognitive skills* or mental processes required to perform those tasks or assignments. After following these three steps and identifying instructional objectives, instructional outcomes, and cognitive skills involved, the teacher is ready to conduct a *preassessment* (or pretest) to determine what students already know.

Instruction is then based on the results of the preassessment with teachers focusing on directly teaching the cognitive skills needed in order for students to perform the task(s). Following instruction, teachers would conduct a *postassessment* (or post-test) to evaluate the results of instruction. Further instruction would be based on the results of the postassessment, that is, whether or not students had achieved expected outcomes, and whether or not teachers had achieved instructional objectives.

Regardless of which theoretical perspective teachers adopt, or if at times, find themselves taking a rather eclectic approach and borrowing elements from several theoretical bases, it is helpful for teachers to consider if they are structuring their classrooms to satisfy learners' needs or merely their own needs as teachers. Furthermore, if the teachers' goal is to increase teaching effectiveness by facilitating learners' knowledge and skill acquisition, then teachers will engage continuously in a process of self-examination and self-evaluation.

METACOGNITION

Self-examination and self-evaluation are both types of *metacognitive* thinking. *Metacognition* is a term used to describe what, how, and why people know what they know when they know it. In short, it is thinking about thinking and knowing about knowing. Cognitive psychologists describe metacognition as a characteristic of higher-ordered, mature, and sophisticated thinking. Generally speaking, as learners achieve higher levels of cognitive skills, they also increase their metacognitive skills. Therefore, not only should teachers engage in metacognitive thinking, they should model this thinking for their students, and encourage their students to develop metacognitive skills.

According to J.H. Flavell, metacognition can be understood in terms of (a) metacognitive knowledge and (b) metacognitive control. Basically, metacognitive knowledge is what learners need to know and metacognitive control is what learners need to do. Metacognitive control, therefore, is in the hands of the learner. Teachers cannot control learners' behavior, although they can encourage or admonish the behavior. The best that teachers can do is help learners expand their metacognitive awareness and knowledge.

Awareness can be increased by talking about metacognition. Flavell has explained that there are three kinds of metacognitive knowledge, those three kinds being (a) person knowledge, (b) task knowledge, and (c) strategy knowledge.

Person knowledge falls into one of three categories: (a) intraindividual knowledge, (b) interindividual knowledge, and (c) universal knowledge. First, intraindividual knowledge is what the learner knows or understands about him- or herself. Therefore, it is important that learners have opportunities to learn about themselves, their interests, abilities, propensities, and so forth. For this reason (among others), it is important that learners have opportunities to learn about their own learning style and their perceptual strengths. It is also helpful for them to have opportunities to examine their personalities, values, and goals.

Furthermore, in a model that recognizes the dynamic nature of instruction, that is, one which recognizes that the learner also knows certain things and can contribute to the classroom, the teacher realizes that he or she is a learner, too. Teachers, then, can benefit from examining their own learning style, perceptual strengths, personalities, values, and goals. Moreover, it can be extremely beneficial for teachers to consider their own instructional style.

MOTIVATION

The teacher understands how motivation affects group and individual behavior and learning and can apply this understanding to promote student learning. Students often say that they like teachers who can motivate them when, in fact, teachers are not responsible for students' motivation. Motivation is a student's responsibility; motivation comes from within the student. However, effective teachers will help students develop self-discipline, self-control, and self-motivation. These skills of self-management can be taught, yet they require a great deal of effort and practice in order for students to gain true proficiency.

When students say that they like or want teachers who motivate them, they are probably referring to some characteristics that teachers possess which are attractive and interesting to learners. So, while it is true that teachers are not responsible for students' motivation, it is also true that teachers can influence motivation—that teachers can promote and/or inhibit motivation in the classroom by their attitudes and their actions.

One researcher, M.B. Baxter-Magolda, has offered three principles to guide teachers that will lead to greater effectiveness in the classroom. Interestingly, each of these principles leads to empowering students and, thus, are motivational in nature.

The first principle is to validate students as knowers. This principle is based on the idea of the active learner who brings much to the classroom (the dynamic view of human development). How can teachers validate students? Baxter-Magolda suggests that teachers display a caring attitude toward students. This means that it is appropriate for teachers to take an interest in students, and to learn about their likes, dislikes, interests, and hobbies, both in school and outside school. This also means that it's okay for teachers to show enthusiasm and excitement for their classes, not only for the subject-matter they teach, but for the students they teach as well. It also means, as Carol Tavris noted, that it's good for teachers to show empathy for students' emotional needs.

Baxter-Magolda also recommends that teachers question authority by example and let students know that they, as teachers, can also be questioned. This means that teachers model critical thinking skills in the classroom. Teachers can question authority when they examine and evaluate readings—whether from textbooks or other sources. Teachers can question authority when they teach propaganda techniques, exposing advertising claims and gimmicks. Teachers can question authority when they discuss the media and how so-called news sources shape and form public opinion. There are numerous opportunities for teachers in dealing with current affairs and public opinion to question authority and inculcate in their students both critical thinking and higher-ordered reasoning skills.

Also, when teachers allow students to question them, teachers are acknowledging that everyone is a learner. Everyone should participate in a lifelong process of continuous learning. It is no shame or disgrace for the teacher to admit that sometimes he or she doesn't know the answer to every question. This gives teachers the opportunity to show students how adults think, how they have a level of awareness (metacognition) when they don't know something, and about how they go about finding answers to their questions. Teachers who admit that they don't have all the answers thus have the opportunity to show students how answers can be found and/ or to reveal to students that there are no easy answers to some of life's most difficult questions.

Third, to validate students as knowers, teachers can value students' opinions, ideas, and comments. Teachers' affirmations include smiles and nods of approval, positive comments (such as, "That's a good answer."), and encouraging cues (such as, "That may seem like a reasonable answer, but can you think of a better answer?" or, "Can you explain what you mean by that answer?"). Validating students as knowers also means supporting students' voices, that is, giving them ample opportunities to express their own ideas, to share their opinions, and to make their own contributions to the classroom. These opportunities can include times of oral discussion as well as written assignments.

JOINTLY CONSTRUCTED MEANING

Another principle in Baxter-Magolda's guidelines for teaching effectiveness is for teachers and students to recognize that learning is a process of jointly-constructing meaning. To explain, Baxter-Magolda says that it is important for teachers to dialogue with students (also an important concept in Piagetian theory), and that teachers emphasize mutual learning. Also in agreement with Piagetian principles, Baxter-Magolda recommends that teachers reveal their own thinking processes as they approach subjects, as they analyze and understand new subjects, and as they solve problems and reach decisions. She further advises that teachers share leadership and promote collegial learning (group work), acknowledging that individual achievement is not the sole purpose or focus for learning. By allowing students to collaborate, they also will learn significant lessons directly applicable to work situations where most accomplishments are the result of team efforts, not the sole efforts of individuals.

Baxter-Magolda's final principle for teachers is to situate learning in the students' own experiences. She suggests that this be done by letting students know that they are wanted in class by using inclusive language (avoiding ethnic and cultural bias and stereotyping, instead using gender-neutral and inclusive language), and focusing on activities. Activities are important for motivation because they give learners things to become actively involved in—arousing their attention and interest, and giving them an outlet for their physical and mental energy. Activities can have an additional benefit in that they can serve to connect students to each other, especially when students are given opportunities to participate in collaborative learning (the way things happen in the "real world"), and to work in groups. Finally, in situating learning in students' own experiences, it is important to consider the use of personal stories in class as appropriate (that is, without violating anyone's right to privacy and confidentiality). Moreover, teachers can share personal stories which allow them to connect with students in a deeper and more personal way.

The child psychologist, Harvard professor, and author of numerous scholarly and popular books, Robert Coles, recently wrote of his experiences teaching in a Boston inner-city high school. He told of his disillusionment and his struggle to claim students' respect and attention so that he could teach them. Finally, there was a classroom confrontation, followed by a self-revelation (that he was able to show his students what he was like as a person). He shared some of his thoughts and feelings about loneliness. He told about his own boyhood experiences of visiting museums with his mother and what she taught him about art. In the end, he too had a revelation. He concluded that when teachers share what we have learned about ourselves with our students, we often can transcend the barriers of class and race. A teacher can change a "me" and a "them" (the students) into an "us." Building camaraderie this way then becomes an optimal starting point for teaching and learning. Dr. Coles' experience was that telling his story to the class was a step toward helping his students claim some motivation of their own.

When students assume responsibility for their own motivation, they are learning a lesson of personal empowerment. Unfortunately, although personal empowerment is probably one of the most important lessons anyone ever learns, it is a lesson infrequently taught in classrooms across the country.

Empowerment has at least four components, one of which is self-esteem. A good definition of self-esteem is that it is my opinion of me, your opinion of you. It is what we think and believe to be true about ourselves, not what we think about others and not what they think about us. Self-esteem appears to be a combination of self-efficacy and self-respect as seen against a background of self-knowledge.

Self-efficacy, simply stated, is one's confidence in one's own ability to cope with life's challenges. Self-efficacy refers to having a sense of control over life or, better, over one's responses to life. Experts say that ideas about self-efficacy are established by the time children reach the age of four. Because of this early establishment of either a feeling of control or no control, classroom teachers may find that even primary grade students believe that they have no control over their life—that it makes no difference what they do or how they act. Therefore, it is all the more important that teachers attempt to help all students achieve coping skills and a sense of self-efficacy.

Control, in this definition of self-efficacy, can be examined in regard to external or internal motivators. For example, external motivators include such things as luck and the roles played by others in influencing outcomes. Internal motivators are variables within the individual. To explain, if a student does well on a test and is asked, "How did you do so well on that test?," a student who relies on external motivators might reply, "Well, I just got lucky," or "The teacher likes me." If the student failed the test and is asked why, the student dependent on external motivators might answer, "Well, it wasn't my lucky day," or "The teacher doesn't like me," or "My friends caused me to goof off and not pay attention so I didn't know the answers on the test." A student who relies on internal motivators and who does well on a test may explain, "I am smart and always do well on tests," or "I studied hard and that's why I did well." On the other hand, even the student who relies on internal motivators can do poorly on tests and then may explain, "I'm dumb and that's why I don't do well," or "I didn't think the test was important and I didn't try very hard." Even though students have similar experiences, in regard to issues of control, what is important is how students explain their experiences. If students have external motivators, they are likely to either dismiss their performance (success or failure) as matters of luck or to credit or blame the influence of others. If students have internal motivators, then they are likely to attribute their performance to either their intelligence and skills (ability) or their effort.

Students who have external motivators need help understanding how their behavior contributes to and influences outcomes in school. Students need clarification as to how grades are determined and precise information about how their work is evaluated. Students who have internal motivators but low self-esteem (such as thinking, "I'm dumb") need help identifying their strengths and assets (something that can be accomplished when students are given information about learning styles). In this way, self-efficacy can be enhanced.

Another factor in empowerment is self-respect. Self-respect is believing that one deserves happiness, achievement, and love. Self-respect is treating one's self at least as nicely as one treats other people. Many students are not aware of their internal voices (which are established at an early age). Internal voices are constantly sending messages, either positive or negative. Psychologists say that most of us have either a generally positive outlook on life, and our inner voice sends generally positive messages ("You're okay," "People like you, "Things will be all right," and so forth) or a generally negative outlook on life, and an inner voice sending negative messages ("You're not okay," "You're too fat, skinny, ugly, stupid," and so forth).

Many students need to become aware of their inner voice and how it can be setting them up for failure. They need to learn that they can tell their inner voice to stop sending negative messages, and that they can reprogram their inner voice to be kinder, gentler, and to send positive messages. However, it does require effort, practice, and time to reprogram the inner voice.

Two tools which can help students in the reprogramming process are affirmations and visualizations. Affirmations are statements describing what students want. Affirmations must be personal, positive, and written in the present tense. What makes affirmations effective are details. For example, instead of saying, "I am stupid," students can be encouraged to say, "I am capable. I do well in school because I am organized, I study daily, I get all my work completed on time, and I take my school work seriously." Affirmations must be repeated until they can be said with total conviction.

Visualizations are images students can create whereby they see themselves the way they want to be. For example, if a student wants to improve his or her typing skills, then the student evaluates what it would look like, sound like, and feel like to be a better typist. Once the student identifies the image, then the student has to rehearse that image in his or her mind, including as many details and sensations as possible. Both visualization and affirmation can restructure attitudes and behaviors. They can be tools for students to use to increase their motivation.

Finally, the fourth component of empowerment is self-knowledge. Self-knowledge refers to an individual's strengths and weaknesses, assets and liabilities; self-knowledge comes about as a result of a realistic self-appraisal (and can be achieved by an examination of learning styles). Achieving self-knowledge also requires that students have opportunities to explore their goals and values.

Students who know what their goals and values are can more easily see how education will enable them to achieve those goals and values. Conversely, students cannot be motivated when they do not have goals and values, or when they do not know what their goals and values are. In other words, without self-knowledge, motivation is impossible. Therefore, teachers who follow Baxter-Magolda's guidelines for effective instruction and who teach their students about personal empowerment are teachers who realize the importance of motivation and who set the stage for students to claim responsibility for their own successes and failures. Such teachers help students to become motivated to make changes and to accomplish more.

Sample

Ben Douglas is a high school history teacher. His class is studying the Korean Conflict when a student brings up a question about the morality of the war in Vietnam. This is not a subject that Mr. Douglas is prepared to teach at the time.

In response to the student's question, Mr. Douglas

(A) tells the student that the day's topic is the Korean Conflict and suggests that the student bring up the question later on in the term.

(B) invites the class to respond to the student's question.

(C) gives the student a cursory response, eliminating the need for any further discussion.

(D) disciplines the student for not paying attention to the topic under discussion.

The correct response is **(B)**. This is the best answer because it acknowledges the student's curiosity and legitimizes the student's right to pursue information by asking questions. It gives approval and recognition to the student's voice of inquiry, and it allows other students to voice their opinions and/or to make relevant comments. The teacher does not have to have a ready answer to every question, and this answer choice recognizes that also. The other three choices (A), (C), and (D) all have the opposite effect of ignoring students' voices and missing an opportunity for students to become active learners, learning something about which they may be genuinely interested. All three of the incorrect choices reflect an autocratic attitude toward teaching, which is the opposite of what Baxter-Magolda recommends for teaching effectiveness.

LEARNING ABOUT THE COMMUNITY

The first staff development for new teachers in a school district is often based upon providing insight into the makeup of the community. Many larger districts have developed videotapes about their communities. Information to help the teacher adjust to a new employment situation, and possibly a new residential and shopping area, is most vital. Sometimes, the district school busses load up the teachers, and a tour of the immediate neighborhood and of the school itself is viewed firsthand, often with helpful commentary by an experienced professional. If such orientation is not provided, the teacher should solicit an informal tour of the community, preferably by someone who has lived there several years. If other new teachers have joined the staff, together they may solicit a guide from the established staff members—a teacher, a secretary, a paraprofessional. Sometimes a volunteer from the organized parents' group of a campus may have the orientation of new staff members as one of their goals.

Chamber of Commerce information can always provide data about the community. This public relations material is important since it projects the image of the community that the community values. Directly or indirectly reflected therein will be the expectation for the school. Real estate brochures are equally informative. Are the schools used as an attracting agent for people considering moving into the general area? What positive factors in the community are used to lure prospective home-buyers or apartment-leasers? If the new teacher is planning to buy or lease living accommodations within the community, calling upon a real estate agent to learn more about the area, as well as assisting in locating potential residential areas, will be useful.

Once the students have started school, the teacher may ask the students to talk about their community. Their perceptions, although certainly reflecting their age biases, still provide insights not otherwise available to a new teacher. Perhaps the teacher will find several students who will spend an hour or two one afternoon or Saturday morning touring the community and pointing out special places—the neighborhood library, nearby public parks, shopping areas, any favorite hangouts of the teenagers. If the teacher is an elementary school teacher, a parent, with one or two of the students, may provide the tour.

Finally, becoming a patron of a few businesses within the community can serve as a source of information about the community, as well as its expectations of and attitudes toward the school. The teacher can take cleaning to a local cleaning establishment, or shop at a grocery store or drugstore, exchanging a few words about the school with the persons who provide service at such establishments. Visiting the local library and talking with the librarian will always provide help as well. If the teacher attends a local church or synagogue, certainly talking to the members can be very informative.

Learning as much as possible about the community that a school serves will assist the teacher in numerous ways throughout the teaching assignment in that community. The teacher, at the same time, may be building allies upon whom to call if a need arises.

STABILIZING STRENGTHS OF THE COMMUNITY

Every community will have established sources of support for the school. Parents' groups such as the Parent-Teacher Association, the Dads' Club, the Band Boosters, the Sports Club, and dozens of other groups have been formed to provide both financial and philosophical support. These groups are often searching for projects to undertake as part of their yearly program of goals.

Retired teachers in the community may provide information that can be invaluable to the new teacher. Finding out the names of respected former teachers can be accomplished by asking other teachers or by seeking names from parents and students. In some cases, the retired teachers not only have advice, but also substantial teaching suggestions, and even materials for an earnest new teacher in search of assistance.

Using the community as subject matter for writing experiences can provide additional information for the teacher's use, while teaching the students to do a variety of activities to gather primary and secondary information about their home area. Students can research the history of the area in several ways. A very young student can interview and record older members of the community as they talk about the past. Often, the elders welcome an invitation to visit a class and talk about their earliest days in the area and retell the stories that their parents may have told them. Gathering letters, photographs, magazines, maps, toys, and other artifacts of days gone by can provide primary documentation that is often quite interesting to students and also to parents when displayed at open house.

Sometimes special interest groups within the community welcome the opportunity to share aspects of their interest with a class. A local storytelling group may visit a class and demonstrate techniques to make a story's retelling truly exciting for the listeners; a writing group may judge creative writing of the students and offer tips for expressive writing. Parents will often attend elementary classes and share work experiences to begin the students' awareness of the world of work. More formal Career Days, frequently planned on secondary campuses, utilize a variety of local people to talk about their vocational choices and respond to students' questions.

All subject areas can find useful activities centered in the community to teach the content more effectively and realistically. Teaching early stages of reading, the teacher requests students to bring in slogans and advertisements associated with popular breakfast cereals. Often, students who do not formally read have become acquainted with such sayings. Sharing them with the class becomes a stimulating activity for everyone. Older language learners can use the community for a variety of language study assignments. Finding errors in spelling or mechanics in the newspaper or on commercial signs, defining the methods used for naming streets in various residential areas of town, collecting the phrases on signs posted about the town—all make reading a real-life activity, not one merely restricted to a textbook in a classroom.

In social studies and literary study especially, as heroes and heroic values are discussed, the teacher can use the community patterns as well to identify contemporary local heroes and heroic values. Open discussion of differences in opinion and style of dress and haircut, conducted in a nonjudgemental environment, allows for the variety of values often found in any community today. Living safely and sanely together is surely an accepted value promoted by most school curricula and cannot be postponed until problems do arise.

COPING WITH PROBLEMS IN THE COMMUNITY

Each community, along with the strengths that can be identified, will have deterrents to the educational process. Some of these negative aspects are not merely local problems, but symptomatic of many communities today—drug and alcohol abuse, unemployment, heavy mobility within the community, and crime and violence, especially as reflected in gang conflicts. Accompanied by the apparent apathy of adults in regard to the educational process, the toll of these problems upon the effectiveness of the schools can be heavy, for students of any age may be affected adversely by one or more of these conditions of contemporary society.

Often when a school exists in an environment affected by one or more of the societal ills of today, the in-service programs for teachers will focus on the relevant problems obviously affecting the student population. The teacher will learn ways to help students in the classroom and will find out about sources of even greater assistance for students through these staff training sessions. The teacher's good judgment will always be required, however, to know to what extent he or she can help with a pervasive problem area. Working at intervention, before a problem area becomes a critical factor affecting the educational process in the classroom, is always a wise course of action.

Young people's familiarity with drugs and alcohol begins very early in some communities. Children as young as nine or ten have become addicted to illegal drugs or alcohol. Certainly by middle-school age, most students have had some personal involvement with alcohol or drugs; either he/she has experimented or know a classmate who has.

Another major factor creating an unstable family structure is the families' employment situation. More and more adults are finding changes in their work necessary. Finding new employment opportunities is seldom easy, and the time during which a parent is searching for work can be most stressful upon all family members. The greater mobility of families throughout the United States is often related to employment changes. Certainly as children move to new schools in new communities, adjustment to a different school can create a problem. Teachers need to find out what a new student has been studying in each content area and try to build upon that familiar base. Records from the former campus often take months to be transferred and may be of little help if the student has moved frequently.

Any community is now vulnerable to greater crime and violence within its boundaries. Such an atmosphere will affect the youth and, therefore, the school environment. Not uncommon today is the requirement for students to enter a school building by passing through a metal detector, one attempt to keep weapons out of the school building. If the community is unfortunate enough to have gangs attracting the teenagers, the rival attitudes and behaviors cannot be blocked out of the building as easily as knives or guns. Staff training in multicultural understanding will assist the new teachers in understanding the characteristics of different ethnic groups. In the classroom, intervention may be successful by studying literary works based upon prejudice. Class discussion may defuse potentially volatile situations in real life as students read about conflicts between rival groups, as in *Light in the Forest, When the Legends Die, The Chosen, Flowers for Algernon,* or other novels based upon religious or ethnic prejudices. The classics can also illustrate groups in conflict, such as in *Romeo and Juliet, A Tale of Two Cities,* or *Animal Farm.* Actual historical incidents, as well as contemporary news stories, provide other examples to discuss in class. The teacher, making good judgment calls, can successfully intervene before a problem occurs in class.

The effective teacher can make a difference, even when the problems in the community seem insurmountable. Using the time and talent available, the teacher can address the problems that seem to affect his or her students in an appropriate way in the classroom and be familiar with sources of more extensive help available on campus and in the community.

The following references were used to write Competency 1. Further reading of these references may enhance understanding of the competency and may also increase performance on the examination.

Baxter-Magolda, M. B. *Knowing and Reasoning in College: Gender-Related Patterns in Students' Intellectual Development.* San Francisco: Jossey Bass, 1992.

Coles, R. "Point of View: When Earnest Volunteers are Solely Tested." *Chronicle of Higher Education.* Vol. A52, May, 1993.

Elkind, D. "Egocentrism in Adolescence." *Child Development.* Vol. 38, p. 1025-34, (1967).

Ellis, D. *Becoming a Master Student.* Rapid City, South Dakota: College Survival, 1991.

Erikson, E. *Childhood and Society.* New York: Horton, 1963.

Flavell, J. H. "Speculations about the Nature and Development of Metacognition." *Metacognition, Motivation, and Learning.* Hillsdale, New Jersey: Erlbaum, 1987.

Maslow, A. *Toward a Psychology of Being.* New York: Horton, 1963.

Piaget, J. *The Psychology of Intelligence.* London: Routledge and Kegan Paul, 1950.

Sternberg, R. J. *Beyond IQ: A Triarchic Theory of Human Intelligence.* Cambridge: Cambridge University Press, 1985.

Tavris, C. Presentation on Coping with Student Conflict Inside and Outside the Classroom at Texas Junior College Teachers Conference, San Antonio, Texas, February 25, 1994.

FTCE

Florida Teacher Certification Exam—
Professional Education Test

Chapter 3
Competency 2

Chapter 3

COMPETENCY 2

DEFINITION OF COMPETENCY

A teacher enhances students' feelings of self-respect and the respect of other people including those from other cultural, economic, ethnic, and linguistic groups.

NATURE AND NURTURE

After experts on both sides of the argument stated their positions, the conclusion seemed to be that both *nature* (the internal variables) and *nurture* (the environment) play equally important roles in determining the outcome of individuals' growth and maturation. Again, it is important to remember the interaction of the individual with his or her environment, recalling that this view is the *dynamic* view of human development.

Before proceeding, teachers would do well to understand that perception plays an important role for learners to the extent that perception creates our individual reality. The world as we know it is a result of our selective perception. We cannot attend to all events and variables in our environment. We select certain events and variables to notice and attend to, and these phenomena which we observe form our perceptions; thus, we create our own reality. External and internal phenomena grab our attention and shape reality for each of us.

Thus, it is one thing for teachers to be aware of and sensitive to the students' environment; it is, however, impossible for teachers to see, feel, and understand the individual's environment in exactly the same way that it is seen, felt, and understood by the student.

Carol Tavris, a social psychologist and author of the book, *Anger the Misunderstood Emotion*, notes that emotion plays a significant role in students' perceptions. For example, guilt is an emotion aroused by thoughts such as, "I should study or my parents will kill (be disappointed in) me." This is easily contrasted with the emotion of fear generated by the thought, "I should study or I will be a failure in life." Furthermore, guilt and fear can be compared to the emotion of anger which is prompted by thoughts such as, "Why should I study when my teacher is out to get me?" Today's student often sees the teacher as an enemy, not as an authority figure or a friend. Tavris has identified anger as a primary emotion experienced by many students today and one which plays a significant role in shaping their academic perceptions which, in turn, forms their reality of classroom experiences.

Explaining further, Tavris observes that unfulfilled expectations lead to anger. For example, if a student is led to believe (by teachers, school administrators, peers, or parents and siblings) that attending class is somehow irrelevant to academic achievement, then the student who is frequently absent still has the expectation of being successful. The student's perception is that absenteeism is compatible with academic achievement. If, because of absenteeism, the student fails to master essential elements of the curriculum and does not succeed, then the student will feel anger, the appropriate and anticipated emotion.

Anger, however, can be diffused by addressing perceptions, correcting false impressions, and establishing appropriate and realistic expectations. To illustrate, if all those individuals significant to the student emphasize the importance of class attendance, then students acquire the correct perception (in this case) that attendance is important for academic achievement and that absenteeism leads to academic failure.

For the sake of illustration only, let's consider what might happen if the teacher stresses attendance and the parents do not. In this case, the best route for the teacher to take is to show empathy for the student's dilemma. The teacher can acknowledge how difficult it is for the student to attend class when the parents are not supporting attendance, but the teacher also must seek to empower the student to make choices and to take responsibility for his or her own behavior.

In the situation described here, the student undergoes stress because of conflicting messages, and stress is faced by students and faculty alike. In fact, in the above example, the teacher is stressed too, in that the teacher faces the conflict between supporting the parents of the student and supporting that which is in the best educational interests of the student.

Stress is the product of any change; both negative and positive changes produce stress. Environmental, physiological, and psychological factors cause stress. For example, environmental factors such as noise, air pollution, and crowding (among others) create stress; physiological factors such as sickness and physical injuries create stress; and, finally, psychological factors such as self-deprecating thoughts and negative self-image cause stress. In addition to the normal stressors that everyone experiences, some students are living in dysfunctional families; some students are dealing with substance abuse and addictions; some are experiencing sexual abuse. There are numerous sources of stress in the lives of students.

Since life is a stressful process, it is important that students and faculty learn acceptable ways to cope with stress. The first step in coping with stress is to recognize the role that stress plays in our lives. A teacher might lead a class through a brainstorming activity to help the students become aware of the various sources of stress affecting them. Next, the teacher could identify positive ways of coping with stress, such as the importance of positive self-talk, physical exercise, proper nutrition, adequate sleep, balanced activities, time-management techniques, good study habits, and relaxation exercises.

Students who are stressed often become angry rather easily; however, students are not just angry. They experience a wide range of emotions and may be sad, depressed, frustrated, afraid, and, on the positive side, happy and surprised. Effective teachers realize that students' emotions as explained in this section and the preceeding section on human development, play a significant role in students' classroom performance and achievement. Thus, effective teachers seek to create a classroom environment supportive of students' emotional needs. They have appropriate empathy and compassion for the emotional conflicts facing students, yet their concern is tempered by a realistic awareness of the importance of students attaining crucial academic and social skills that will grant them some control over their environment as they become increasingly independent and, eventually, must be prepared to be productive citizens.

Effective teachers recognize the effects of students' perceptions on the learning process and the effects of many environmental factors; as a result, they plan instruction to enhance students' self-esteem and to promote realistic expectations. It is important that teachers be able to differentiate positive and negative environmental factors, maximizing the positive variables and minimizing the negative ones. The teacher has the primary responsibility of creating a classroom environment that recognizes the different environmental factors affecting each student and that encourages each learner to excel, to achieve his or her personal best. Effective teachers work hard at creating learning environments in which all students are ready to learn—where students feel safe, accepted, competent, and productive.

DIVERSITY

The effective teacher appreciates human diversity, recognizing how diversity in the classroom and the community may affect learning and creating a classroom environment in which both the diversity and uniqueness of individuals are recognized and celebrated. Effective teachers realize that students bring to the classroom a variety of characteristics, both personal and social, that create within the classroom a microcosm reflective of American society at large. Indeed, America has long held to the notion of being a "melting pot" whereby members of various racial, ethnic, religious, and national origin groups contributed to the wealth of our culture.

Ethnocentrism is a sociological term used to describe the natural tendency of viewing one's own cultural or familial way of doing things as the right, correct, or best way. Because ethnocentrism is a natural tendency, all people are likely to engage in ethnocentric thinking and behaviors at times.

Some social critics have pointed out that ethnocentrism has played a notable role in American education. They assert that educational institutions often have been guilty of assuming a Eurocentric viewpoint, that is, solely recognizing the contributions of European writers, artists, scientists, philosophers, and so forth, at the expense of those from other cultures. These critics have also noted that the contributions of men often are disproportionately recognized over like achievements of women.

In fact, David and Myra Sadker (1994) have found that teachers, both male and female, at all grade levels, are more likely to call on male than female students, are more likely to give positive reinforcement to males' correct responses than to those of females, and to provide more coaching or instructional help to males when their responses are incorrect than to females. Their research has led them to conclude that teachers are usually unaware of gender bias in their teaching, but that such bias is pervasive in American schools. Their research also has persuaded them that bias can be eliminated once teachers become sensitive to its debilitating effects on students.

The point made here is that ethnocentrism, in any form, can be damaging because it is exclusive rather than inclusive. Eurocentric, Afrocentric, and other ethnocentric perspectives are equally limited in that they narrowly focus attention on one set of ideas at the neglect of others. Therefore, effective teachers will wisely expend a degree of effort in avoiding ethnocentric thinking and behaviors. Effective teachers will attempt to include all students in all classroom activities. The race, ethnicity, religion, national origin, and gender of learners will be viewed as strengths which enable students to learn with and from each other.

Historically speaking, educational experiments have demonstrated the importance of teachers avoiding bias and ethnocentric thinking. The *Hawthorne effect*, or the phenomenon whereby what teachers expected became reality, was demonstrated when teachers were told that some students in their classes were extremely intelligent whereas others were extremely slow or mentally retarded. In fact, all students had normal range intelligence. Nonetheless, at the end of the experiment, students who had been identified to the teachers as being extremely intelligent all had made significant academic progress and were not only at the top of their class, but also performing at the top on national achievement tests. Those students who had been identified as retarded had made no progress at all; in fact, they had lost previously-made gains. Thus, it was demonstrated that teachers' expectations for students often become self-fulfilling prophecies.

In today's society, there is a considerable reference to multiculturalism. Multiculturalism, if it serves merely to separate and distinguish the accomplishments of select cultural and ethnic groups, has the potential of separating and alienating Americans. To view multiculturalism in a positive light is to acknowledge a kind of multiculturalism which embraces the accomplishments of all cultural and ethnic groups, thereby strengthening our country and society instead of fragmenting it.

Because multiculturalism and/or cultural diversity can be a controversial issue with many sides to consider, a reasonable approach to diversity for the classroom teacher is to distinguish between cultural diversity and learning diversity and to focus on diversity in learning. This approach transcends cultural boundaries and recognizes that all people have distinct learning preferences and tendencies. Furthermore, this approach acknowledges that all preferences and tendencies are equally valid and that each style of learning has strengths. The teacher who understands learning styles can validate all students in the class.

Environmental Factors

Many factors play a role in determining a student's learning style. Among those most often cited in the research literature on learning style are environmental, emotional, sociological, physiological, and psychological factors. Although there are several different models for understanding learning differences and many good instruments for assessing learning styles, the Dunn and Dunn (1993) model is one widely used in public schools with versions suitable for students in elementary and secondary classrooms. It will serve as the basis for the following discussion.

Environmental factors include students' reactions to stimuli such as sound, light, temperature, and room design. Do students prefer to study and learn with or without sound, with bright or soft lights, in warm or cool rooms, and/or with standard classroom furniture or alternative seating? Classroom teachers observe that some students are easily distracted by any noise and require absolute quiet when studying or working on assignments. On the other hand, some students seem to learn best when they can listen to music. Some researchers have found evidence that students who prefer sound learn best when classical or instrumental music is played in the background.

Light is another environmental factor with students' preferences for light appearing to be basically inherited, with family members often exhibiting the same preference. Some students prefer bright, direct illumination, while others prefer dim, indirect lighting.

Temperature and design are two other environmental factors affecting learning style. Some students will prefer warmer temperatures whereas others will prefer cooler temperatures. Finally, some students will prefer to sit in straight-backed chairs at desks while others may prefer to sit on soft, comfortable chairs or to sit or recline on the floor.

Although traditional classrooms are structured to provide quiet, brightly illuminated study and work areas with straight-backed chairs and desks, classroom teachers will observe that this environment meets the needs of only some of the learners in the class. An effective teacher will take into consideration the learning styles of all students and experiment with different room designs and study centers creating different environments in the classroom. Although classroom temperature may seem to be beyond the control of the teacher, students can be advised to dress in layers so that they can remove outer garments when they are too warm and put on more layers when they are too cool.

Emotional Factors

According to Rita and Kenneth Dunn, emotional factors include motivation, persistence, responsibility, and structure. To explain, some students are motivated intrinsically: they undertake and complete tasks because they see the value in doing so. Other students are motivated extrinsically: they undertake and complete tasks because they desire to please others or to earn good marks. In regard to persistence, some students, when they undertake assignments, become totally and completely engaged in their work; they seem to lose track of time and can work for long periods without interruption or without feeling fatigued. Other students seem to work in short spurts of energy, needing to take frequent breaks.

When it comes to responsibility, some students are nonconforming, always doing the unexpected (and sometimes unwanted), whereas other students are conforming, always following the rules. Structure refers to whether or not students need detailed and precise instructions. Some students have lots of questions about how assignments should be done, and they desire detailed, step-by-step instructions on each phase of the assignment. Other students, however, seem to work from general concepts and are usually eager to begin assignments, often beginning their work before the directions have been given.

Sociological factors include whether or not students are social learners—preferring to work in pairs or in groups—or whether they are independent learners—preferring to work alone. Another sociological factor is whether or not students work best under the close guidance and supervision of an authority figure, be it teacher or parent, or whether they work best with a minimum of adult guidance and are best left primarily on their own to do their work.

Physiological factors include students' preferences for food or drink while they study, what time of day they learn best, their mobility needs, and their perceptual strengths. Briefly, some students may need to eat or drink in order to effectively and efficiently learn. Rita Dunn says that to make sure that students do not abuse this privilege, she allows them to eat only carrot or celery sticks (cooked so that the snacks will not crunch when eaten by students) and to drink water. This way, she is certain that only students who really need intake when they are learning will take advantage of this concession.

Some students may learn best early in the morning, some later in the morning, some in early afternoon, and some later in the afternoon.

Researchers have found that merely manipulating the time of day that certain students take tests can significantly affect their test performance.

Mobility needs refer to the fact that some students need to move around when they study, whereas other students can sit still for longer periods of time. Although all of these factors are important, and a growing body of literature tends to support the idea that these factors play a significant role in increasing students' performance and in increasing teachers' effectiveness with students, perhaps one of the most important elements in understanding learning style is to identify students' perceptual strengths. Perceptual strengths refer to students' learning modalities, such as whether they are visual, auditory, tactile, or kinesthetic learners. Basically, these perceptual modalities refer to whether students learn best by seeing, hearing, or doing.

Some students can be given a book or handout to read and then perform a task well, based on what they have read. These students tend to have visual (iconic or semantic) perceptual strength. Other students are visual learners, too, but they tend to learn best from images. These are the students who seem to recall every event, even minor details, from films, videos, or classroom demonstrations.

Although evidence indicates that less than 15 percent of the school-age population is auditory, much of the classroom instruction takes the form of teachers telling students information. Most students do not learn auditorially. Therefore, these students must be taught how to listen and learn from oral instructions and lecture.

Teachers who rely on telling students the information that is important would do well to remember that females are more likely to learn auditorially than males. Teachers should also keep in mind that whether or not students benefit from lectures is likely to depend on several other elements as well, such as whether or not the students are auditory learners, whether or not the students like the teacher, whether or not they think the information being presented is important, or whether or not they think that listening to the teacher will help them to achieve their goals.

On the other hand, there are students who do not seem to benefit much from lectures, textbook assignments, or visual aids. These students' perceptual strengths are tactile and kinesthetic. They learn from movement and motion—being able to touch, handle, and manipulate objects. Often these students may have been identified as having learning disabilities. Sometimes they have been relegated to shop or cooking classes or have found their success in athletics, music, or art. Interestingly, many of the "hands on" skills that often identify a student for a career as an auto mechanic are also important skills for mechanical engineers and surgeons.

The following references were used to write Competency 2. Further reading of these references may enhance understanding of the competency and may also increase performance on the examination.

Baxter-Magolda, M. B. *Knowing and Reasoning in College: Gender-Related Patterns in Students' Intellectual Development*. San Francisco: Jossey Bass, 1992.

Dunn, R. Presentation on the Productivity Environmental Preferences Scale (PEPS) at Learning Styles Institute, Lubbock, Texas, June 5–9, 1993. (Sponsored by Education Service Center, Region XVII).

Dunn, R. & K. Dunn. Presentation on Using Learning Styles Information to Enhance Teaching Effectiveness at Learning Styles Institute, Lubbock, Texas, June 5–9, 1993. (Sponsored by Education Service Center, Region XVII).

Sadker, M. & D. Sadker. *Failing at Fairness: How America's Schools Cheat Girls*. New York: Charles Scribner's Sons, 1994.

Tavris, C. Presentation on Coping with Student Conflict Inside and Outside the Classroom at Texas Junior College Teachers Conference, San Antonio, Texas, February 25, 1994.

FTCE

Florida Teacher Certification Exam—
Professional Education Test

Chapter 4
Competency 3

Chapter 4

COMPETENCY 3

DEFINITION OF COMPETENCY

The teacher organizes the physical environment to facilitate instruction and ensure the safety of his or her students.

PHYSICAL ENVIRONMENT

While there are certain physical aspects of the classroom that cannot be changed (size, shape, number of windows, type of lighting, etc.), there are others that can be. Windows can have shades or blinds which distribute light correctly and which allow for the room to be darkened for video or computer viewing. If the light switches do not allow part of the lights to remain on, sometimes schools will change the wiring system. If not, teachers can use a lamp to provide minimum lighting for monitoring students during videos or films.

Schools often schedule maintenance, such as painting and floor cleaning, during the summer. Often school administrators will accede to requests for a specific color of paint, given sufficient time for planning.

All secondary school classrooms should have a bulletin board used by the teacher and by the students. The effective teacher has plans for changing the board according to units of study. Space should be reserved for display of student work and projects, either on the bulletin board, the wall, or in the hallway. (Secondary teachers who need creative ideas can visit elementary classrooms.)

Bare walls can be depressing; however, covering the wall with too many posters can be visually distracting. Posters with sayings that promote cooperation, study skills, and content ideas should be displayed, but the same ones should not stay up all year because they will seem invisible when they become too familiar.

Most classrooms have movable desks, which allow for varied seating arrangements. If students are accustomed to sitting in rows, this is sometimes a good way to start the year. Harry K. Wong has described his method of assigning seats on the first day of school, which is to assign each desk a column and row number, then give students assignment cards as they come into the room. Another method is to put seating assignments on an overhead, visible when students enter the room. Once students are comfortable with classroom rules and procedures, the teacher can explain to students how to quickly move their desks into different formations for special activities, then return them to their original positions in the last 60 seconds of class.

The best place for the teacher's desk is often at the back of a room, so there are few barriers between the teacher and the students and between the students and the chalkboards. This encourages the teacher to walk around the classroom for better monitoring of students.

SOCIAL AND EMOTIONAL CLIMATE

The effective teacher maintains a climate which promotes the lifelong pursuit of learning. One way to do this is to practice research skills which will be helpful throughout life. All subject areas can promote the skills of searching for information to answer a question, filtering it to determine what is appropriate, and using what is helpful to solve a problem.

Here is an example. Most English teachers require some type of research project, from middle school through the senior year. Ken Macrorie's books on meaningful research can guide English teachers as they develop a project which can answer a real-life issue for students. For instance, a student who is trying to decide which college to attend could engage in database and print research on colleges that have the major characteristics he or she is interested in, conduct telephone or written interviews with school officials and current students, review school catalogs and other documents, and find magazine or journal articles that deal with the school. At the end of the process, students will have engaged in primary as well as secondary research, plus they will have an answer to a personal question.

The English teacher and any other subject area teacher can team up to collaborate on a joint research project. The resulting product satisfies both the need of the English teacher to teach research skills and the need of the subject area teacher to teach content knowledge as well as research skills.

Primary research can be done through local or regional resources such as business owners, lawyers, physicians, and the general public. Research questions could include: (1) What effects do artificial sweeteners have on the human body's functioning (biology)? (2) What process is used to develop the platform of a political party (history)? (3) What happens when a business is accused of Title IX violations (business)? (4) What effects have higher medical costs had on family budgets (economics)? (5) How has the popularity of music CDs affected the music industry and businesses that sell records and tapes (music and business)?

The effective teacher also facilitates a positive social and emotional atmosphere and promotes a risk-taking environment for students. He or she sets up classroom rules and guidelines for how he or she will treat students, how students will treat him or her, and how students will treat each other. In part this means that he or she doesn't allow ridicule or put-downs, either from the teacher or among the students. It also means that the teacher has an accepting attitude toward student ideas, especially when the idea is not what he or she was expecting to hear. Sometimes students can invent excellent ideas that are not always clear until they are asked to explain how they arrived at them.

Students should feel free to answer and ask any questions that are relevant to the class, without fear of sarcasm or ridicule. Teachers should always avoid sarcasm. Sometimes teachers consider sarcasm to be mere teasing, but because some students often interpret it negatively, effective teachers avoid all types and levels of sarcasm.

ACADEMIC LEARNING TIME

The effective teacher maximizes the amount of time spent for instruction. A teacher who loses five minutes at the beginning of class and five minutes at the end of class wastes ten minutes a day that could have been spent at educational activities. Ten minutes may not seem like a lot of time to lose. However, this is equivalent to a whole period a week, four classes a month, and 25 periods a year.

Academic learning time is the amount of allocated time that students spend in an activity at the appropriate level of difficulty with the appropriate level of success. The appropriate level of difficulty is one which challenges students without frustrating them. Students who have typically been lower achievers need a higher rate of success than those who have typically been higher achievers.

One way to increase academic learning time is to teach students procedures so they will make transitions quickly. Another is to have materials and resources ready for quick distribution and use. Another is to give students a time limit for a transition or an activity. In general, time limits for group work should be slightly shorter than students need, in order to encourage time on task and to prevent off-task behavior and discipline problems. It is essential for the teacher to have additional activities planned should the class finish activities sooner than anticipated. As students complete group work, they should have other group or individual activities so they can work up until the last minute before the end of class.

FTCE

Florida Teacher Certification Exam—
Professional Education Test

Chapter 5
Competency 4

Chapter 5

COMPETENCY 4

DEFINITION OF COMPETENCY

A teacher can detect overt signs of emotional distress in students and has knowledge of suitable intervention and referral procedures.

CLASSROOM BEHAVIOR

The effective teacher realizes that having an interesting, carefully planned curriculum is one of the best ways to promote desired student behavior and to prevent most discipline problems. Teachers maintain a system of classroom rules, consequences, and rewards to guide students toward proper classroom behavior with the goal of keeping them engaged and on-task. Inevitably, students misbehave and test the techniques and procedures that teachers use to guide students back on-task. Some student behaviors will not respond to the standard procedures used by the effective teacher. If a student continues to misbehave frequently or in a disturbing manner, the effective teacher observes the student with the intent of determining if any external influences are causing the misbehavior that may require additional intervention from the student's teacher and family.

When under stress, students may be inclined to act out or to behave differently for the duration of the stress-inducing event. Students may react to events in the classroom or in their homes in a manner that violates the established policies of the classroom. For example, nervousness caused by a test or a school play audition may cause a student to speak out of turn or appear skittish. The loss of a loved one may cause a student to become depressed. Such behaviors are normal reactions to stress. However, teachers must pay attention to these situations and observe if the misbehavior occurs for an extended period of time. Unusual and/or aggressive student behavior may indicate that the student is suffering from severe emotional distress. Teachers must be careful to note the frequency, duration, and intensity of the student's misconduct.

Atypical behaviors, such as lying, stealing, and fighting, should be recorded if they transpire frequently. The teacher should attempt to determine the motivation behind the behavior. Is the child lying to avoid a reprimand? Is the student telling false stories to hide feelings of insecurity? Does the student cry during a particular subject, or at random moments during the school day? These are some of the many questions the teacher needs to consider.

Misbehaving may be a sign that a student is losing control of his or her actions and is looking for help. The role of the teacher in these situations is to help determine if the student is acting out as a reaction to a particular issue, or if there is a deeper emotional problem. Some students may require various forms of therapy to treat the emotional disturbances that cause the misbehavior. Therapy can also be used to examine the possibilities of a more severe cause for the student's behavior.

If concerned that a student is suffering from emotional stress, the teacher should contact, and then remain in constant discussion with, the student's parents. It is particularly important in these situations to establish an open dialogue with the student's family to facilitate the student's treatment. When combined, the parents and teacher will be able to provide important and unique insights into the student's situation.

School professionals are another valuable resource for advice, assistance, and support when dealing with students' emotional disturbances. Guidance counselors, school psychiatrists, and other specialists are able to aid in the counseling of these students and make recommendations for the parents and teacher. Together, with the student's family, these professionals may develop or recommend a particular program or therapy for treatment.

When working with a class of students with emotional disorders, the management of the classroom must be flexible to aid in the student's development. While the goal of any management system is to prevent misbehavior, the teacher must be prepared to provide an area or opportunity for the student to regain control, should an emotional episode occur.

Teachers should also be aware that drug therapy is often used as a form of treatment. Prescribed by medical doctors, the drug treatments available can help students gain independence from their disorder. However, these drugs treat the symptoms, rather than the cause of the disorder, and can have severe side effects. Drug treatments should not be taken lightly. Their use should also be closely monitored by the classroom teacher and the school nurse.

BEHAVIOR PATTERNS

Established behavior patterns that teachers must be aware of include neurotic disorders, psychotic disorders, and autism.

Neurotic Disorders

Neurotic disorders, or neuroses, are characterized by various emotional and physical signs. Depression can manifest itself in an overall lack of interest in activities, constant crying, or talk of suicide. Anxiety or obsessive thoughts are another indication of a possible neurotic disorder. Physical signs include a disruption in eating or sleeping patterns, headaches, nausea and stomach pain, or diarrhea. These difficulties need to be addressed by the teacher as a cause for serious concern and treatment.

Psychotic Disorders

Psychotic disorders, such as schizophrenia, are serious emotional disorders. These disorders are rare in young children and difficult to diagnose. One of the warning signs for this disorder is a student who experiences a complete break from the reality of his or her surroundings. Schizophrenics may have difficulty expressing themselves, resulting in unusual speech patterns or even muteness. Schizophrenics, who are more likely to be boys than girls, may also exhibit facial expressions that are either markedly absent of emotion or overly active.

Early Infantile Autism

Infantile autism is a serious emotional disorder that appears in early childhood. It is characterized by withdrawn behavior and delayed or absent language and communication skills.

Symptoms of autism can appear in children between four and eighteen months of age. Autistic children will usually distance themselves from others and may be unable to experience empathy. In addition, they often cannot distinguish or appreciate humor. These symptoms are frequently misdiagnosed as mental retardation, hearing/auditory impairment, or brain damage.

Autistic children may have a preoccupation with particular objects, or may perform particular activities repeatedly. While autistic children can range in all levels of intelligence, some children can be extremely skilled in particular and focused areas, such as music or math.

Treatment for autistic children may involve therapy, drugs, or residential living. However, only five percent of autistic children become socially well-adjusted adults.

FTCE

Florida Teacher Certification Exam—
Professional Education Test

Chapter 6
Competency 5

Chapter 6

COMPETENCY 5

DEFINITION OF COMPETENCY

The teacher distinguishes signs of alcohol and drug abuse in students and demonstrates awareness of appropriate intervention and referral procedures.

Dr. Elaine M. Johnson, Director of the Center for Substance Abuse Prevention, recently wrote, "...We must prevent substance abuse if we really hope to reduce crime, violence, school failure, teen pregnancy, unemployment, homelessness, HIV/AIDS, diminished productivity and competitiveness, highway death, and escalating health care costs." In this single statement, the risks to society of substance abuse are encapsulated.

Substance abuse prevention focuses on the promotion of healthy, constructive lifestyles for individuals without the use of drugs. Prevention reduces the risk of danger in society and fosters a safer environment. Successful prevention programs have led to reductions in traffic fatalities, violence, HIV/AIDS and other sexually transmitted diseases, rape, teen pregnancy, child abuse, cancer and heart disease, injuries and trauma, and many other problems associated with drug abuse.

The backbone of substance abuse prevention is education. Every professional educator should be aware of the behaviors and characteristics that indicate a tendency toward the use of drugs and/or alcohol and the physical and behavioral signs indicating that students are under the influence of drugs and/or alcohol. Moreover, teachers must be able to make immediate referrals when any student is suspected of using drugs and/or alcohol in order to protect other students and to secure assistance for the abuser. Finally, teachers must be equipped to provide accurate information to students concerning substance abuse.

BEHAVIORS THAT INDICATE A TENDENCY TOWARD SUBSTANCE ABUSE

Drug and alcohol problems can affect anyone, regardless of age, sex, race, marital status, place of residence, income level, or lifestyle. However, certain risk factors for substance abuse have been identified. Risk factors are those characteristics that occur statistically more often for those who develop alcohol and drug problems, either as adolescents or as adults, than for those who do not develop substance abuse problems. Recent research studies have identified a number of such factors, including individual, family, and social/cultural characteristics.

Individual Characteristics

Studies have shown that certain personality characteristics or traits are associated with problems of substance abuse. These personality characteristics include the following: a) aggressiveness; b) aggressiveness combined with shyness; c) decreased social inhibition; d) emotional problems; e) inability to express feelings appropriately; f) hypersensitivity; g) inability to cope with stress; h) problems with relationships; i) cognitive problems; j) low self-esteem; k) difficult temperament; and i) overreacting.

Other important personal factors are whether the individual is the child of an alcoholic or other drug abuser, whether there is less than two years between the child and older/younger siblings, and whether the child has any birth defects, including possible neurological and neurochemical dysfunctions. The presence of physical disabilities, physical or mental health problems, and learning disabilities can also add to the student's vulnerability to substance abuse. In many ways, students who are at risk academically are also susceptible to substance abuse problems.

In adolescence, other factors emerge that are statistically related to problems with substance abuse. These factors are a) school failure and attrition (dropping out); b) delinquency; c) violence; d) early, unprotected sexual activity; e) teen pregnancy/parenthood; f) unemployment or underemployment; g) mental health problems; and h) suicidal tendencies. Teachers should be alert to these factors as they may be symptomatic of a number of negative adolescent behaviors and experiences, including: a) a failure to bond with society through family, school, or community; b) rebellion and nonconformity; c) resistance to authority; d) a strong need for independence; e) cultural alienation; f) feelings of failure and a fragile ego; g) lack of self-confidence and low self-esteem; and h) the inability to form positive, close relationships and/or an increased vulnerability to negative peer pressure.

Family Characteristics

Many family characteristics are also associated with substance abuse among youth. First, and perhaps most important, is the alcohol or other drug dependency of a parent or both parents. This characteristic might be linked with another significant factor—parental abuse and neglect of children. Antisocial and/or mentally ill parents are also factors that put children at risk for drug and/or alcohol abuse. In addition, high levels of family stress (including financial strain), large, overcrowded family conditions, family unemployment or underemployment, and parents with little education or socially isolated parents are also risk factors. Single parents without family or other support, family instability, a high level of marital and family conflict or violence, and parental absenteeism due to separation, divorce, or death can also increase children's vulnerability. Finally, other important factors to consider are the lack of family rituals, inadequate parenting, little child-to-parent interaction, and frequent family moves. These factors describe children without affiliation or a sense of identity with their families or community. All of these family factors can present risks for substance abuse.

Social and Cultural Characteristics

Living in an economically depressed area with high unemployment, inadequate housing, a high crime rate, and a prevalence of illegal drug use are social characteristics that can put an individual at risk of substance abuse. Cultural risk factors include minority status involving racial discrimination, differing generational levels of assimilation, low levels of education, and low achievement expectations from society at large.

While these are recognized as risk factors, they are only indicators of the potential for substance abuse. Although these factors can be helpful in identifying children who are at risk or vulnerable to developing substance abuse problems and useful to teachers in helping them develop prevention education strategies, they are not necessarily predictive of an individual's proclivity to drug or alcohol abuse. Some children who are exposed to very adverse conditions grow up to be healthy, productive, and well-functioning adults. Yet, if teachers recognize these risk factors in some of their students, there are certain things that teachers possibly can do to increase the chances that the youngster or adolescent will resist the lures of illegal and dangerous alcohol and drug abuse.

Experts suggest that children have a better chance to grow up as healthy adults if they can learn to do one thing well that is valued by themselves, their friends, or their community. Teachers certainly can help assure that students achieve this goal by teaching them the crucial reading, writing, and math skills that will enable them to become independent learners. By presenting lessons that require the development of effective communication and critical thinking skills, teachers can help students acquire important life skills.

Other important strategies for educators to consider are listed below:

- Require children to be helpful as they grow up;

- Help children learn how to ask for help themselves (develop assertiveness skills);

- Help children elicit positive responses from others in their environment (enable children to develop a sense of community in their classrooms and to work collaboratively and/or in cooperation);

- Assist children in developing a healthy distance from their dysfunctional families so that the family is not their sole frame of reference;

- Encourage children to form bonds with the school and to identify with the school as an important and integral part of the community.

Finally, the teacher can be a caring adult who provides students with consistent caring responses and messages. Researchers have identified this as a crucial element in preventing substance abuse among children exposed to multiple risk factors.

PHYSICAL AND BEHAVIORAL CHARACTERISTICS OF STUDENTS UNDER THE INFLUENCE OF DRUGS

Sometimes it can be difficult to tell if someone is using illegal drugs or alcohol. Usually, people who abuse drugs or alcohol (including young people) go to great lengths to keep their behavior a secret. They deny and/or try to hide the problem. However, there are warning signs that can indicate if someone is using drugs or drinking too much alcohol.

Some of the signs that substance abuse is a problem include: a) lying about things; b) avoiding people who are longtime friends or associates; c) giving up activities that once brought pleasure and positive feedback (ranging from failing to turn in homework assignments to giving up extra-curricular activities such as sports, drama, band, and so forth); d) getting into legal trouble; e) taking risks (including sexual risks and driving under the influence of alcohol and/or drugs); f) feeling run-down, hopeless, depressed, even suicidal; g) suspension from school for an alcohol- or drug-related incident; and h) missing work or having poor performance.

Teachers should be alert to these signs in their students' behavior at school. When students stop coming to class, stop doing their work (or start performing poorly), avoid making eye contact with the teacher, have slurred speech, smell of alcohol or drugs (such as marijuana), complain of headaches, nausea, or dizziness, fall asleep in class and/or have constant difficulty in staying awake and participating in class activities—a teacher's suspicions should be awakened. These examples, in and of themselves, are insufficient to confirm a substance abuse problem, but in combination and when displayed with consistency over time, they are strong indicators. Teachers should record their observations, keeping written reports of the behavioral changes they witness. Moreover, they should report their suspicions to the appropriate school authorities.

THE USE OF REFERRALS

Schools should adopt zero tolerance policies for guns and drugs. For safer schools and a higher quality of education, schools should provide effective anti-drug and substance prevention programs, including programs that teach responsible decision making, mentoring, mediation, and other activities aimed at changing unsafe, harmful, or destructive behaviors.

Teachers should report suspicious behaviors to the appropriate school authorities. Florida State Law requires that school personnel "report to the principal or the principal's designee any suspected unlawful use, possession, or sale by a student of any controlled substance, any alcoholic beverage or model glue." The law further states that:

> School personnel are exempt from civil liability when reporting in good faith to the proper school authority such suspected unlawful use, possession or sale by a student. Only a principal or the principal's designee is

authorized to contact a parent or legal guardian of a student regarding this situation. (Florida State Law, Chapter 232.277, Item 1)

Teachers should not delay in taking action, since substance abuse has the potential for great harm. Authorities can investigate and verify or allay the teacher's concerns.

In addition to school resources, students with substance abuse problems can find help in a number of community resources. These community resources can include community drug hotlines, community treatment centers and emergency health care clinics, local health departments, Alcoholics Anonymous, Narcotics Anonymous, Al-Anon and Alateen, and hospitals.

TEACHING ABOUT THE DANGERS OF SUBSTANCE ABUSE

Teachers will find a number of helpful resources for teaching students about the dangers of substance abuse and for promoting prevention by contacting different agencies or organizations, including those listed below:

American Council for Drug Education

136 East 64th Street

New York, NY 10021

(800) 488-3784

Center on Addiction and Substance Abuse

Columbia University

152 West 57th Street

New York, NY 10019

(212) 841-5200

National Clearinghouse for Alcohol and Drug Information

P.O. Box 2345

Rockville, MD 20847-2345

(800) 729-6686

In addition, the Internet offers a number of sites with useful information. The National Clearinghouse for Alcohol and Drug Information (http://www.health.org) and the National Institute on Drug Abuse (http://www.nida.nih.gov/) have excellent web sites with links to updated statistics, reports, and educational materials.

Prevention education promotes healthy and constructive lifestyles that discourage drug abuse and fosters the development of social environments that facilitate and support drug-free lifestyles. Successful prevention means that underage youth, pregnant women, and others at high risk do not use alcohol, tobacco, or other drugs. Education for prevention does work. Research studies show that in 1979, 37 percent of all adolescents aged 12–17 drank alcohol in the past month; by 1992, that number dropped to 16 percent. The incidence of cirrhosis of the liver, a product of alcohol abuse, has dropped significantly, and 14,000 lives have been saved that would have been lost in alcohol-related traffic fatalities, with credit given to minimum drinking age laws. Teachers play an important role in drug and alcohol education and abuse prevention.

The following references were used to write Competency 5. Further reading of these references may enhance understanding of the competency and may also increase performance on the examination.

Breaking New Ground for Youth at Risk: Program Summaries. OSAP Technical Report 1 BK 163, 1990.

Florida State Law, Chapter 232.277.

Johnson, Elaine M. *Making Prevention Work.* Center for Substance Abuse Prevention, 1998.

National Clearinghouse for Alcohol and Drug Information. *Straight Facts About Drugs and Alcohol,* 1998.

FTCE

Florida Teacher Certification Exam—
Professional Education Test

Chapter 7
Competency 6

Chapter 7

COMPETENCY 6

DEFINITION OF COMPETENCY

The teacher is aware of the overt physical and behavioral indicators of child abuse and neglect, knows the rights and responsibilities regarding reporting, and understands how to interact appropriately with a child after a report has been made.

During an observation, you see that the teacher is getting nowhere with Belinda, the child who sits in the third row, center, of the classroom. No matter how many times her teacher, Mr. Smith, smiles at her, she flinches. If he waves his hands while illustrating a point, she flinches. If he raises his voice to ask for quiet, she flinches. He's taken the few extra minutes he finds in his teaching day to sit with her independently, but she doesn't seem to want this. Is it his fault? Is it the child's? Maybe there's another question to ask: Is it the fault of another who may be abusing or neglecting her?

Despite all the media attention given to child abuse and neglect, many teachers still believe that it can't happen to their students. They may think, "This is a nice neighborhood," or "Most of these students have both a mother and father living at home with them," or "The children are too outspoken to allow that to happen." However, abuse and neglect happen to children all the time, possibly even to some of those who will be in your classroom.

SYMPTOMS OF ABUSE

Contemporary research has led scientists to believe that modifications of both the chemistry of the brain and a child's neurological structure may be caused during abuse and, worse yet, that these effects are permanent. The child suffers from chronic shock, which is a result of increased hormones and electrical impulses. Each time the child is abused, a modification in the child's brain and its systems occurs. It's the stress accompanying the abuse that causes the child to become hypersensitized to the abuse; this hypersensitizing then causes brain and body modification.

This process may also explain why Belinda involuntarily flinches when her teacher smiles at her—she may believe he's singling her out and, in her experience, not necessarily in a positive way. When he makes sudden motions with his hands—as is done when striking a person—or raises his voice, which may also be a precursor to rage, Belinda associates these behaviors with patterns of abuse. The effects of child abuse may not be as evident when dealing with an older child (possibly as a result of being told he or she "asked for it" or being threatened with dire consequences if he or she tells), but may be clearer in the child's peer interactions. At times, the teacher may become overly sensitive and may see child abuse/neglect in every bruise and mood change. But, through practice and by discussing suspicions with other teachers, one can become adept at recognizing signs that suggest child abuse.

While the abused child may be angry, "wired," unruly, and/or belligerent (in a word, "overstimulated"), the neglected child acts differently. All he or she may want is to be left alone. Common symptoms of neglect include being unsociable, sedate, withdrawn—all of which point to understimulation. It is thought that this behavior is taught at home during periods of neglect. The child's affect has been changed by the neglect, but the range is wide, varying from almost flat—registering no emotion—to anger. While poor attention, tears, violence, and languid behavior may be indicators of either abuse or neglect, the children usually have feelings of hopelessness and cannot adequately control their thoughts. Students either become obsessed by the neglect or refuse to acknowledge that the neglect is really happening.

Darnell looks like he isn't getting enough to eat, yet he eats everything—including the other children's leftovers at lunch—but remains underweight. He's a loner who seems shy and always looks rundown. He seems oblivious to his appearance, but the teacher notices he is often absent due to colds and other minor ailments. What the teacher may not know is that these are symptoms of neglect; it's poor nutrition that causes these illnesses. It's important for the teacher to see that Darnell's immunizations are up-to-date since he is so susceptible to illness. Darnell's sad affect may be another clue to the neglect he has experienced.

VISIBLE SIGNS OF ABUSE

There are visible signs of child abuse. Among those are red welts on the body that are caused by being hit. This may be proof that the child is being abused and teachers must report the evidence. It is also one of the ways teachers separate the real abuse cases from those which are unfounded. While marks from the hand, fist, or belt are usually recognized, other marks in geometric shapes—eating utensils, paddles, coat hangers, and extension cords—can signify child abuse. If, for example, a boy in your class has unrecognizable bruises on his arms and legs, they could be the result of whippings; furthermore, if he constantly has bruises on his neck and head and always tells you they are from falling, be prepared to report suspicion of child abuse—this could be the result of hitting, possibly even choking. Teachers need a basis for their reports, so they must notice capillary ruptures (reddened areas) in any bruise, which indicate a strong hit. If a bruise is shaded on its outer borders, it may still be a result of hitting—just a softer hit. It may help to establish the charge of abuse if the teacher also reports the size and shape of the bruises, since they may indicate what was used to create such bruises. Teachers should be alert to any suspicious marks or signs of abuse and neglect.

Teachers must be aware of children who are prematurely interested in sex acts. Children who are prepubertal and act in a sexual manner have been taught, by example, to act this way. They are possible victims of sexual abuse. For example, young children who have been known to masturbate in the classroom or to attempt to foist sexual behavior on their classmates are simply not sexually developed nor mature enough to understand the consequences of their actions. A sudden show of promiscuity may follow molestation. Kissing, usually seen as a positive interaction between parent and child, if done in a sexual manner, is also abuse, as are leers and sexual stares. Parents are not the only ones to commit sexual abuse of children; grandparents, family friends, and siblings may also be the perpetrators of criminal abuse.

HOW TO REPORT SUSPICIONS OF ABUSE

Teachers may want to comfort the child after he or she admits to being sexually abused. However, they must be careful not to interview the child, but to wait for the professional trained to deal with abuse. Otherwise, teachers may inadvertently delay or even damage the possibility of a conviction and potentially cause more harm to the child. As a state-licensed teacher, educators must report suspicion of child abuse/neglect.

Reports are required by anyone—especially educators—in any case of suspected child abuse. The child is the one who needs help. Teachers must report suspicions so that an investigation can be made. Failure to report suspicions may adversely affect the child's life. Teachers have the right to keep the report confidential, but including their name may save time and effort if more information becomes necessary. Failure to file a report of suspicion of child abuse/neglect has consequences; it may result in a fine, criminal charges, or revocation of teacher certification or license to teach.

The State of Florida Department of Health and Rehabilitative Services maintains a 24-hour-per-day reporting phone number, which is (800) 962-2873. It is important for teachers to use this number, if necessary, since there is not a specified waiting time to confirm suspicions. This means that a delay in reporting solid suspicions of child abuse/neglect may be cause for action against the teacher. Solid suspicion does not mean proof; it means that the suspicion is reasonable. Once again, the onus of deciding if this is child abuse/neglect is on the counselor—not the teacher. If it is deemed necessary—by the counselor, not the teacher who reports the suspicion—an investigation will be immediately initiated. If an immediate threat to the child is not found, an investigatory team will be sent out within 24 hours to collect further evidence.

Once the report is made, the teacher may want to interact with the child. The teacher should realize that the child—already needing support—may feel that his/her private life has been exposed. While accepting the child's feeling of betrayal, the teacher can explain that the report had to be filed. The teacher should assure the child that he/she can be protected against reprisals for telling about the abuse. Sometimes the child may benefit from just knowing that an adult does care about his/her well-being.

Once the report is filed, the teacher should avoid the person suspected of the abuse/neglect. Should the teacher be harassed or persecuted by this person, the teacher should go to the police. If the report turns into a legal issue, the teacher would be wise to retain an attorney. While the teacher's rights as the reporter are protected, legal matters can take unusual directions and a teacher may require legal advice to avoid becoming another victim of criminal behavior.

Teachers need to know that suspected sexual abuse creates special situations for the teacher. The teacher should ask for permission before patting a student on the back or holding a student's hand. The student has the right to decide whether he or she wants to be touched, and the teacher must acknowledge this decision. Often, the most important action for the teacher to take after reporting suspected abuse is to offer his/her support.

FTCE

Florida Teacher Certification Exam—
Professional Education Test

Chapter 8
Competency 7

Chapter 8

COMPETENCY 7

DEFINITION OF COMPETENCY

The teacher develops a standard for student behavior in the class-room.

Jaime Escalante, called "America's greatest teacher" by President Reagan and the subject of the motion picture *Stand and Deliver*, tells a story about having two students named Johnny in his class. He says that one, "good Johnny," was a dedicated and responsible student, courteous, polite, and high-achieving. The other Johnny, "bad Johnny," seldom came to class, and when he did, he created discipline problems. "Bad Johnny" wouldn't listen, wouldn't do his work, and wouldn't cooperate.

On the night of the annual open house, a very nice woman came to Mr. Escalante's classroom and introduced herself, "I am Johnny's mother." Mr. Escalante assumed she was "good Johnny's" mother. He said, "Oh, I am so glad to meet you. You must be very proud of your son. He is an exceptional student, and I am pleased to have him in my class."

The next day, "bad Johnny" came to class. After class, he approached Mr. Escalante and asked, "Hey, why did you tell my mother those things last night? No one has ever said anything like that about me." It was then that Mr. Escalante realized his mistake.

He didn't admit his error to Johnny, and the strangest thing happened next. "Bad Johnny" stopped being bad. He started coming to class. He started doing his work. He started making good grades. Mr. Escalante concludes his story by saying, "I ended up with two 'good Johnnys' in my class."

This anecdote emphasizes an important aspect of teaching: Teacher perception is ultimately significant. Students may be what their teachers think them to be. What's more, students may also become what their teachers believe them to be. Teachers report that when they treat their students like responsible young adults, most students rise to the occasion.

COGNITIVE DEVELOPMENT AND MORAL DECISION MAKING

Of course, teachers of young children may have to contend with some different issues, but all teachers should be aware of age and maturational differences among students. Jean Piaget, whose ideas on cognitive development have greatly influenced American education, thought that children younger than eight years of age (because of their egocentric thought) were unable to take the perspective of another individual. Thus, Piaget concluded that children under the age of eight made decisions about right and wrong on the basis of how much harm was caused. For example, children might say that a child who ate two forbidden cookies was less guilty than the child who ate six forbidden cookies. Children over the age of eight, however, were able to take into consideration whether or not the individual acted purposely or accidentally. For example, a child who broke a toy by accident was not as guilty of misbehavior as the child who broke the toy on purpose. Researchers who have tested Piaget's ideas have found that children younger than age eight are able to engage in moral reasoning at much more complex levels than Piaget thought possible.

The term *standards*, when used with regard to behavior, evokes issues of right and wrong, sometimes referred to as ethical or moral decisions. With regard to moral development, teachers should be familiar with the concepts of Lawrence Kohlberg. Kohlberg, following the example of Piaget, developed a scenario to quiz children and teens. Kohlberg told a story about a man whose wife was so seriously ill that she would die without medication, yet her husband had no money to buy her medicine. After trying various legal means to get the medicine, her husband considered stealing it. Kohlberg asked if it was wrong or right to steal the drug and to explain why it was either wrong or right. Kohlberg did not evaluate whether the respondent said it was wrong or right to steal the drug; he was interested in the reasons given to justify the actions.

On the basis of the responses he received, Kohlberg proposed six stages of moral development. Stage one, punishment and obedience, describes children who simply follow the rules so as to escape punishment. If these children, for example kindergarten-age students, are told not to talk or they'll lose their chance to go outside for recess, they will not want to lose their playground privileges, so they will not talk. On the other hand, stage two, individualism and change, refers to children who follow the rules, not only to escape punishment, but also when they think there is some reward in following the rules. These children, for example older primary-grade children, seek not only to escape punishment, but also to receive a reward or benefit for their good behavior.

Kohlberg's stage three is described as mutual interpersonal expectations and interpersonal conformity; at this stage, children want to please the people who are important to them. Junior high students, for example, may behave in a manner that gains the approval of their peers or their idols. At stage four, Kohlberg said that adolescents become oriented to conscience, and they recognize the importance of established social order. Teens at this stage obey the rules unless those rules contradict higher social responsibilities. In other words, most high school students realize that rules are necessary, and they will obey most rules if the rules are based on basic social values, such as honesty, mutual respect, courtesy, and so forth.

Post-conventional morality was the term Kohlberg gave to stages five and six. At stage five, individuals recognize the importance of both individual rights and social contracts, but believe that people should generally abide by the rules to bring the greatest good to the majority. Kohlberg believes that about one-fifth of adolescents reach stage five. Therefore, Kohlberg would have expected that few high school students would be operating at this level.

Finally, Kohlberg would not have expected high school students to reach stage six, since he believed that very few individuals ever reached this stage. Stage six is characterized by universal principles of justice. Individuals at this stage believe that most rules should be obeyed because most rules are based on just principles; however, if rules violate ethical principles, then individuals have a greater obligation to follow their conscience even if that means breaking the rules. Social reformers, such as Martin Luther King, Jr., would be an example of stage six moral reasoning.

Kohlberg's theory describes the progression of children's moral reasoning from school entry at kindergarten (stage one) to graduation from high school (stages four and five, for some). Kohlberg's theory has been widely taught and applied in school settings, but not without controversy.

Some have contended that Kohlberg's theory is limited and biased because of his research techniques (getting reactions to a scenario) and because his theory was based on a study of white, middle-class males under the age of 17. Many would say that his ideas have limited application to other ethnic groups, socioeconomic groups, or females.

One theorist interested in applying Kohlberg's theory to women is Carol Gilligan, a student of Kohlberg's, who developed an alternative theory of moral development in women. Gilligan found that women, unlike the men at Kohlberg's stages five and six, tend to value caring and compassion for others above abstract, rational principles. Therefore, when women make decisions, they base their conclusions on how others will be affected by their choices and actions.

Gilligan posited that women pass through three levels of moral reasoning, although like Kohlberg, not all reach the third level. At the first level, the individual is concerned only about herself. At level two, the individual sacrifices her own interests for the sake of others. Finally, at the third level, the individual synthesizes responsibilities to both herself and to others.

An effective teacher may want to consider the implications of these theories for the behavior of students in their classes, in particular, how students will respond to rules of behavior. Although students taking the exam will not be tested on these specific theorists, their theories are, nonetheless, a valuable resource for assessing student behavior. For example, according to Kohlberg, younger students are more concerned about punishments and rewards; older students are more concerned about reasonable rules based on principles of fairness and equality. According to Gilligan, female students may be thinking about how rules affect their friendships. To illustrate, according to these theorists, a male student might be offended by someone cheating (because cheating is wrong) and report the individual to the teacher. Female students, on the other hand, might value their friendship with the cheater more than the principle of honesty; therefore, females might be less likely to report cheating to the teacher.

LEARNING STYLES AND PERSONALITY TYPES

Information about learning styles and personality types essential to effective teaching can also shed light on how individuals make ethical and moral decisions. For example, research indicates that the population is fairly evenly distributed between people who make decisions based on rational, logical, and objective data—thinking types—and those who make decisions based on feelings—feeling types. Slightly more males than females are thinking types.

The feeling half of the population tends to make decisions based on how those decisions may affect others, avoiding conflict and promoting harmony; slightly more females than males are feeling types.

In addition to this aspect of type, that is, how people make decisions, is the aspect of type that deals with how people learn or process information. Most people (approximately 76 percent) are the sensing type, those who learn through sensory experiences; they are linear learners who enjoy facts and details. They like sequential organization and memory tasks. They often work slowly and methodically, taking great care to finish each project before beginning another one.

On the other hand, however, are the minority (approximately 24 percent) who are the intuitive type. This type learns not through experience, but by insight and inspiration. These students are bored by facts and details, preferring global concepts and theories. They dislike memory work. Generally, they are quick to grasp ideas and catch on to the gist of things; this means they can be disruptive because they have already learned their lesson or finished their assignment. While they generally perform well on tests, they also daydream and lose interest quickly in the things that they deem uninteresting or dull. They like to do several things at once and find it tedious to have to slow down or wait for others to finish.

STANDARDS FOR CLASSROOM BEHAVIOR

Teachers who understand these characteristics and ways of thinking, whether it is in regard to information processing or moral decision making, can use this information to establish standards for classroom behavior. Standards should reflect community values and norms and should take into consideration students' ethnicity (i.e., what language they speak at home), socioeconomic status, and religious beliefs. These factors are important when formulating a dress code, determining how to address authority figures, defining the use of appropriate language, examining interactions between males and females, or developing school safety procedures. An important part of the teacher's role is to educate the students about school policies and/or district and state policies with regard to these issues.

What are common values across cultural, ethnic, religious, and social strata? Honesty, mutual respect, consideration, and courtesy are among those virtues that have widespread acceptance. Students (and their parents) should know about standards for attendance, grades, and student behavior.

Students should know how to dress for school, how to address their teachers and other school employees, and what is appropriate language for school (limiting the use of slang or vulgarities). They should know rules for turning in homework, rules for making up missed assignments, and rules for handing in work late (if it is accepted). They should know what they can and cannot bring to school (certain kinds of materials and tools). They should know what will happen if they break the rules.

Psychological research on behavior modification and reducing aggression shows that modeling acceptable and nonaggressive behaviors is more effective than catharsis and punishment. Teachers are most effective when they follow the rules and exemplify the standards of conduct themselves. Teachers who are courteous, prompt, enthusiastic, in control, patient, and organized provide examples for students through their own behavior. They send the message "Do as I do," not "Do as I say."

The Florida Department of Education states in its "Code of Ethics and the Principles of Professional Conduct" that teachers shall a) make reasonable efforts to protect students from conditions that would harm learning or mental and physical health and safety; b) not restrain students from independent action in pursuit of learning; c) not deny students' access to diverse points of view; d) not intentionally suppress or distort information regarding students' academic program; e) not expose a student to unnecessary embarrassment or disparagement; f) not violate or deny students' legal rights; g) not harass or discriminate against students on the basis of race, color, religion, sex, age, national or ethnic origin, political beliefs, marital status, handicapping condition, sexual orientation, or social and family background, and make reasonable efforts to assure that students are protected from harassment and discrimination; h) not exploit a relationship with a student for personal gain or advantage; and i) shall keep information in confidence or as required by law (Florida State Board of Education, Rule 6B-1.006, FAC). Teachers who honor this code will be modeling the appropriate standards of behavior for their students.

In addition to modeling appropriate behaviors, another effective way of treating misbehavior (that is, more effective than catharsis and punishment) is the use of incompatible responses. Effective teachers learn how to employ these responses. Some studies have even suggested that open body language (arms open, not crossed) and positive facial expressions (smiling) can be used by teachers to diffuse student anger.

RULES AND THE STUDENT'S ROLE IN DECISION MAKING

Some educational experts have suggested that standards and rules are most effective if students play a role in formulating them. This doesn't mean that students make all the rules, but it means that they can contribute ideas. Stephen Covey, author of the best-selling *The Seven Habits of Highly Effective People,* suggests that people who desire to be effective or successful should be proactive. He explains that being proactive means anticipating everything that can go awry before it does; teachers can think about what could go wrong in class concerning a student's conduct and be prepared if it ever happens. Of course, a teacher may not be able to predict everything that a student may attempt, but trying to analyze many possibilities may provide a teacher some level of comfort in dealing with misbehaviors. Covey also uses the term *proactive* to stress the importance of self-direction, not only for teachers, but for students, as well.

Allowing students to have a voice in establishing standards and formulating codes provides students with an excellent opportunity to exercise their problem-solving skills and critical-thinking abilities. Although one key purpose of education is often purported to be graduating students who are responsible citizens capable of participating thoughtfully in a democratic society, educational practices have had a tendency to foster dependency, passivity, and a "tell me what to think and do" complacency.

Older students especially can benefit from participating in the decision-making process. American industries and businesses have attained greater success, efficiency, and effectiveness through principles of Total Quality Management (TQM). Many TQM principles have also been applied to American education with great success.

One of the key ingredients of TQM is information sharing, so that all partners in an endeavor are aware of goals and objectives. If education is the endeavor, then applying TQM principles means that teachers and students, parents and principals, and other supporting players are all partners in the endeavor. Following TQM principles also means that if all partners have information concerning goals and objectives, then they can form a team to work cooperatively with greater efficiency and effectiveness to achieve goals and objectives.

These ideas require teachers to share authority with students, allowing students a voice in decision making. For some teachers, learning to share control with students may be difficult. Helping students to make some of their own decisions will conflict with some teachers' training, as well as their own ideas and expectations about being in charge. But the many benefits of shared decision making, already described, are worth the struggle to adjust.

Although this may not sound like the perfect classroom to every teacher, Covey describes what, for him, was his most exciting learning experience:

> As a teacher, I have come to believe that many great classes teeter on the very edge of chaos.... There are times when neither the teacher nor the student knows for sure what's going to happen. In the beginning, there is a safe environment that enables people to be really open and to learn and to listen to each other's ideas. Then comes the brainstorming, where the spirit of evaluation is subordinated to the spirit of creativity, imagining, and intellectual networking. Then an absolutely unusual phenomenon begins to take place. The entire class is transformed with the excitement of a new thrust, a new idea, a new direction that's hard to define, yet it's almost palpable to the people involved.

Covey describes a dynamic classroom, not one in stasis; however, there are important requirements for the classroom. First, the students have to feel safe, not only safe from physical harm, but safe from mental harm—from mockery, intimidation, unfair criticisms, threats—from teachers or, especially, other classmates. These features describe a classroom where there is mutual respect and trust between teacher and students and among the students themselves.

THE TEACHER'S ROLE

One experienced teacher of seventh- and eighth-grade students has suggested the following guidelines for teachers in managing their classes:

- Let students have input whenever you can, and when you can't, let them think they are giving input;

- Listen to students; they have surprising insights and viewpoints;

- Be consistent with expectations and consequences;

- Don't make exceptions to school rules, even if you don't agree with them;

- Don't correct or reprimand a student in front of a class. Quickly establish that your classroom is a safe place and can be a fun place, but that disrespect for learning, others, or property will not be tolerated and there will be no further warnings;

- Do not begin teaching until everyone is ready to learn;

- Do consult with colleagues and administrators for advice;

- Make sure that students know their rights and their responsibilities.

Blanchard and Johnson, the authors of *The One Minute Manager,* another best-selling book for those wanting to achieve success, describe one-minute goal-setting as: a) deciding on goals; b) identifying what good behaviors are; c) writing out goals; d) reading and re-reading goals; e) reviewing goals every day; and f) determining if behaviors match goals. This list is applicable to the classroom teacher who needs to decide on behavioral goals and identify behaviors both expected and unacceptable.

Another good technique offered by these authors is the "one-minute praise," by which they encourage catching people (in this case, students) doing something right. Blanchard and Johnson suggest to praise people immediately, telling them what they did right. In applying this principle to students, the teacher would tell students how he or she feels about their behavior and how it has helped others in class and helped the success of the class. The teacher would stop for a moment after the praise to let the student feel good about the praise. Finally, the teacher would encourage the student to continue behaving in this manner, shaking hands with the student.

Likewise, the one-minute reprimand could also be useful. However, the teacher should reprimand the student after class, avoiding interrupting a lesson whenever possible. Specifically, the teacher should tell the student what was done wrong. After correcting the student, the teacher should stop and let the student think about the situation for a moment. Then, the teacher should shake hands with the student and remind the student that he or she is valued and affirmed as a person, even though his or her behavior was inappropriate. It is important to distinguish between the individual student (who deserves respect) and the individual's actions (which may be disrespectful and/or unacceptable).

As final advice, Blanchard and Johnson admonish, "When it's over, it's over." After correcting the student, the teacher should not harbor a grudge or ill-will toward the student or dwell on the infraction, but move on to the next task at hand. The authors conclude their book by stating, "Goals begin behaviors, [sic] Consequences maintain behaviors."

When teachers discipline students, they do well to remember that the word *discipline* comes from the Latin word for teaching. The whole point of disciplining a student should be to teach the student what is right and correct, not to embarrass, humiliate, or shame a student.

Teachers should make sure that students understand the rules and that they understand the consequences for breaking the rules. Teachers, like parents, should carefully choose their battles. They should not make rules that they do not want to enforce. Consequences for breaking rules should be certain and swift. Consequences should be appropriate in scope and severity to the infraction.

Budd Churchward, creator of *The Honor Level System: Discipline by Design,* describes a system of discipline with four stages. Step one is a reminder. He explains that a reminder is not a reprimand. A reminder can be directed at an individual or the entire class. Churchward stresses that many students will learn quickly to respond to reminders, but he points out, "Some teachers may complain that they should not have to remind children over and over. We remind the children because they ARE children."

Step two is a reprimand, approaching a student and issuing a verbal or written reprimand. Verbal warnings are not given across the room, but delivered personally to the student. The teacher comes close to the student and tells him or her what to do; the student is asked to identify the next step (step three). Written warnings, however, are described as being even more effective. The teacher approaches the student and gives the student an infraction slip. The teacher has checked an item on the slip and tells the student that if no further problem occurs, the student can throw the slip away at the end of the class or period. If the misbehavior continues, the slip will be collected and turned in (to the principal's office). Churchward emphasizes that it is important that the child have possession of the slip and know that he or she is in control of the slip and what happens to it next (fostering and encouraging internal locus of control, or a feeling of being in charge, being self-directed, or proactive, as Covey would say).

Step three is collecting the infraction slip. If the student is approached again, he or she is reminded that a warning already has been issued. If the student received a verbal warning, an infraction slip now is sent to the office. If the student has the infraction slip, it is taken up. The student is then asked to identify the next step.

The next step, the final step, is to send the offender to the office, removing the student from class. Churchward advises that if the first three steps are followed faithfully, the last step is rarely required. However, if things do go this far, he insists that the teacher can stay calm and unemotional, perhaps saying something such as, "Tomorrow we will try again. I'm sure that we can work this out."

Churchward recommends that these steps be posted in several places in the classroom, as well as posting three to five selected classroom rules important to teaching. The list should be short and stated in a positive way. For example, instead of writing, "Students will not ask for repeated directions," the teacher should write, "Students will follow directions the first time they are given." By taking time to go over the rules and the steps with students, they will know that they can always look on the wall if the teacher asks them what the next step will be. Churchward says it is important to let students know that they may be asked to identify the next step if they get in trouble; also, students should know that the teacher has the right to skip steps in extreme cases if there are certain behaviors that cannot be tolerated. Teachers should be specific about the behaviors that are not tolerated and give students exact examples of what is meant.

Some other practices, which may encourage good classroom behaviors, are a) monitoring; b) low-key interventions; c) "I" messages; and d) positive teaching. Briefly, monitoring refers to walking around the room to monitor what students are doing. After a teacher gives an assignment, he or she should wait a few minutes to give students time to get started and then the teacher should move around the room, checking to make sure that all students have begun their work. Thus, the teacher can also give individualized instruction as needed. Students who are not working may be motivated to begin as they see the teacher approaching. The teacher should not interrupt the class during monitoring, but should use a quiet voice to show personal attention.

Low-key interventions are quiet and calm. Effective teachers are careful that students are not rewarded for misbehavior by becoming the focus of attention. By being proactive, teachers have anticipated problems before they occur. When teachers correct misbehaving students, the teachers are inconspicuous, making sure not to distract others in the class. When they lecture, effective teachers know to frequently mention students by name to bring the students' attention back to class.

"I" messages are an effective communication technique, whatever the situation; however, they can be used with particular success in the classroom. The message begins with the word "I" and contains a message about feelings. For example, a teacher might say, "I am very frustrated about the way you are ignoring instruction. When you talk while I am talking, I have to stop teaching and that is very frustrating."

Finally, positive discipline refers to the use of language to express what the teacher wants instead of the things that students cannot do. Instead of saying, "No fighting," a teacher can say, "Settle conflicts using your words." Taking a positive approach with language also means using lots of praise. An effective teacher is quick to praise students for their good behavior, using lots of smiles and positive body language, as well as laudatory words.

RULES AND SCHOOL SAFETY ISSUES

The importance of a safe school environment for promoting good behavior has been mentioned already; however, statistics indicate that school safety is a vital concern for all educators. More than 100,000 students bring weapons to school each day. Every day, 40 students are killed or wounded with these weapons. One out of every five students is afraid to go the restroom at school for fear of victimization. In addition to student fears, more than 6,000 teachers are threatened by students each year.

Research shows that the following factors contribute to school violence and antisocial behaviors: overcrowding, poor design and use of school space, lack of disciplinary procedures, student alienation, multicultural insensitivity, rejection of at-risk students by teachers and peers, and anger or resentment at school routines. On the other hand, the following characteristics contribute to school safety: positive school climate and atmosphere, clear and high performance expectations for all students, practices and values that promote inclusion, student bonding to school, high levels of student participation and parent involvement in school activities, and opportunities to acquire academic skills and develop socially.

Effective teachers need to be alert to the signs of potentially violent behavior, acknowledging that signs can easily be misinterpreted and misunderstood. Warning signs should be used to get help for children, not to exclude, punish, or isolate them. Experts also emphasize that warning signs should not be seen as a checklist for identifying, labeling, or stereotyping children, and that referrals to outside agencies based on early warning signals must be kept confidential and, except for those suspected of child abuse or neglect, must have parental consent.

The American Psychological Association has identified four "accelerating factors" that increase the risk of violence. These four factors are a) early involvement with drugs and alcohol; b) easy access to weapons, especially handguns; c) association with antisocial, deviant peer-groups; and d) pervasive exposure to media violence. Longitudinal studies (studies following groups over time) have shown youth violence and delinquency to be linked with situations in which a) one or more parents have been arrested; b) the child has been the client of a child-protection agency; c) the child's family has experienced death, divorce, or another serious transition; d) the child has received special-education services; and/or e) the youth exhibits severe antisocial behavior.

Along somewhat analogous lines, the U.S. Department of Education and Department of Justice have compiled a long list of possible early warning signs. These signs include a) social withdrawal (often associated with feelings of depression, rejection, persecution, unworthiness, and lack of confidence); b) excessive feelings of isolation and being alone; c) excessive feelings of rejection; d) being a victim of violence—including physical or sexual abuse; e) feelings of being picked on and persecuted; f) low school interest and poor academic performance; g) expression of violence in writings and drawings; h) uncontrolled anger; i) patterns of impulsive and chronic hitting, intimidating, and bullying behaviors; j) history of discipline problems; k) history of violent and aggressive behaviors; l) intolerance for differences and prejudicial attitudes; m) drug use and alcohol use; n) affiliation with gangs; o) inappropriate access to, possession of, and use of firearms; and p) serious threats of violence.

In addition to these early warning signs are what the Departments of Education and Justice called imminent warning signs, requiring an immediate response. Imminent warning signs are a) serious physical fighting with peers or family members; b) serious destruction of property; c) rage for seemingly minor reasons; d) detailed threats of lethal violence; e) possession and/or use of firearms and weapons; and f) other self-injurious behaviors or threats of suicide. Immediate intervention by school authorities and possibly law enforcement officials is required if a child has presented a detailed plan to harm or kill others or is carrying a weapon, particularly a firearm, and has threatened to use it. In situations where students present other threatening behaviors, parents should be informed immediately.

Violence prevention strategies at school range from adding social-skills training to the curriculum to installing metal detectors at the entrances to buildings. Educational experts recommend that schools teach all students procedures in conflict resolution and anger management, in addition to explaining the school rules, expectations, and disciplinary policies.

The federal Gun-Free Schools Act of 1994 required every state to pass zero-tolerance laws on weapons at school or face the loss of federal funds. Every state has complied with this law and requires school districts to expel students for at least a year if they bring weapons to school.

The U.S. Department of Education and the Department of Justice have produced a joint report recommending actions to promote school safety. First, an open discussion of safety issues is essential. "Schools can reduce the risk of violence by teaching children about the dangers of firearms, as well as appropriate strategies for dealing with feelings, expressing anger in appropriate ways, and resolving conflicts. Schools also should teach children that they are responsible for their actions and that the choices they make have consequences for which they will be held accountable." Also recommended is treating students with equal respect, creating ways for students to share their concerns, and helping children to feel safe when expressing their feelings.

In review, effective and safe schools develop and enforce consistent rules that are clear, broad-based, and fair. Effective schoolwide disciplinary policies include a code of conduct, specific rules, and consequences that can accommodate student differences on a case-by-case basis when needed. School policies need to include anti-harassment and anti-violence policies and due process rights. Rules should reflect the cultural values and educational goals of the community. School staff, students, and families should be involved in the development, discussion, and implementation of fair rules, written and applied in a nondiscriminatory manner, and accommodating cultural diversity. Consequences for violating rules must be commensurate with the offenses, and negative consequences must be accompanied by positive teaching for socially appropriate behaviors. Finally, there must be zero-tolerance for illegal possession of weapons, drugs, or alcohol.

The following references were used to write Competency 7. Further reading of these references may enhance understanding of the competency and may also increase performance on the examination.

American Psychological Association, 1998.

Blanchard, K. and S. Johnson. *The One Minute Manager.* New York: Berkley Books, 1981.

Border, L. *Morphing: A Quintessential Human Capability.* National Teaching and Learning Forum, Vol. 7 (4).

Churchward, B. *The Honor Level System.* 1995.

Covey, Stephen. *The Seven Habits of Highly Effective People.* New York: Simon and Schuster, 1989.

ERIC Clearinghouse on Educational Management. *Trends and Issues: School Safety and Violence Prevention.* 1998.

Florida State Board of Education. *The Code of Ethics and the Principles of Professional Conduct of the Education Profession in Florida.* 1998.

Gilligan, C. *In a Different Voice: Psychological Theory and Women's Development.* Cambridge, Massachusetts: Harvard University Press, 1982.

Kohlberg, L. "The Psychology of Moral Development: The Nature and Validity of Moral Stages." *Essays on Moral Development* (Vol. 2), 1984.

McDaniel, T. R. "A Primer on Classroom Discipline." *Phi Delta Kappan.*

Myers, I. B. *Gifts Differing.* Palo Alto, California: Consulting Psychologists Press, 1980.

Sternberg, R. *In Search of the Human Mind.* Ft. Worth, Texas: Harcourt Brace, 1995.

U.S. Department of Education and Department of Justice. *Early Warning, Timely Response.* Washington, D.C.: U.S. Government Printing Office, 1998.

FTCE

Florida Teacher Certification Exam—
Professional Education Test

Chapter 9
Competency 8

Chapter 9

COMPETENCY 8

DEFINITION OF COMPETENCY

A teacher deals with various misconduct in a manner that promotes and maintains instructional momentum.

Teachers must be "with it" in a classroom to prevent misbehavior that will interrupt the flow of learning. The level of "with it"-ness must extend beyond the obvious events of the classroom. A teacher needs to understand the dynamics behind the actions that occur in the classroom, and then proceed accordingly.

There are many factors that influence student behavior. Young children will generally follow the rules of the classroom out of a desire to please their teachers. Misbehavior that occurs in a classroom may be the result of a conflict that is occurring elsewhere. Teachers should be aware that these conflicts can occur between peers, between students and the teacher, or as a result of events in the student's family or out-of-classroom experiences.

"WITH IT"-NESS IN THE CLASSROOM

The goal of "with it"-ness is to prevent misconduct in the classroom. Through everyday interactions, the teacher develops a sense of an individual student's normal behavior and general mental state. The "with it" teacher also develops a sense of the relations between the students in a class and within the school. If the beginning of a conflict between individuals in a class is noticed, the "with it" teacher is able to mediate the students to a resolution that avoids the disruption of class time.

The desired behavior for the students should be well-explained and clearly displayed in a classroom. Posted rules provide a constant guide and reminder of classroom rules. Teachers can also use these displays as a reference when discussing expected behavior, either individually or with the class as a whole.

Teachers should self-monitor their interactions with the misbehaving students. Children may act out if they feel they are threatened, disliked, or treated unfairly. A "with it" teacher knows which particular students are causing the class disruption and works to curb this behavior without punishing the class as a whole. The class momentum can be disrupted either by the teacher's response to the behavior or by the teacher allowing the misbehavior to persist.

Both the individual student and the class as a whole are affected by how the teacher handles classroom misconduct. The effective approach is when the teacher compliments the positive behavior modeled by other students in the classroom, rather than individually reprimanding student misbehavior. If certain students are not properly addressing the task at hand, the teacher can say, "I like the way Glen is working in his math book" or "Belinda, I like the way you are quietly raising your hand and waiting your turn." By doing so, the teacher is reinforcing the desired behavior for the class without directly addressing and calling attention to the misbehavior. The individual student has an opportunity to monitor his or her own behavior, and class momentum is not lost.

Teachers can also guide a student toward appropriate behavior by stating the student's name, or explaining what task he or she should currently be working on. Non-verbal cues include walking toward the student, making eye contact, or gently touching the student's desk or shoulder. These techniques can be used without disrupting the flow of the classroom.

Teachers must clearly voice their expectations without yelling or being angry. Quiet and controlled reprimands have been shown to be very effective. Maintaining control without involving punitive measures lowers the tension in the entire classroom. Students should not be made to feel uncomfortable because the teacher is angry. This is especially important when teachers are working with small groups, or when working on simultaneous tasks. Individualized instruction should not suffer when the teacher must reprimand another student. When a teacher demonstrates "with it"-ness, students do not feel that they have an opportunity to misbehave just because the teacher's attention is not focused directly on them.

PARENT-TEACHER COMMUNICATION

If a student is misbehaving, the teacher should examine if the misbehavior is caused by a conflict in the classroom. If the cause cannot be determined based on classroom experience, there may be a problem at home. When a child is not responding to the teacher's efforts to stop the behavior, the teacher should contact the parents. This will allow the teacher and parents to discuss any problems that may help explain the misbehavior. The parents may be facing similar difficulties at home, or may not even be aware of a problem. Such a discussion enables the teacher and parents to work together at getting the child back on track. It is important for the teacher to express his or her feelings of concern to the parents. The parents should also be assured that the child's educational welfare and personal well-being are continuing primary concerns of the teacher.

The teacher can contact the parents using a written note, a telephone call, a meeting outside of school hours, or even a home visit if the administration approves. During the conference, the teacher should mention the incidents of misbehavior, the record of the student's daily effort if failure to accomplish assignments is the problem or part of it, the attempts made to change the negative performance, and the suggestions for solving the problem. In turn, the teacher should ask the parents about the child's attitude toward school, comments, and behavior at home. Having the student present is sometimes a useful strategy, especially if the student is omitting part of the story when talking about it at home. The parents and teacher must develop a partnership to focus on the student's well-being.

The end of any conference should include writing down the actions each participant—teacher, parent, and student—will take to improve the situation. A tentative date for meeting again, or at least for communication between the teacher and parents, should be established before the meeting ends. Within a few days, the teacher must try to find an opportunity to provide feedback to both the parents and the student about the matters discussed, especially if improvement of a negative situation is noted.

If the initial consultation with the parents is not successful at ending the misbehavior, there are a few techniques that the teacher and parents can try. A daily report may be used to provide frequent contact between the teacher and the student that allows the parents to monitor the student's behavior in the classroom. The teacher sends home a report of the student's behavior, positive and/or negative, for the parents to review, sign, and return back to the teacher the next day. This also provides the parents a way to add their own feedback to the situation. If the behavior improves, the reports can be sent less frequently, until the student's behavior is consistently positive.

If the combined efforts of the parents and the teacher are unable to resolve the situation, they may need to consult with a school or community professional. Family or individual counseling may be another route to end the student's conflict and guide him or her back into the classroom momentum.

FTCE

Florida Teacher Certification Exam—
Professional Education Test

Chapter 10
Competency 9

Chapter 10

COMPETENCY 9

DEFINITION OF COMPETENCY

A teacher determines the entry-level understanding and ability of students for a given set of educational objectives using diagnostic tests, teacher observations, and/or student records.

PURPOSES OF ASSESSMENT

The effective teacher understands the importance of ongoing assessment as an instructional tool for the classroom and uses both informal and formal assessment measures. Informal measures may include observation, journals, written drafts, and conversations. More formal measures may include teacher-made tests, district exams, and standardized tests. Effective teachers use both formative and summative evaluation. Formative evaluation occurs during the process of learning, when the teacher or the students monitor progress in obtaining outcomes, while it is still possible to modify instruction. Summative evaluation occurs at the end of a specific time period or course, usually by a single grade used to represent a student's performance.

TEACHER-MADE TESTS

The effective teacher uses a variety of assessment techniques. Teacher-made instruments are ideally developed at the same time as the goals and outcomes are planned, rather than at the last minute after all the lessons have been taught. Carefully planned objectives and assessment instruments serve as lesson development guides for the teacher.

Paper and pencil tests are the most common method for evaluation of student progress. There are a number of different types of questions: multiple-choice, true/false, matching, fill-in-the-blank, short answer, and longer essay. The first five tend to test the knowledge or comprehension levels. Essays often test at the lower levels, but are suitable for assessing learning at higher levels. Projects, papers, and portfolios can provide assessment of higher-level thinking skills.

If the purpose is to test student recall of factual information, a short objective test (multiple-choice, true/false, matching, fill-in-the-blank) would be most effective and efficient. The first three types of questions can be answered on machine-scorable scan sheets to provide quick and accurate scoring. Disadvantages are that they generally test lower levels of knowledge and don't provide an opportunity for an explanation of answers.

If the purpose is to test student ability to analyze an event, compare and contrast two concepts, make predictions about an experiment, or evaluate a character's actions, then an essay question would provide the best paper/pencil opportunity for the student to show what he or she can do. A teacher should make the question explicit enough so that students will know exactly what he or she expects. For example, "Explain the results of World War II" is too broad; students won't really understand what the teacher expects. It would be more explicit to say, "Explain three results of World War II that you feel had the most impact on participating nations. Explain the criteria you used in selecting these results."

Advantages of an essay include the possibility for students to be creative in their answers, the opportunity for students to explain their responses, and the potential to test for higher-level thinking skills. Disadvantages of essay questions include the time needed for students to formulate meaningful responses, language difficulties of some students, and the time needed to evaluate the essays. Consistency in evaluation is also a problem for the teacher, but this can be alleviated by using an outline of the acceptable answers. Teachers who write specific questions and who know what they are looking for will be more consistent in grading. Also, if there are several essay questions, the effective teacher grades all student responses to the first question, then moves on to all responses to the second, and so on.

AUTHENTIC ASSESSMENTS

Paper and pencil tests or essays are only one method of assessment. Others include projects, observation, checklists, anecdotal records, portfolios, self-assessment, and peer assessment. Although these types of assessment often take more time and effort to plan and administer, they can often provide a more authentic assessment of student progress.

Projects are common in almost all subject areas. They promote student control of learning experiences and provide opportunities for research into a variety of topics, as well as the chance to use visuals, graphics, videos, or multimedia presentations in place of, or in addition to, written reports. Projects also promote student self-assessment because students must evaluate their progress along each step of the project. Many schools have science or history fairs for which students plan, develop, and display their projects. Projects can also be part of business, English, music, art, mathematics, social sciences, health, or physical education courses.

The teacher must make clear the requirements and the criteria for evaluation of the projects before students begin them. He or she must also assist students in selecting projects which are feasible, for which the school has learning resources, and which can be completed in a reasonable amount of time with little or no expense to students.

Advantages of projects are that students can demonstrate their visual, graphic, art, or music abilities; students can be creative in their topic or research; and the projects can appeal to various learning styles. Disadvantages include difficulty with grading, although this can be overcome by devising a checklist for required elements and a rating scale for quality.

Observations may be made for individual or group work. This method is very suitable for skills or for effective learning. Teachers usually make a list of competencies, skills, or requirements, then check off the ones that are observed in the student or group. An office skills teacher wishing to emphasize interviewing skills may devise a checklist that includes personal appearance, mannerisms, confidence, and addressing the questions that are asked. A teacher who wants to emphasize careful listening may observe a discussion with a checklist which includes paying attention, not interrupting, summarizing another person's ideas, and asking questions of other students.

Anecdotal records may be helpful in some instances, such as capturing the process a group of students uses to solve a problem. This formative data can be useful during feedback to the group. Students can also be taught to write an explanation of the procedures they use for a project or a science experiment. An advantage of an anecdotal record is that it can include all relevant information. Disadvantages include the amount of time necessary to complete the record and difficulty in assigning a grade. If used for feedback, then no grade is necessary.

Advantages of checklists include the potential for capturing behavior that can't be accurately measured with a paper and pencil test, i.e., shooting free throws on the basketball court, following the correct sequence of steps in a science experiment, or including all important elements in a speech in class. One characteristic of a checklist that is both an advantage and a disadvantage is its structure, which provides consistency but inflexibility. An open-ended comment section at the end of a checklist can overcome this disadvantage.

Portfolios are collections of students' best work. They can be used in any subject area where the teacher wants students to take more responsibility for planning, carrying out, and organizing their own learning. They may be used in the same way that artists, models, or performers use them to provide a succinct picture of their best work. Portfolios may be essays or articles written on paper, video tapes, multimedia presentations on computer disks, or a combination. English teachers often use portfolios as a means of collecting the best samples of student writing over the whole year. Sometimes they pass on the work to the next year's teacher to help assess the needs of his or her new students. Any subject area can use portfolios, since they contain documentation that reflects growth and learning over a period of time.

Teachers should provide or assist students in developing guidelines for what materials should be placed in portfolios, since it would be unrealistic to include every piece of work in one portfolio. The use of portfolios requires the students to devise a means of evaluating their own work. A portfolio should be a collection of the student's own best work, not a scrapbook for collecting handouts or work done by other individuals, although it can certainly include work by a group in which the student was a participant.

Some advantages of portfolios over testing are that they provide a clearer picture of a student's progress, they are not affected by one inferior test grade, and they help develop self-assessment skills in students. One disadvantage is the amount of time required to teach students how to develop meaningful portfolios. However, this time can be well spent if students learn valuable skills. Another concern is the amount of time teachers must spend to assess portfolios. However, as students become more proficient at self-assessment, the teacher can spend more time in coaching and advising students throughout the development of their portfolios. Another concern is that parents may not understand how portfolios will be graded. The effective teacher devises a system which the students and parents understand before work on the portfolio begins.

STANDARDIZED TESTING

In *criterion-referenced tests*, each student is measured against uniform objectives or criteria. CRTs allow the possibility that all students can score 100 percent because they understand the concepts being tested. Teacher-made tests should be criterion-referenced because the teacher should develop them to measure the achievement of predetermined outcomes for the course. If teachers have properly prepared lessons based on the outcomes, and if students have mastered the outcomes, then scores should be high. This type of test may be called noncompetitive because students are not in competition with each other for a high score, and there is no limit to the number of students who can score well. Some commercially developed tests are criterion-referenced; however, the majority are norm-referenced.

The purpose of a *norm-referenced test* is to provide a way to compare the performance of groups of students. This type of test may be called competitive because a limited number of students can score well. A plot of large numbers of NRT scores will resemble a bell-shaped curve, with most scores clustering around the center and a few scores at each end. The midpoint is an average of data; therefore, by definition, half of the population will score above average and half below average.

The bell-shaped curve was developed as a mathematical description of the results of tossing coins. As such, it represents the chance or normal distribution of skills, knowledge, or events across the general population. A survey of the height of sixth-grade boys will result in an average height, with half the boys above average and half below. There will be a very small number with heights way above average and a very small number with heights way below average, with most heights clustering around the average.

NRT scores are usually reported in percentile scores (not to be confused with percentages), which indicate the percent of the population whose scores fall at or below the score. For example, a group score at the 80th percentile means that the group scored as well as or better than 80 percent of the students who took the test. A student with a score at the 50th percentile has an average score.

Percentile scores rank students from highest to lowest. By themselves, percentile scores do not indicate how well the student has mastered the content objectives. Raw scores indicate how many questions the student answered correctly and are, therefore, useful in computing the percentage of questions a student answered correctly.

A national test for biology is designed to include objectives for the widest possible biology curriculum, for the broadest use of the test. Normed scores are reported so that schools can compare the performance of the students with the performance of students who the test developers used as its norm group. The test will likely include more objectives than are included in a particular school's curriculum; therefore, that school's students may score low in comparison to the norm group. Teachers must be very careful in selecting a norm-referenced test, and should look for a test that includes objectives which are the most congruent with the school's curriculum.

Schools must also consider the reliability of a test, or whether the instrument will give consistent results when the measurement is repeated. A reliable bathroom scale, for example, will give identical weights for the same person measured three times in a morning. An unreliable scale, however, may give weights that differ by six pounds. Teachers evaluate test reliability over time when they give the same, or almost the same, test to different groups of students. Because there are many factors which affect reliability, teachers must be careful in evaluating this factor.

Schools must also be careful to assess the validity of a test, or whether the test actually measures what it is supposed to measure. If students score low on a test because they couldn't understand the questions, then the test is not valid because it measures reading ability instead of content knowledge. If students score low because the test covered material which was not studied, the test is not valid for that situation. A teacher assesses the validity of his or her own tests by examining the questions to see if they measure what was planned and taught in his or her classroom.

A test must be reliable before it can be valid. However, measurements can be consistent without being valid. A scale can indicate identical weights for three weigh-ins of the same person during one morning, but actually be 15 pounds in error. A history test may produce similar results each time it is given, but not be a valid measure of what was taught and learned. Tests should be both reliable and valid. If the test doesn't measure consistently, then it can't be accurate. If it doesn't measure what it's supposed to measure, then its reliability doesn't matter. Commercial test producers perform various statistical measures of the reliability and validity of their tests and provide the results in the test administrator's booklet.

PERFORMANCE-BASED ASSESSMENT

Some states and districts are moving toward performance-based testing, which means that students are assessed on how well they perform certain tasks. This allows students to use higher-level thinking skills to apply, analyze, synthesize, and evaluate ideas and data. For example, a biology performance-based assessment may require students to read a problem, design and carry out a laboratory experiment, then write a summary of his or her findings. He or she would be evaluated on both the process used and the output he or she produced. A history performance-based assessment may require students to research a specific topic over a period of several days, make presentations of their findings to the rest of the class, then write a response which uses what the students have learned from their own research and that of their classmates. The students are then evaluated on the process and the product of their research. An English performance-based test may require students to read a selection of literature, then write a critical analysis. A mathematics test may state a general problem to be solved, then require the student to invent one or more methods of solving the problem, use one of the methods to arrive at a solution, then write the solution and an explanation of the processes he or she used.

Performance-based assessment allows students to be creative in solutions to problems or questions, and it requires them to use higher-level skills. This type of assessment can be time-consuming; however, students are working on content-related problems, using skills that are useful in a variety of contexts. This type of assessment also requires multiple resources, which can be expensive. It also requires teachers to be trained in how to use this type of assessment. Nonetheless, many schools consider performance-based testing to be a more authentic measure of student achievement than traditional tests.

FTCE

Florida Teacher Certification Exam—
Professional Education Test

Chapter 11
Competency 10

Chapter 11

COMPETENCY 10

DEFINITION OF COMPETENCY

The teacher identifies long-range goals for subject areas that are appropriate to student needs.

All successful teachers begin the term with a clear idea of what they expect students to learn in a given course. Establishing long-range goals for a course—goals that are age-appropriate and reflect student ability and needs—help to clarify the knowledge and skills that teachers and students will work toward during the school year.

Long-range goals can be established for the classroom by the Board of Education, by knowledgeable curriculum specialists, or by a single teacher or group of teachers. Stated in clear, concise language, these goals define the knowledge that students will achieve or the skills that they will acquire through specific instructional activities. For example, a language arts instructor might state the following long-range goals for high school students:

- The student is able to identify major American poets and authors of the twentieth century;

- The student is able to write narrative, informative, and persuasive essays;

- The student is able to properly cite research references;

- The student is able to identify important themes in literature;

- The student is able to identify with multicultural perspectives on the American experience.

After developing a list of potential goals for a course, it is necessary to evaluate those goals against the following criteria:

Importance: The resulting learning must be significant and relevant enough for students to aim for.

Instruction: Appropriate classroom activities must be able to support the learning of the stated goal.

Evaluation: Students must be able to demonstrate the achievement of the goal.

Suitability: The goal must be challenging, as well as reachable, for all students.

Importance

There are many ways to evaluate the importance of selected goals. Teachers can judge goals on the basis of whether the stated outcome is necessary to gain advanced knowledge of a particular field of study, as in the following goal: Students will memorize the letters of the alphabet or master the use of punctuation. Goals can be evaluated on the basis of whether or not their achievement will lead students to become better citizens, such as: Students will apply their knowledge of the constitution to judge a contemporary court case. Goals can also be judged on the basis of whether or not their achievement will lead students to become well-adapted members of society or competitive in the workforce, as in the following: Students will be able to demonstrate their ability to use the Internet to locate information. Finally, goals can be selected on the basis of whether or not their achievement will help prepare students for college admissions standards.

Instruction

In order to ensure that students achieve the stated goal, appropriate classroom activities must be chosen to support its learning. When students have completed these activities, they should be able to successfully demonstrate the knowledge or skills that they have achieved.

Evaluation

Through the successful completion of writing assignments, tests, projects, or activities, students must be able to demonstrate that they have achieved the stated long-range goals.

Suitability

All goals for a given course must be achievable for the entire class, while leaving room to challenge students to master new skills. In order to determine if long-range goals are appropriate, teachers can refer to a number of resources, including student files which may include the results of basic skills tests and reading level evaluations, as well as writing samples.

FTCE

Florida Teacher Certification Exam—
Professional Education Test

Chapter 12
Competency 11

Chapter 12

COMPETENCY 11

DEFINITION OF COMPETENCY

The teacher constructs and sequences related short-range goals for a given subject area.

IDENTIFIES KNOWLEDGE, SKILLS, AND ATTITUDES

After identifying long-range goals for a given subject, it is necessary to recognize the short-range goals that are essential to achieving the larger objective. In order to do this, teachers must be aware of the underlying skills needed to successfully achieve the stated long-range objective. For example, in order to write an essay, a language arts teacher must ensure that students are able to compose complete sentences and paragraphs, develop a coherent outline of ideas, create a thesis, write an introduction, advance the stated thesis through supporting ideas in the body paragraphs, and form a logical conclusion. If students are unable to master these basic skills, they will be unable to achieve the long-range goals of producing an essay.

Likewise, a biology teacher, whose long-range goal is for students to understand the process of photosynthesis, will identify another list of necessary skills. For example, students must know basic elements like hydrogen, oxygen, and carbon, and students must understand how these elements combine to form water (H_2O) and carbon dioxide (CO_2). Moreover, a geometry teacher would know that in order for students to find the area of a triangle or the circumference of a circle, they must know how to compose and solve basic geometric problems.

CONSTRUCTS OR ADAPTS SHORT-RANGE OBJECTIVES

Short-range objectives should be stated in simple terms and should outline identifiable behaviors and skills. When constructing short-range objectives for a course of study, teachers must make certain that each objective leads to the realization of a long-range goal and that the skill or knowledge is easily observable. For example:

- Students will be able to demonstrate an understanding of Shakespearean language;

- Students will be able to list the pros and cons of various forms of energy, including nuclear energy, natural gas, solar energy, dams, and coal;

- Students will be able to solve advanced word problems involving multiplication and division;

- Students will be able to complete a diagram outlining the processes involved in digestion; or

- Students will be able to recite a poem by a well-known twentieth-century poet.

When short-range objectives have been supplied by the Board of Education or the local school system, teachers must be able to interpret and adapt them, making certain that they are appropriate to the age and ability of their own students. For example, a high school senior might be able not only to list the positive and negative implications of nuclear fusion as an energy source, but also to write a persuasive essay, arguing for or against nuclear energy. While an elementary school student might find reciting a poem from memory to be a formidable task, he or she might be appropriately challenged by the assignment of selecting a poem and reading it aloud to the class.

ORGANIZES AND SEQUENCES SHORT-RANGE OBJECTIVES

As learning is achieved by moving from basic skills and knowledge to the understanding of complex ideas and functions, it is important for teachers to sequence short-range objectives according to their appropriate place in the development of higher-order thinking. For example, a history student might first be introduced to the life and achievements of Einstein through a documentary film, later studying his most famous equation for the production of energy ($E=mc^2$). Later, that student might be introduced to the top-secret Manhattan Project that involved hundreds of physicists in the race to turn Einstein's equation for energy into an atomic weapon. Still later, the disastrous results of the atomic bomb in Hiroshima and Nagasaki might be introduced through first-hand accounts from survivors. Finally, he or she might be required to study current treaties surrounding the control of nuclear proliferation. The students might conclude their course of study with a class debate on nuclear proliferation and how it promotes or threatens chances for global peace. From the study of historical events like the Manhattan Project and basic terms like nuclear proliferation to the application of this knowledge in a classroom debate, the short-range goals that guide the activities of this history class have been sequentially ordered to allow students the opportunity to gradually develop and demonstrate higher-order thinking skills.

Other examples of the sequencing of short-range objectives to build upon knowledge can be found in the very clear development of skills outlined in the study of mathematics. From the simple memorization of numbers beginning in the first grade, to the mastery of addition, subtraction, multiplication, and division studied throughout elementary school, through more complicated functions in middle school like algebra and the application of these skills in advanced word problems, to the study of geometry, trigonometry, and calculus in high school—mathematical studies are clearly delineated to build upon previously acquired skills. Without knowledge of multiplication, the idea of division would be impossible to master. Without an understanding of division, fractions would be beyond the reach of students. Inasmuch as no decent math teacher would consider asking students to give the area of a triangle without first ensuring that the students know basic algebra, all teachers must be aware of the basic skills necessary to achieve higher-order skills, and must arrange classroom activities and short-range goals in the order that best promote learning.

FTCE

Florida Teacher Certification Exam—
Professional Education Test

Chapter 13
Competency 12

Chapter 13

COMPETENCY 12

DEFINITION OF COMPETENCY

A teacher chooses, adapts, and develops materials for a given set of educational objectives and for the learning needs of his or her students.

The effective teacher continually seeks materials which help instigate and enhance student learning. In some instances, the teacher may select instructional materials from those readily available based on the appropriate age level for his or her students. In other instances, he/she will need to adapt available materials to better serve individual needs and learning styles. And in yet other instances, the teacher will need to design and develop materials specifically suited to his or her learning objectives and the needs of the students. Such acquiring, adapting, or creating of materials will primarily be done prior to the beginning of the school year. However, some of it will need to occur while the class is in progress, as particular learning challenges arise and as individual student needs are discovered. A considerable proportion of the time invested in locating and shaping these materials will bear dividends, since materials which prove to be well-suited to a particular unit are eligible for repeated use.

EDUCATIONAL RESOURCES

The teacher uses a variety of educational resources (including people and technology) to enhance both individual and group learning. The effective teacher includes resources of all types in the curriculum planning process. He or she should be very familiar with the school library, city/county library, education service center resources, and the library of any college or university in the area. The teacher should have a list of all audiovisual aids which may be borrowed, for example, kits, films, filmstrips, videos, laser disks, and computer software. All audiovisual aids should be related to curricular objectives. Many librarians have keyed their resources to objectives in related subject areas so the teacher can incorporate them with ease into the lessons. However, resources should never be used with a class unless they have been previewed and approved by the teacher. The list of resources to be used in a lesson or unit should be included in the curriculum guide or the lesson plan for ease of use.

Planning for Resources

The effective teacher determines the appropriate place in the lesson for audiovisual aids. If the material is especially interesting and thought-provoking, he or she may use it to introduce a unit. For example, a travel video on coral reefs or snorkeling might be an excellent introduction to the study of tropical fish and plants. The same video could be used at the end of the study to see how many fish and plants the students can recognize and name. Computer software that "dissects" frogs or worms may be used after a discussion of what students already know about the animals and how their internal organs compare with those of humans. A video of a Shakespearean play could be intermixed with discussion and class reading of scenes from the play.

Videos, films, and filmstrips may be stopped for discussion. Research reveals that students comprehend better and remember longer if the teacher introduces a video or film appropriately, then stops it frequently to discuss what the students have just seen and heard. This method also helps keep students' attention focused and assists them in learning note-taking skills.

Print Resources

The most common print material is the textbook, which has been selected by teachers on the campus from a list of books approved by the state. Textbooks are readily available, economical, and written to match state curriculum requirements. However, the adoption process is a long one, and textbooks (particularly science and history) can become out-of-date quickly; therefore, the teacher must use additional resources with recent dates.

Local, state, and national newspapers and magazines should not be overlooked. Some newspapers and magazines have special programs to help teachers use their products in the classroom for reading and writing opportunities as well as for sources of information. Local newspapers may be willing to send specialists to work with students or act as special resource persons.

A limitation of textbooks is their tendency to provide sketchy or minimal treatment of topics, partly because publishers are required to include such a broad range of topics. An ineffective teacher may use the "chapter a week" theory of "covering" a textbook. This method pays no consideration to the importance of information in each chapter or its relevance to the overall district curriculum. Neither does it promote critical thinking on the part of the teacher or the student. Students tend to believe the textbook is something to be endured and not employed as a tool for learning. The effective teacher chooses sections from the textbook that are relevant to his or her learning goals and omits the rest. He or she also supplements the sketchy treatments by using an abundance of other resources.

VISUAL MATERIALS

The most available visual tools in classrooms are the chalkboard and the overhead projector. There are several principles which apply to both. The teacher must write clearly and in large letters. Overhead transparencies should never be typed on a regular typewriter because the print is too small. Computers allow type sizes of at least 18 points, which is the minimum readable size. Also, both boards and transparencies should be free of clutter. Old information should be removed before new information is added. These tools work more effectively if the teacher plans ahead of time what he or she will write or draw on them. Using different colors will emphasize relationships or differences.

Posters and charts can complement lessons, but the walls should not be so cluttered that students are unable to focus on what's important for the current lesson. Posters and charts can be displayed on a rotating basis. Filmstrips, films, and videos are appealing to students because they are surrounded by visual images on television, computers, and video games. Films and filmstrips have the advantage of being projected on a large screen so all students can see clearly. Videos and computers can be connected to large displays or projected on large screens, but these projection devices are rather expensive. If the available screen is too small for large-group viewing, then the teacher might break the class into groups and have several different projects for them to do on a rotating basis.

Some of the best graphic aids will be those developed by individual students or by groups of students. Along with learning about subject area concepts, students will be learning about design and presentation of information. Students can take pictures of their products to put in a portfolio or scrapbook.

Videodisc and Interactive Video

Videodiscs provide a sturdy, compact system of storage for pictures and sound. They can store more than 50,000 separate frames of still images, up to 50 hours of digitized stereo music, or about 325 minutes of motion pictures with sound. An advantage of videodisc over videotape is that each frame can be accessed separately and quickly. The simplest level of use involves commands to play, pause, forward, or reverse. Individual frames can be accessed by inputting their number.

These programs can become interactive by linking them to a computer. The teacher can then individually access, sequence, and pace the information from the interactive system. An art teacher with a collection of pictures of the world's art treasures can choose which pictures to use and the order in which to show them, then design custom-made lessons which can be used repeatedly or easily revised. He or she might decide to develop a program on landscapes as portrayed in art during a certain period of time. By using the videodisc's reference guide, the teacher determines which pictures to use and the length of time he or she wants each displayed. He or she can develop numerous lessons from one videodisc.

More comprehensive interactive programs can use the computer to present information, access a videodisc to illustrate main points, then ask for responses from the student. A multimedia production run by the computer can include images, text, and sound from a videodisc, CD-ROM, graphics software, word processing software, and a sound effects program. Teachers can develop classroom presentations, but students can also develop learning units as part of a research or inquiry project.

The cost of a multimedia system remains relatively high, but students can use it to develop high-level thought processes, collaborative work and research skills, as well as content knowledge and understanding.

HUMAN RESOURCES

Parents and other members of the community can be excellent local experts from which students can learn about any subject—mathematics from bankers, art and music from artists, English from journalists, history from club or church historians or librarians, business from owners of companies. The list can be endless. Effective teachers make sure that any guest who is invited to speak or perform understands the purpose of the visit and the goals or objectives the teacher is trying to accomplish. Preparation can make the class period more focused and meaningful.

Field trips are excellent sources of information, especially about careers and current issues such as pollution control. One field trip can yield assignments in mathematics, history, science, and English, and often art, architecture, music, or health. Teachers can collaborate with each other to produce thematic assignments for the field trip or simply to coordinate the students' assignments. Often a history report can serve as an English paper as well. Data can be analyzed in math classes and presented with the aid of computers.

FTCE

Florida Teacher Certification Exam—
Professional Education Test

Chapter 14
Competency 13

Chapter 14

COMPETENCY 13

DEFINITION OF COMPETENCY

A teacher chooses, develops, and sequences learning activities that are suitable to instructional objectives and student needs.

One of the most challenging and important synthesizing activities of the teaching professional is determining how to match what needs to be taught with the specifications of those who need to learn it. The successful teacher spends considerable time becoming familiar with required instructional objectives, curriculum, and texts. This should be done well in advance of the start of the school year. In addition to general knowledge about the intellectual and social developmental levels of students, the particular needs which characterize any specific group of students, including their individual learning styles, are more apparent to the teacher after the first few days and weeks of school. The effective teacher must then be organized enough to choose and sequence learning activities before the school year begins, but flexible enough to adapt these activities after becoming acquainted with the special needs and learning styles of specific students.

PROCEDURES FOR LEARNING SUCCESS

There are several steps the teacher should follow to ensure success for student learning: a) know and start at the proper level of the students; b) share with students learning objectives and the processes chosen to attain them; c) prepare for the successive steps in the learning process—from instruction, through guidance and support, to feedback; d) choose relatively small steps in which to progress, and include regular assessments of these progressions; e) distinguish between the learning a student can do independently and that which is best facilitated and monitored by the teacher, and choose methods appropriate to content and skills; and

f) include a variety of activities and methods which appeal to the full range of student learning styles and preferences.

ORGANIZING ACTIVITIES

Instructional objectives necessitate that the skill or knowledge to be taught should be valuable on its own, or should clearly lead to something else which is valuable. When the class begins, these long-range objectives should be shared with students as part of the teacher's planned "idea scaffolding," to acknowledge learning as a mutual enterprise. Sharing these objectives is the first important learning activity because this serves as the basis for the communal task of "making sense" of the learning in progress.

Since teachers are expected to be professionally prepared to recognize the cognitive and social levels of students, a simple review of the generally accepted theories of Piaget, Erikson, and other research theorists may be necessary to recall specific characteristics appropriate to various developmental levels. Familiarity with the learning objectives and material to be mastered, as well as the level of the students, enables the teacher to choose and develop a wide range of appropriate activities and to tentatively sequence them in ways that facilitate learning.

A high school language arts teacher, for example, who wishes to convey to his or her students the excitement and value of closely reading literary texts will, at the start of the year, address this learning objective with them. The teacher may also include a personal experience of close reading that is inspiring and revealing. He or she can then plan a series of short-term goals, such as "Students will be able to read carefully enough to gather important details of plot" and "Students will be able to read sensitively enough to notice the connotative dimensions of words and appreciate the nuances suggested by cumulative connotation." Naturally, recognizing denotative details will precede appreciating connotative dimensions. Both will precede the students' ability to identify and appreciate the author's choice of point of view.

Careful, incremental goal-setting allows for considerable flexibility in pace and methods, and leads to further valuable sequencing of strategies. For example, a variety of activities may be used to enhance close reading: the teacher may model close reading of a very short story; the teacher may assign small group work with close reading of paragraphs where one student identifies an important detail, and another student suggests its relevance to the details; the teacher can show the class an overhead color-marking of important descriptive words from one page of a short story or poem; students can work on individual in-class color-marking for the next page, followed by a group discussion of student results; the teacher can assign homework assignments to color-mark a short story or poem; and students can work on group assignments graphing elements of literary text.

Such preliminary planning is enhanced for any specific group of students by a perceptive teacher's growing awareness of individual student learning styles. Since students do not fall precisely into theoretical stages, activities must be designed for a range of developmental levels and learning styles. This includes concrete as well as abstract dimensions, opportunities for instruction by the teacher, and exploration and discovery by individual students and groups.

Once the learning enterprise is launched, the teacher's continued instruction, support, regular assessment, and feedback help maximize the potential of learning opportunities.

OUTCOME-ORIENTED LEARNING

Effective teachers plan carefully so that outcome-oriented activities will produce students who are self-directed learners, in group or individual environments. He or she knows how to plan so that the curriculum guides, lesson plans, actual lessons, tests, and assessments are correlated. Effective teachers plan in advance, explain the unit's goals and objectives to the students, then choose activities which will help the class reach the desired outcomes.

In outcome-oriented learning, teachers define outcomes, or what they want students to know, do, and be when they complete a required course of study. The teachers set high but realistic goals and objectives for their students, then plan instructional activities which will assist students in achieving these goals.

The key to effective outcome-oriented planning is to consider what outcomes must be achieved, then determine which teacher and student behaviors will improve the probability that students will achieve the outcomes.

Outcome-based planning starts with the end product—what must be learned or accomplished in a particular course or grade level. For example, an algebra teacher may decide that the final outcome of his or her algebra course would be that students use quadratic equations to solve problems. He or she then works "backwards" to determine prerequisite knowledge and skills students need to have in order to accomplish this outcome. By continuing to ask these questions about each set of prerequisites, the teacher finds a starting point for the subject or course, then develops goals and objectives. The outcomes should be important enough to be required of all students.

An outcome-oriented system means that students are given sufficient time and practice to acquire the knowledge and skills. It also means that teachers take into account students' various learning styles and time required for learning, and make adaptations by providing a variety of educational opportunities.

FTCE

Florida Teacher Certification Exam—
Professional Education Test

Chapter 15
Competency 14

Chapter 15

COMPETENCY 14

DEFINITION OF COMPETENCY

A teacher manages his or her time in the classroom efficiently.

PLANNING AND PERFORMANCE OF THE CLASSROOM TEACHER

The amount of time in which effective learning and instruction occur depends on a number of variables, but the planning and performance of the classroom teacher is a major factor. The time available for instruction can be determined by calculating the amount of allocated time in the schedule. For example, a class that meets five times a week from 10:00 A.M. to 10:50 A.M. has an allocation of 225 minutes per week for that subject. Students will not interact academically with their teacher and/or the content of the subject 100 percent of that time. There are time "leaks" that reduce the allocated time. However, the most effective teachers have learned how to minimize those leaks and maximize the amount of time spent by students on academic learning tasks.

A major difference between effective and ineffective teachers is found in the amount of time they arrange for their students to engage in productive "on task" learning. Effective teachers also recognize the difference between successful and unsuccessful engagement in academic learning. Time spent on learning does not provide any assurance that learning will take place unless student comprehension also takes place. Optimum learning occurs when students experience a high success rate when engaged with the content. Thus, productive "on task" student behavior requires the additional dimension of high comprehension that accompanies student interaction with content.

This section provides a discussion of the teacher behaviors that increase the efficient use of time which leads to higher achievement through increased student engagement in learning.

BEGINNING CLASSWORK PROMPTLY

Effective teachers are skilled in beginning classwork promptly. Prompt beginnings include teacher planning that provides rules and norms for students that clarify their expected classroom behavior. These rules include basic requirements about where students should be when the class period begins. Effective teachers are also punctual and begin classwork promptly. Depending on the subject of study, classroom rules may call for students to be in their seats, at their computers, at a learning station, with a team of students, at a laboratory station, lined up in rows, and so forth. Clear directions and enforcement regarding student responsibility for the beginning of each class set the tone for the entire class period and help to avoid distracting delays.

STUDENT ACTIVITY

A second element that teachers must provide is student activity that initiates the learning experiences planned for that class period. Merely requiring students to be at a certain physical location in the learning environment, without a concurrent activity to initiate their learning, is inadequate to promote efficient use of class time. The burden for initiating classroom learning should be shared between students and their teacher. However, the teacher must assume responsibility by taking the following actions:

1. Have materials prepared and organized for students.

2. Check attendance efficiently as students enter the room or by some other expeditious method.

3. Maintain eye contact instead of organizing other materials, or being diverted to other activities at his/her desk or on the bulletin board.

4. Provide opening prompts or directions to students to help them get started with their responsibilities.

It is the responsibility of the teacher to see that the focus of teacher and student talk is on academic subject matter. The daily objectives of each class session require that learning activities, teacher presentations, class discussions, and seatwork must be related directly or indirectly to the content or skills to be learned in that session. Distracting activities, especially discussion by either the teacher or the student that strays significantly from the topic, must be minimized or eliminated. Teachers can tactfully refocus students whose diversionary tactics are off task without demeaning student participation. Teachers must recognize when a diversion is too intrusive and develop in advance ways to suggest how another time or topic might be a more appropriate way to inject the activity or remark. When diversions have no productive value and waste learning time, they must be tactfully eliminated. Such elimination may be handled by a direct response to the students, or it may be handled in a private conversation if the diversions are repeated by particular students. The teacher must also be careful to avoid unproductive digressions. The classroom does provide an opportunity for teachers and students to express anecdotes, experiences, and opinions, but they should relate to the content of the lesson as examples, clarification, or contextual materials.

As each class period unfolds, events usually flow from one topic or activity to another. The effective teacher manages these transitions in a systematic, academically oriented way. The variety of events that occur and pose the threat of a disruption of learning include a) shifting from one activity to another; b) wait time when some students finish before others; c) interruptions that result from tardiness or from students who failed to bring their supplies; d) routine housekeeping tasks; e) setting up equipment; and f) significant changes in the topic under discussion or study.

TRANSITIONS

The effective teacher is aware of these potential interruptions and anticipates them by preparing solutions for them in advance. Each transition calls for methods that will minimize the loss of learning time. When shifting from one activity to another, it is crucial to reach closure on the first activity and to make it clear to students that a new activity is underway. This means that any materials or issues that related to the initial activity are shelved, even if temporarily, to give complete attention to the new activity. The teacher can help with this transition by stating that the class will engage in a new activity and then provide instruction, materials, and any other element needed to help students focus on the new activity.

When students are given time to complete an assignment in class, some students will finish first. Unless plans are made for a productive activity for these students, valuable time for these students will be wasted.

When an assignment for class work is made, the teacher should provide an attractive activity for those who finish early. The activity might be an opportunity to work on a homework assignment and reduce the time the student will spend at home that night on schoolwork. It might be an extra credit task or it may be study time for another subject. In any event, the teacher should avoid asking students who have completed their assignments to wait until everyone is finished.

Tardy students or students who forget books or materials should not disrupt classroom learning. Regular procedures should be established for these common events. For example, it could be a rule that tardy students who bring a tardy slip from the office should enter the room and give the teacher the slip without comment, go to their seat, and the nearest student will quietly show them where the class is in the lesson. Such a policy simplifies an occurrence that has the potential to interrupt the flow of the classroom.

Equipment for the classroom should always be set up in advance and tested to make certain that it works. Valuable time can be lost replacing a burned-out bulb, hunting for an extension cord, or setting up a screen on a tripod that suddenly broke.

Routine classroom events include passing out papers, getting books, writing on the board, distributing materials, and taking attendance. Pre-planning enables the teacher to expedite each of these activities and preserve valuable learning time. Papers can be pre-sorted by rows and given to the first person in each row to hand back to other students. Distributing books might be accomplished by delegating this task to one student in each group (row, team). Information can be written on the board ahead of time and covered with newsprint until it is used. Possibly the information could be put on a transparency and presented with an overhead projector. Some classrooms may have computers on a network, and, therefore, the board or transparency may not be needed.

One of the more difficult transitions to make is to know when to shift from one topic to another. This may be difficult because any topic may reach a boring stage if it continues too long, but if it ends too soon, it may leave some students frustrated. Teacher judgment based on professional observation must determine when to continue or cease a discussion. However, teachers must be sensitive to student interests and respect their needs in making a transition to a new topic. When flowing into another topic, the teacher can offer to meet with students at another time if they have more to say, or the topic might be included at another appropriate time. The purpose of the classroom activity is to meet specific goals, and once those goals are met, it is best to move on to achieve additional goals rather than linger and lose valuable time.

SUMMARY

The efficient use of time requires teacher leadership and student behavior that maximizes the use of time and optimizes learning. This can be accomplished by a punctual and effective beginning to each class, a focus on academic subject matter, and provision for smooth transitions and minimal effect from interruptions.

FTCE

Florida Teacher Certification Exam—
Professional Education Test

Chapter 16
Competency 15

Chapter 16

COMPETENCY 15

DEFINITION OF COMPETENCY

A teacher communicates effectively both verbally and nonverbally.

PRINCIPLES OF VERBAL COMMUNICATION

There are several principles which apply to written and oral messages in the classroom. The message must be accurate. As Mark Twain said, "The difference between the right word and the almost right word is the difference between lightning and the lightning bug." Teachers in particular must be careful to use very specific words that carry the appropriate denotation (literal meaning) as well as connotation (feelings, associations, and emotions associated with the word). Content teachers must carefully teach vocabulary related to the subject area.

It is possible to be completely accurate, however, without being clear. At times a teacher may use an excessive amount of jargon from his or her subject area. While students must learn vocabulary related to the subject area, the teacher must ensure that he or she teaches the words and then reviews them so the students have practice using them. At other times a teacher may assume that students understand difficult words. Many students are hesitant to ask what a word means; teachers must be alert to nonverbal signs that students don't understand a word (confused looks, pauses in writing a word down, failure to answer a question containing the word, etc.). Taking a couple of seconds to ask students to define a word will help them understand the larger content area concepts.

Words should also be specific or concrete. The more abstract a word, the more ambiguous it will be. For example, "physical activity" is very general; "Little League baseball" is much more specific. Although students need to learn abstract words, explaining them in a concrete manner will increase their understanding. Saying that a war causes economic difficulties is general; being more specific would be to say that it reduces the amount of tax money available to cities because of money spent on munitions.

A teacher's communications must also be organized. Students will not be able to follow directions which are given in jumbled order, interrupted with, "Oh, I forgot to tell you." Effective teachers plan their directions carefully, writing them down for the students or making notes for themselves so they will give directions or explain concepts in appropriate order.

Other communication strategies include monitoring the effects of a message, or making sure that the audience actually received and understood the message. A teacher may encourage students to be active and reflective listeners by having each student summarize what another has said before making his or her own contribution.

VOICE

The way a teacher uses the voice conveys prejudices, feelings, and emotions. When a teacher's words convey one meaning and his or her tone of voice conveys another, the students will believe the tone rather than the meaning. Students immediately know the difference between "That's a great idea" said in a low voice with a shrug, and "That's a great idea!" said with energy and a smile. A teacher's tone of voice can tell a student, "I'm asking you, but I don't think you can answer this." Messages can be modified by varying the loudness or softness, by varying the tone, by using high or low pitch, and by changing the quality of speech.

NONVERBAL COMMUNICATION

Even when the verbal or written message is accurate, clear, specific, and organized, nonverbal communication can confuse the message. Sometimes the nonverbal aspect of communication can carry more weight than the verbal. Nonverbal messages can be sent by the way teachers dress, the way they use their facial expressions, and the way they use their voice. Experienced educators realize that students respond better when teachers dress professionally. Most people find it easier to take seriously someone dressed in neat, clean clothes than someone in wrinkled, ill-fitting clothing. Also, students behave better when they themselves are dressed better.

EYE CONTACT

Facial expressions communicate a world of emotions and ideas. Teachers use many voluntary facial expressions. All students have seen "the look" from a teacher, usually when a student does something out of order. A frown or raised eyebrow can also be very effective. Although positive involuntary expressions such as smiles and laughter are appropriate, teachers should guard against involuntary negative facial expressions that convey contempt, anger, or dislike to a student.

Eye contact can be used to control interactions. Teachers often look directly at students to encourage them to speak, or look away to discourage them from speaking. "The stare" can be part of "the look" which teachers use for discipline reasons. Making eye contact with students is important when the teacher is giving instructions, sharing information, or answering questions. Many people make a habit of scanning the room with their eyes and pausing briefly to meet the gaze of many members of an audience. However, eye contact should last about four seconds to assure the person in the audience (or classroom) that the speaker has actually made contact.

Students also use their eyes, making contact with the teacher when they want to answer a question, but often looking at the floor or ceiling when they want to avoid being called on. However, teachers must be careful in making assumptions about eye contact. Research has revealed that students who are visually oriented tend to look upward while they are thinking about a response; kinesthetic learners tend to look down while they are thinking; auditory learners may look to the side. The teacher who says to a student, "The answer's not written on the floor!" may not understand the student's mode of thinking. Effective teachers who are encouraging higher-level thinking may find a classroom filled with eyes that look in various directions.

Cultural factors may also contribute to confusion about eye contact. Many cultures teach children that it is very disrespectful to look an adult in the eye; therefore, these students may stand or sit with downcast eyes as a gesture of respect. Forcing the issue only makes the students and teacher uncomfortable and actually hinders communication.

BODY LANGUAGE

Body language can also convey feelings and emotions to students. A teacher can emphasize points and generalizations by gesturing or tapping something on the chalkboard. If a teacher gestures too often or too wildly, students find it difficult to determine what the teacher is trying to emphasize. Too many gestures can also cause the students to watch the gestures instead of attending to the information.

Beginning teachers especially need to convey a relaxed but formal body posture, which denotes strength, openness, and friendliness. Hiding behind the desk or crossing the arms indicates timidity or even fear. A teacher who meets students at the door with a smile and even a handshake shows students he or she is confident and in control.

MEDIA COMMUNICATION

Media communication has become a vital part of the classroom process. Effective teachers use a variety of audio-visuals in every class, including posters, graphs, overhead transparencies, films, videos, CD-ROMs, and laser disks.

SUMMARY

A teacher's expectations for student behavior can be revealed through a combination of verbal and nonverbal communication. Jere Brophy and others have researched the relationship between teacher expectations and student behavior. This research shows that teachers often communicate differently when dealing with high-achievers and low-achievers. This behavior is not always deliberate or conscious on the part of the teacher, but it can communicate negative expectations. When dealing with high-achievers, as opposed to low-achievers, teachers tend to listen more carefully, give them more time to answer, prompt or assist them more, call on them more often, give more feedback, and look more interested. The effective communicator will be careful not to differentiate communication based on a student's achievement level.

FTCE

Florida Teacher Certification Exam—
Professional Education Test

Chapter 17
Competency 16

Chapter 17

COMPETENCY 16

DEFINITION OF COMPETENCY

A teacher creates and preserves academic focus by using verbal, nonverbal, and media communication.

PLANNING PROCESSES

Madeline Hunter describes a planning model which requires teacher decisions about content, teacher behavior, and student behavior. The three parts of this model overlap and are related to each other; a decision in one category influences a decision in another. Decisions about content are often made at the state or district level. Teachers use frameworks from the state, curriculum documents developed by the district, and materials from district-chosen textbooks as bases for planning lessons.

A teacher using this model would make decisions about content, including goals and objectives for a lesson or unit, length of lesson or unit, emphasis of lesson, textbooks, and additional resource materials. Decisions about his or her own behavior include teaching strategies, accommodations for various learning styles, types of activities, sizes of groups, uses of technology and other resources, and room arrangements. Decisions about students' behavior include individual or group responses, format of responses, ways students will demonstrate learning, and products of activities.

Robert Gagné outlines nine external events which are important in planning an appropriate sequence of instruction. They are: gaining attention; informing students of the lesson objectives; stimulating recall of previous learning; presenting stimuli with distinctive features; guiding learning; eliciting student performance; providing informative feedback; assessing student performance; and enhancing the retention and transfer of learning.

The term "lesson cycle" has been applied to processes of lesson planning developed by a variety of people because the process repeats itself continually. These planning processes usually include the development of objectives and a focus for attention, a design for instructional input, constant monitoring of student understanding, provision for rehearsal and practice of knowledge, and opportunities for enrichment or follow-up.

Teachers choose objectives for a lesson from a curriculum guide, or develop their own from their knowledge of their subject area and the needs of students. These objectives are clearly communicated to the students in terms of what they will learn (not activities they will do) during the lesson. In a deductive lesson, these objectives are explained to students at the beginning; in an inductive lesson, objectives are clarified at the end of the lesson. Teachers develop a focus or introduction to the lesson (called an anticipatory set by Hunter) which should hook the students' interest and focus attention toward the upcoming activities. Instruction may take a variety of forms. The teacher provides instructional activities which will produce the desired outcomes in the students. A wide variety of instructional methods may be used for input, from mastery lectures or labs to cooperative learning or several different types of inductive strategies. The teacher is constantly monitoring student behavior, checking for understanding, and modifying the instruction as necessary.

After or during instructional input, the students rehearse or apply what they've learned. In guided practice, the teacher watches carefully to make sure students have grasped the material correctly. Because the teacher is on hand to assess student responses, he or she is able to provide correction or additional input if necessary. During independent practice, students work independently. At the end of each lesson (or at the end of the class), the teacher or students summarize or review what has been learned. An additional feature is enrichment, which should be for all students, not only the faster ones. Enrichment means that students either delve deeper into a subject they've been studying, or broaden their understanding of the general topic. For example, students who have been studying the stock market could research the history of its development, or they could study the market in other countries.

Lesson cycles are repeated for additional blocks of content. A lesson may last anywhere from a few minutes to several days; it isn't limited by the period or the bell.

SELF-DIRECTED LEARNING

Effective teachers not only set goals for their students, but also teach students to set and accomplish their own goals, both individually and in groups. Students need to learn how to plan for their individual learning as well as for learning with a group of students. If students are unaccustomed to setting goals, the effective teacher begins by modeling the process. The teacher explains how he or she develops goals and objectives for the class. One way of encouraging students to set goals is to ask students to set a performance standard for themselves in regard to time needed to complete a project. For example, students might determine they will need 15 minutes to answer five questions, writing one paragraph of at least five sentences for each question. In order to accomplish this goal, the students must focus their attention very carefully and limit themselves to about three minutes per question. The teacher should then ask questions to help students determine whether the goal was realistic, and if not, what adjustments he or she needs to make.

Other steps could be to ask students to develop their own questions about material to be learned or to plan activities to accomplish the goals of the lesson. The highest level is to have students determine the goals for their own learning. For example, a science teacher might introduce the topic of earthquakes, then help students determine what they need to know about earthquakes and the activities and resources which will help them learn. Students also need to develop plans for products which will show that they have met their goals.

Another way to encourage self-directed thinking and learning is to use higher-level questioning strategies and to teach students to use them as well.

FTCE

Florida Teacher Certification Exam—
Professional Education Test

Chapter 18
Competency 17

Chapter 18

COMPETENCY 17

DEFINITION OF COMPETENCY

A teacher displays forms of knowledge such as ideas, rules, principles, and values.

DEDUCTIVE STRATEGIES

Methods can be divided into two categories: deductive and inductive. Deductive methods are those in which teachers present material through mastery lecture, or students teach each other through presentations. In deductive lessons, the generalizations or rules are taught from the beginning, then examples and elaboration are developed which support the generalizations or rules. Deductive thinking often requires students to make assessments based on specific criteria which they or others develop.

Inductive methods are those in which teachers encourage students to study, research, and analyze data they collect, then develop generalizations and rules based on their findings. During inductive lessons, a hypothesis or concept is introduced at the beginning, but generalizations are developed later in the lesson and are based on inferences from data.

The lecture is a deductive method, whereby information is presented to students by the teacher. New teachers are especially attuned to lecture because that is the usual mode of instruction in college classes. An advantage of lecture is that large amounts of information can be presented in an efficient manner; however, effective teachers avoid dumping loads of information through lectures. Mastery lectures should be short, usually no more than 10 or 15 minutes at a time, and constantly interrupted with questions to and from students. Questions during a lecture tend to be lower-level ones, where the teacher is building a foundation of knowledge for students to use in later activities. The effective teacher, however, uses higher-level questions even during lectures.

Information sessions must also be supplemented with an array of visual materials that will appeal to visual learners as well as auditory ones. Putting words or outlines on the board or a transparency is very helpful; however, this is still basically a verbal strategy. Drawings, diagrams, cartoons, pictures, caricatures, and graphs are visual aids for lectures. Teacher drawings need not be highly artistic, merely memorable. Often a rough or humorous sketch will be more firmly etched in students' minds than elaborate drawings. Using a very simple sketch provides a better means of teaching the critical attributes than a complicated one. The major points stand out in a simple sketch; details can be added once students understand the basic concepts. For example, a very simple sketch of the shapes of the snouts of alligators and crocodiles can fix the difference in students' memory; identification from pictures then becomes easier.

Teachers should also be careful to include instruction on how to take notes while listening to a speaker, a skill that will be useful during every student's career, whether listening to instructions from a supervisor or a speaker at meetings and conferences. One way a teacher can do this is to show students notes or an outline from the mini-lecture he or she is about to present, or to write notes or an outline on the board or overhead while the teacher is presenting the information. This activity requires careful planning by the teacher and will result in a more organized lecture. This type of structure is especially helpful for sequential learners, those who like organization. It will also help random learners develop organizational skills. A web or map or cluster is a more right-brained method of connecting important points in a lecture or a chapter. The effective teacher will use both systems and teach both to students, so they have a choice of strategies.

INDUCTIVE STRATEGIES

Inquiry or discovery lessons are inductive in nature. Inquiry lessons start with a thought-provoking question for which students are interested in finding an explanation. The question can be followed by brainstorming a list of what the students already know about the topic, then categorizing the information. The categories can then be used as topics for group or individual research. Deductive presentations by students of their research can follow.

Some advantages of inductive lessons are that they generally require higher-level thinking by both teacher and students, and they usually result in higher student motivation, interest, and retention. They are also more interesting to the teacher, who deals with the same concepts year after year. Disadvantages include the need for additional preparation by the teacher, the need for access to a large number of resources, and additional time for students to research the concepts. The teacher spends a great amount of time in planning the lessons, then acts as facilitator during classes.

Generally, the greater the amount of planning and prediction by the teacher, the greater the success of the students. This does not mean that the activity must be tightly structured or set in concrete, but the effective teacher tries to predict student responses and his or her reactions to them. The need for purchasing additional resources has been moderated by computerized bibliographic services, interlibrary loan, and CD-ROMs with all types of information. Because inductive, research-oriented units require more class time, subject-area teachers must work together to determine what concepts are essential for students to understand; other nonessential concepts are omitted.

An English teacher wishing to introduce an inductive study of *Julius Caesar* might ask students what would happen if a group of United States senators and representatives banded together to kill the current president and take control of the government. After brainstorming ideas about causes and effects of the assassination, students could categorize the ideas (political, irrational, economic, etc.), then work in cooperative groups to develop their predictions about each area. Groups could also research the assassinations of Lincoln, McKinley, and Kennedy, then study *Julius Caesar* for comparison of motives and effects. A culminating activity could be to write a scenario of what might happen in an assassination of the current president. English and history teachers who want to team-teach could develop this project together.

A computer science teacher could ask students if they think there will ever be a computer that's smarter than a human being. This would lead to a definition of terms, investigation into human intelligence, artificial intelligence, computer languages, and films such as *2001: A Space Odyssey*, along with demonstrations of computer programs related to artificial intelligence.

Books such as *The Timetables of History* or *The People's Chronology* can be used as a reference for history, English, science, business, and the arts. Students can analyze ten-year periods to discover what was happening in Western Europe and the Americas, then look for connections. Is literature connected to political events? Do art and music reflect current events? What effects do scientific discoveries have on economics? Does the U.S. "Black Friday" of October 28, 1929, have any relationship to the

"Black Friday" in Germany in 1927? What predictions does William Beveridge make in his 1942 "Report on Social Security"? A major class project could be to extend a section of the timetables to include African and Asian events. Over a period of several years, this could become a valuable resource for the school.

A science teacher has numerous opportunities for inductive approaches; in fact, he or she could develop his or her complete curriculum around problems to solve. He or she could ask students to brainstorm a list of everything they can think of that runs by electrical power, then to predict what the world might be like today if electricity had not yet been discovered, or if it hadn't been discovered until 1950. Would there have been any world wars? Atomic weapons? Movies? Pollution? Their study could include effects on the people in the time it was discovered (including violent reactions), resulting devices which use electricity, ecological issues, possible future uses of electrical power, etc.

Science teachers could also lead a discussion of ethical issues in science during a study of cell biology. What would happen if biochemists discover how to clone people, and a dangerous criminal steals the formula and clones himself or warlike leaders of nations? What effects might this have on law and order, peace and war? Should there be laws to stop scientific experiments of certain types?

Teachers of mathematics could introduce a lesson on place value or number systems by asking students how mathematics might be different if people had eight or twelve fingers instead of ten. Students could then investigate number systems and even invent one of their own.

Art or music teachers could show a selection of paintings or play several recordings and ask students in what decade they were created. Students must explain their reasons for giving a particular date. Research could lead to discussion on what paintings or music of a particular decade had in common, their countries of origin, the influence of religion on art or music, and whether political events influence art and music. They could also be asked to predict what art will look like or how music will sound in the year 2050. Students could do projects based on how someone in the year 2050 might write about current art or music. Content area teachers can team with an art teacher to discuss mathematics in art and music, the influence of historical events on the arts, poems, or plays related to the art or music world, or the science of sound. Art or music students could develop original projects as part of subject-area class assignments.

Business teachers might ask students what kind of business they would like to own if money were no object. Students would need to explain their reasons, then research the business they chose. The class could brainstorm questions for study, then categorize them to determine general areas of research. Students who choose the same business could work together; resource people from the business community could visit the class to explain business concepts, answer questions, and predict what business will be like in 10, 20, or 50 years.

COOPERATIVE STRATEGIES

Cooperative learning lessons may be developed as deductive or inductive. Deductive activities include practice and review of information through games or tournaments and presentations made by the teacher or by students. Inductive activities include research, analysis, and synthesis of information.

DISCUSSION STRATEGIES

Discussions are often thought of as unstructured talk by students sitting around in a circle, answering the basic question, "What do you think about _____?" However, profitable discussions are carefully planned, with specific objectives leading to understanding of specific concepts.

Discussion lessons may be deductive or inductive, depending on the emphasis. Deductive lessons will be more structured, often with clear answers which the teacher expects and leads the students to provide. Inductive lessons will be less structured, but very well planned. Teachers ask open-ended questions and accept a variety of answers which are well supported by information or inferences from the text. The effective teacher plans a variety of questions, with learner outcomes in mind, and leads the discussion without dominating it. He or she also will make certain that all students participate and have an opportunity to contribute. Students may also plan and lead discussions, with careful assistance from the teacher.

An English teacher may plan a discussion of *Our Town*. All students write a variety of questions, e.g., based on levels of Bloom's taxonomy. Half the class discusses among themselves the questions presented by the other half of the class; roles change for the last half of the period or the next class period. The teacher's main role is to facilitate and make sure students follow the guidelines.

An important advantage, which is also a disadvantage, is the amount of time required by genuine discussion. The advantage is that all students have opportunities to contribute to learning and, therefore, feel a greater sense of ownership; the disadvantage is that productive discussion takes a great deal of time.

COMPARISON/CONTRAST

An important higher-order thinking skill is the ability to compare and contrast two things or concepts which are dissimilar on the surface. Thomas Gordon has described a process of synectics whereby students are forced to make an analogy between something that is familiar and something that is new; the concepts seem to be completely different, but through a series of steps, students discover underlying similarities. For example, a biology teacher might plan an analogy between a cell (new concept) and a city government (familiar concept). Although they seem impossibly different, they both have systems for transportation, disposal of unwanted materials, and parts that govern these systems. By comparing something new with something familiar, students have a "hook" for the new information, which will help them remember it as well as better understand it. For example, students trying to remember functions of a cell would be assisted by remembering parts of the city government.

FTCE

Florida Teacher Certification Exam—
Professional Education Test

Chapter 19
Competency 18

Chapter 19

COMPETENCY 18

DEFINITION OF COMPETENCY

The teacher implements directions for carrying out instructional activity.

Just as students have learning styles, teachers also have learning styles as well as teaching styles. Since teachers, naturally, prefer their own learning style (a learning style is a set of preferences), they may teach according to their personal way of learning. Many teachers end up teaching the way they were taught when they were students—whether or not their own teachers were using effective methods!

When a teacher becomes aware of his or her own learning and teaching styles, then the teacher has the freedom of choice. The teacher can choose the most effective methods to reach all the students in class. Thus, it is worthwhile for each teacher to learn more about his or her learning and teaching styles.

This chapter focuses on giving directions so that students can complete instructional activities. Directions are an important part of the information that teachers dispense to their students, and it is important to develop strategies and techniques for giving good directions.

TEACHING STYLES

A teacher may give some thought to his or her basic approach to teaching. Is the teacher a sympathetic and friendly teacher, or a realistic, pragmatic, and practical teacher? On the other hand, the teacher may be more logical, intellectual, and knowledge-oriented, or curious and imaginative. Out of a teacher's basic approach to teaching comes the teacher's values. For example, Silver and Hanson describe four categories of teachers: a) nurturers who value interaction and collaboration and tend to stress role-playing, teamwork or team games, group projects, and so forth; b) trainers who value knowledge and skills and stress drills, observations, demonstrations, and time on task; c) intellectuals who value logic and critical thinking and who stress inquiry, concept development, problem-solving, and analysis; and d) facilitators who value creative expression and flexibility and who stress inductive learning, divergent thinking, hypothesis formation, and metaphoric expression. It follows that these different categories of teachers will choose different instructional activities to achieve educational objectives held in common by all teachers.

With regard to giving directions, however, some teachers will choose to be more directive, giving more commands and orders and less room for the student to make choices concerning activities and behaviors, whereas other teachers will choose to be less directive, giving few commands and allowing students to make more choices for themselves. These are differences in teaching style. These differences reflect the different values and priorities of the teachers and should be considered equally valid; no one style, in general, is superior to another. Nonetheless, there are times when most teachers will find that they must be open to adopting the most effective teaching style for accomplishing the objectives at hand. In other words, sometimes teachers adopt a strategy that is not their natural preference in order to be more effective.

To illustrate this point further, consider the tools a carpenter may have in a toolbox. A hammer is not necessarily a better tool than a saw or a screwdriver. However, there are some tasks that may require a hammer and neither a saw nor a screwdriver can do the job or perform the task as well as a hammer. Likewise, teachers have natural preferences or styles, but, if they understand the characteristics of their own style, they can select the tools or approaches that will allow them to be most effective.

This information about teaching styles explains the importance of giving directions effectively and efficiently and meeting the many needs of diverse learners. Even as some teachers may be directive and others less directive or nondirective, so there are some students who demand detailed, step-by-step, precise, and definite directions; that is their learning style. Likewise, there are some students who prefer to make more decisions for themselves, and they need very general directions, preferring to fill in the details for themselves. For example, the teacher may tell the class, "I want you to write a five-paragraph theme about anything you choose." Some students will pick up their pens and begin to write. Other students may ask, "What should we write about?" Those students would benefit by the teacher simply saying, "If I were you, I might write about ..." and providing some suggestions.

DIRECTIONS

Every teacher knows that some students are more easily motivated than others. Some students receive directions and they busily get to work. Other students resist. Some students ask, "Why are we doing this?" Such a question should not be thought impertinent or obstreperous. Students who ask this question really need to know why. Unless they can see some personal benefit or reasonable justification for the activity, they will resist. Taking the time to explain the nature of the activity and just why it is important and what it will lead to next is well worth the investment when it comes to the dividend of seeing a motivated student perform at his or her best.

Some studies suggest that analytic, left-brain students need step-by-step, sequential directions. They need to begin at the beginning, proceed methodically, step by step through the information, and finally derive the conclusion. On the other hand, global, right-brain learners need to hear the conclusion first; they need to know the goal or outcome before they begin. Instead of progressing step-by-step, global learners work in random, sporadic patterns; analytic types might even call it haphazard. However, the nonlinear approach works for global learners.

An effective teacher will attempt to accommodate the needs of all students in class. This is one reason effective teachers give verbal announcements, send home written reminders, put signs on the wall and in the hall, write messages on the board, and direct students to take notes. The more ways the teacher can find to communicate the information, the more likely the message will get through.

Sometimes the teacher is most effective when starting directions by saying, "This is what we are going to do today in order to ..." and then telling what the objective of the learning activity is. This will satisfy the needs of the global learners. Then, the teacher can say, "Now the way we are going to do this is, first, ..." and then give the steps, one by one. This way the teacher can address the needs of the sequential learners. Teachers who are aware of preferences in teaching and learning styles can give more successful directions.

OBJECTIVES

In addition to giving students general directions and specific instructions about academic tasks and instructional activities, teachers need to announce and explain objectives. Teachers also need to announce all formal tests or assessments, giving students and their parents complete and accurate information.

The more information a teacher can provide about a test, the better the student can prepare for and perform on the test. Teachers need to tell students when they will have to take the test. Just announcing the test topic or the chapters to be covered on the test is insufficient. Teachers need to thoroughly describe the test: How many questions will be on the test, how much time will students have to answer the questions, what kind of questions—multiple-choice, fill-in-the-blank, true or false, matching, or essay? All of these questions should be answered so that conscientious students can adequately prepare for each test. The point value of each question or of each section of the test should be made clear.

To help those students who may be more sensitive or prone to test anxiety, the teacher should also be careful in making speculative or prejudicial comments about tests. The teacher who says, "Oh, this test is really going to be hard," may cause come students to panic and suffer increased anxiety about their test performance.

When teaching a lesson, an effective teacher gives clear, complete, and concise instructions, making certain that students understand why they are doing the lesson (the objectives). When preparing students for a test, an effective teacher provides complete and thorough details concerning the test, making sure that students have had an opportunity to acquire the skills or knowledge the test will measure.

PERFORMANCE STANDARDS

In addition, effective teachers describe performance standards so that there is no mystery about what a student must do in order to be successful. Performance standards are the criteria against which success is measured. For example, if grades are awarded, what makes a paper an "A" paper versus a "B" paper or a "C" paper? What must a student do in order to score 95 percent on the test versus 75 percent? Students should know what constitutes above-average, average, and below-average performance. Criteria should be discussed and explained. The value of every assignment should be discussed at the time it is assigned. At the beginning of the academic year, teachers should thoroughly explain the grading scale.

Students should also have opportunities to learn about their performance and how their performance compares to the established standards. They should be provided with information to help them improve their performance. Students need to know what it is that they must do in order to demonstrate proficiency. Teachers of younger children need to take special care to communicate objectives, assessment information, and information about performance standards to parents who often are eager to work with their children to help them achieve school success.

SUPPLIES

Informing students about the materials needed for learning and how to use those materials is also an important part of teaching. At the beginning of the school year, teachers and school districts should provide students and their parents with a list of the routine materials that will be needed: pencils, pens, notebook paper, notebooks, crayons, scissors, and so forth.

If the teacher needs to bring special materials to class, he or she will probably find it helpful to include a list of materials needed on the lesson plan. If students need special materials, in addition to their routine school supplies, the teacher should give them a list to take home to give their parents or send a message to the parents.

Students usually have a great deal on their minds, so they need frequent reminders to bring special supplies to class. If students need a dictionary in order to complete the day's lesson, they must know in advance to bring their dictionaries or they will end up wasting a day of precious instruction and time on task.

When a student uses a tool for the first time (the dictionary, for example), the teacher should spend time carefully introducing the tool and explaining its use. With the dictionary, the effective teacher will talk about how the dictionary is organized (alphabetical order), its standard features (pronunciation keys, etymologies, definitions, sentence examples), and special features (appendices with biographies, geographical information, tables, and so forth).

Most experienced teachers have learned firsthand the costs of assumptions. A teacher should not assume that a student knows how to use a calculator or computer or even a ruler. The teacher, paying attention to details to meet the special needs of all students in the class, should carefully explain whatever tools or materials will be used.

CLASSROOM ASSESSMENT

Teachers spend a great deal of their time explaining and giving directions. To some, that seems to be what teaching is all about. But, despite all the effort that teachers expend and all the expertise they develop in explaining and instructing, some students ignore instructions. Some experts even suggest that some students' learning styles intentionally skip the directions or avoid instructions. For these reasons, teachers must check to make sure that students do understand the directions and are, in fact, following instructions.

"Does everyone understand? Are there any questions?" are probably two of the most misused and unproductive questions that teachers ask. Seldom does the student who doesn't understand ask a question. There are better ways to check comprehension.

The teacher can give the students a chance to get started on the work and then check each student's progress. Sometimes a teacher may want to call on a student to ask a specific question or to "say back" an important piece of information.

Angelo and Cross, authors of *Classroom Assessment Techniques*, recommend classroom assessment techniques as being most effective at checking comprehension. They further recommend that classroom assessment can a) increase students' active involvement in learning; b) promote students' metacognitive development; c) foster student cooperation and a sense of community in the classroom; d) increase student satisfaction with learning; and e) may even improve students' performance.

A simple classroom assessment technique is to ask students to write a summary of the information or instructions given. The teacher can then quickly read the summaries to determine if there have been misunderstandings or incomplete understanding.

The teacher could give the students a feedback form, asking the students questions about the test they took (Did you think it was a fair test? Did you enjoy one part more than another? What kind of test do you prefer? Why?) or a reading they have completed (How well did you read this? How useful was this reading assignment in helping you understand the topic? How well did you understand the reading?). Asking students to do something (write or talk or draw) to demonstrate that they have understood instructions is a much more effective method of checking comprehension than simply asking what has become to many students (and maybe even some teachers) nothing more than a rhetorical question, "Do you understand?"

The following references were used to write Competency 18. Further reading of these references may enhance understanding of the competency and may also increase performance on the examination.

Angelo, T. A. and K. P. Cross. *Classroom Assessment Techniques*. San Francisco: Jossey Bass, 1993.

Dunn, R. Presentation on Using Learning Styles Information to Enhance Teaching Effectiveness at Learning Styles Institute, Lubbock, Texas, June 5-9, 1993.

Lawrence, G. *People Types and Tiger Stripes*. Gainesville, Florida: Center for Applications of Psychological Type, 1993.

Silver, H. F. and J. R. Hanson. *Learning Styles and Strategies*. Princeton, New Jersey: The Thoughtful Educational Press, 1980.

FTCE

Florida Teacher Certification Exam—
Professional Education Test

Chapter 20
Competency 19

Chapter 20

COMPETENCY 19

DEFINITION OF COMPETENCY

A teacher stimulates and guides student thinking, and verifies student comprehension through suitable questioning techniques.

QUESTIONING

There are many ways that teachers can ask questions that elicit different levels of thinking, although studies of teachers' skills in questioning often reveal frequent use of lower-level questions and infrequent use of higher-level ones.

A simple method is to divide questions into two types, closed and open. An example of a closed question is, "What was the main character's name?" There is usually only one right answer to a closed question. Often students can point to a phrase or sentence in a book to answer a closed question.

An open-ended question requires students to think carefully about the answer. There may be more than one appropriate answer to an open-ended question. An example is, "What do you think was the most important contribution of Pascal to the field of mathematics?" Teachers who ask open-ended questions are not looking for one specific answer, rather they are looking for well-supported responses. Asking an open-ended question but requiring one specific answer will discourage rather than encourage thinking.

An example of a closed math question is, "What is 5×5?" An example of an open-ended math question is, "What is the best way to solve this problem?" The open-ended question assumes that the teacher will accept all reasonable methods of solving the problem, provided the students can explain why their method is best.

There are other ways to categorize questions. Benjamin Bloom, et al., developed a taxonomy of educational objectives for the cognitive domain. Teachers have used this taxonomy for a variety of purposes in addition to writing objectives, including categorizing questions and activities.

THE SIX LEVELS OF TAXONOMY

There are six levels in the taxonomy, each one building on the previous level. The first level is knowledge. This is similar to the closed question, with one right answer which should be obvious to students who have read or studied. Words which often elicit recall or memory answers include who, what, when, and where. Examples of knowledge-level questions include: Who developed the first microscope? What were the names of Columbus' ships? When was South Carolina first settled? Where is Tokyo?

The next level is comprehension, which also elicits lower-level thinking and answers. The primary difference from the first level is that students must show that they understand a concept, perhaps by explaining in their own words. The question "What does obfuscate mean?" would be answered on a knowledge level if students repeat a memorized definition from the dictionary and on a comprehension level if students explain the term in their own words.

The first higher-level category is application. Students take what they've learned and use this knowledge in a different way or in a different situation. A simple example of this level is using mathematics operations —add, subtract, multiply, and divide—to solve problems. Another example is translating an English sentence into Spanish, or applying what the students have learned about Spanish vocabulary and grammar to develop an appropriate and correct response. Another form of application is changing the format of information, e.g., create a graph from a narrative description of a survey. The key to this level is the use or application of knowledge and skills in a similar but new situation.

The next level is analysis, which involves taking something apart, looking at all the pieces, and then making a response. An example of an analytical question is, "How are these two characters alike and how are they different?" This question requires students to examine facts and characteristics of each individual, then put the information together in an understandable comparison. Another example is, "What are the advantages and disadvantages of each of these two proposals?" Another example might be, "Compare the wolves in *The Three Little Pigs* and *Little Red Riding Hood.*"

The next level is synthesis, which involves putting information together in a new, creative way. Developing a new way of solving problems, writing a short story, and designing an experiment are all creative ways of synthesizing knowledge. For example, fourth-grade science students may develop and conduct research on food waste in the cafeteria and make recommendations for changes. An example of a synthesis question is, "What do you predict will happen if we combine these two chemicals?" This question assumes students will have factual knowledge. Their predictions must be reasonable and based on prior reading and/or discussion.

The highest level is evaluation. This level involves making value judgments and very often involves the question "Why?" or a request to "Justify your answer." For example, students may be asked to use their analysis of two possible solutions to a problem to determine which is the better solution. Their response must be reasonable and well supported.

Evaluation-level activities must build on previous levels. Skipping from knowledge-level to evaluation-level questions will result in ill-conceived and poorly supported responses. Although teachers might use an evaluation question to provoke interest in a topic, they should make sure that students have opportunities to work at other levels as they develop their responses.

This type of questioning promotes risk-taking and problem-solving, where the teacher has established a safe environment where students are encouraged and not ridiculed for creative or unusual responses. The teacher does not expect only one specific answer, but allows students to ponder several reasonable possibilities.

Effective teachers also appreciate cultural dimensions of communication and are aware that some cultures teach their children not to question adults. These teachers explain to students that they expect questions, encourage students to ask them, but do not force the issue if students are very uncomfortable. Sometimes students may be willing to write down and turn in questions for the teacher. Teacher attitude can promote or deter questions, even by so simple a tactic as changing, "Does anybody have any questions?" to "What questions do you have?" The first question implies that no one should have questions; the second assumes that there will be questions.

FTCE

Florida Teacher Certification Exam—
Professional Education Test

Chapter 21
Competency 20

Chapter 21

COMPETENCY 20

DEFINITION OF COMPETENCY

The teacher provides appropriate practice to promote learning and retention.

It is obvious that in virtually any human activity we learn by practice. Whether we are trying to learn to play tennis or to speak a second language, we quickly realize how much we need to practice in order to make progress in the new skill. And yet, it is sometimes easy for teachers to neglect the importance of practice because they themselves are so familiar with the material they teach. It is so clear and plain to them that they forget what is was like to learn it as new and different. However, it became clear and plain only through long familiarity and practice.

Students need not only to understand a lesson; they need practice in using and applying their new knowledge. A child may "learn" one day that $4 \times 25 = 100$, but may not fully master that knowledge until he or she has several times given or received four quarters for a dollar. He or she may learn that valiant means brave, but the child may not remember the meaning or use the word until he or she has seen or heard it used many times.

The practice a teacher provides must be appropriate—that is, it must promote the objective established by the teacher or the prescribed curriculum. For example, if the objective is for students to be able to locate specific states on a map of the United States, practice in spelling the names of the states is inappropriate for that particular objective. The student must have practice in trying to do the very thing that is expected. To take another example, if the objective is to enable students to carry on simple conversations in Spanish, they must practice listening to and speaking Spanish; practice in reading Spanish would not be appropriate for that objective.

VARY PRACTICE ACTIVITIES

Numerous studies have shown that variety in teaching methods and styles promotes student achievement and helps maintain attention.

The nature of practice activities, therefore, should be varied. At one time, the teacher may have the students respond in unison; at another time, the teacher may have students work in pairs, where they ask one another questions; still another time, he or she may call on individuals or have all the students do written exercises at their seats.

Perhaps the most common of all practice activities is recitation, whereby the teacher poses questions to the class and calls on individuals to answer. Once a pupil has answered, the teacher responds to the answer and either calls on another pupil in the event that the question has been answered incorrectly, or goes on to another question if the student's answer is correct.

There are, however, many alternatives to recitation that teachers can and should use:

- demonstrations by the teacher of a student,
- oral reports,
- slides,
- movies,
- television,
- radio, and
- recordings.

Small group activities, such as the following, can all help provide practice in newly learned material:

- debates,
- role-playing sessions,
- panel discussions,
- project construction, and
- discussions of test answers.

The duration of practice should be varied according to the difficulty of the material. Grammatical concepts of subject-verb-object may need considerable repetition and practice exercises, while the concept of size (large/small) may need only brief practice before it is mastered.

The duration of practice should vary also according to the ability of the learner. Some students will catch on right away to the idea of subject-verb-object; others will need considerable practice with it. Teachers need to determine which students are "getting it" quickly and which ones need to spend more time learning the material so that they grasp it fully. This may mean that the teacher gives most of the class a new activity while he or she works individually or in small groups with those who require help and practice.

One of the teacher's weightiest responsibilities is to pay close attention to the progress of individual students, providing more practice for those who have not yet mastered the material and introducing new or related challenges to those who have mastered it.

REINFORCE RETENTION OF SPECIFIC INFORMATION

A geography teacher is trying to help his/her students learn the names and locations of the major regions and countries in Africa. He or she can ask the students individually to come up to the map and point to Egypt or South Africa. The teacher can also ask individuals to name the country or the region to which he/she points. Or, the teacher can have the whole class call out the names of the countries and regions as he/she points to them in turn. If the teacher uses a variety of these methods, he/she is more likely to keep students' attention longer, and hence increase the learning that takes place in that session.

Varying the method is important for another reason—each method has its own benefits. Individual student responses give the spotlight to particular students, increasing their involvement in the class and developing their ability and comfort in speaking in a group. Group response ensures that everyone is involved. Of course, the teacher should watch for the student who is not responding and encourage him or her to participate.

In calling on and responding to individual students in class, teachers must be especially mindful of personal biases to which everyone is susceptible. Do you tend to call on boys more than girls, or vice versa? Do you tend to call only on those who raise their hands? Should you ignore "call-outs"? The last question has no easy answer. If a student who is usually nonparticipatory calls out an answer on one occasion, it may be better to reward that student's willingness to participate by acknowledging the response. On the other hand, if a student frequently calls out without raising his/her hand, it is probably better to ignore the response until the student raises his/her hand and waits to be recognized.

PROVIDE A VARIETY OF ACTIVITIES TO PROMOTE RETENTION

Repetition is the mother of learning. Unfortunately, it can also be the father of boredom. To prevent practice exercises from becoming monotonous and unproductive, the teacher needs to vary the kinds of repetitive practice.

If, for example, students are to learn 20 new vocabulary words, the teacher may use some or all of the following practice activities:

- fill in the blanks in sentences with the appropriate vocabulary words,

- create your own sentences using the vocabulary words,

- match the vocabulary words to synonyms or antonyms,

- match the vocabulary words to definitions,

- find the vocabulary words in a word-search puzzle,

- complete a crossword puzzle whose answers are the vocabulary words, and

- write a brief story of speech using the vocabulary words.

To practice material that has been explained by the teacher and discussed in class, students can work in pairs or small groups, asking questions of one another. In foreign language classes, for example, students can practice simple conversations in pairs, using newly learned words and phrases.

In mathematics classes, practice need not be limited to homework assignments of number problems and word problems. If, for example, students are learning to add fractions, they might be asked to make up their own word problems using real-life situations, exchanging problems with their classmates, and solving one another's problems. Such an activity not only gives the students practice in adding fractions, it also engages their imaginations since they have to think about situations in their own lives where fractions are used and need to be added.

ASSIST STUDENTS DURING SEATWORK

One common and potentially effective way to give students practice in the material is to assign them seatwork—reading, writing, or some other individual activity done by the student at his or her desk. It is estimated that elementary school students spend 300-400 hours a year doing seatwork in language arts alone. It is obviously important, then, that seatwork be well designed and appropriate to the learning goal and the learner, and that the teacher explain clearly:

- what is to be done,

- how to do it, and

- what the student should learn from doing it.

Unfortunately, many teachers neglect the last two instructions, telling the students only what they are to do.

With seatwork, the teacher's job is to make sure that individual students are

- staying on task,

- understanding what they are doing (not just going through the motions), and

- receiving help when they need it.

The teacher should be especially watchful for low achievers who often do poorly on seatwork assignments, answering questions without really understanding the material. For example, a student may perform arithmetical operations with the numbers in word problems without having any idea what particular operation (addition, subtraction, multiplication, or division) is called for.

The teacher can prevent children from wasting time by carefully overseeing what they are doing in their workbooks or on their activity sheets. Also, since these practice materials often fail to require higher levels of comprehension, such as reasoning and drawing conclusions, the teacher would be well advised to use them sparingly.

For seatwork, some good alternatives to workbooks and worksheets are the following:

- silent reading,

- answering open-ended questions,

- writing an alternate ending to a story, and

- writing an ending for another student's story.

Sometimes it is good to have students work together on seatwork. You may want to have them debate an issue in a story, compare endings that they have written, and so forth.

PRACTICE ACTIVITIES PROMOTE LONG-TERM RETENTION

One way to vary practice exercises is to alternate between massed and distributed activities. A massed activity is a single activity done by the whole class; a distributed activity is one that is divided into a number of parts, each part assigned to a different group or individual.

Let us suppose, for example, that you have been teaching your class about the elements of a story: plot, character, setting, theme, conflict, and so on. You could have the whole class first do a massed activity—all pupils write out in their own words what is meant by plot, character, setting, etc. Once they have done that, you could have them do a distributed activity by dividing the class into as many groups as there are elements of a story. Each group would be assigned a story element and would describe that element in a story they have recently read. Group A would describe the plot of the story, Group B would name and describe the main characters, and so forth.

Once all the groups have completed their work, a spokesperson for each group could read to the whole class the description that group wrote. This last activity would combine massed and distributed activities: the whole class is listening, but each group is reporting on a different story element.

The combination of massed and distributed activities promotes long-term retention through repetition (several activities all about the elements of a story) and variation (individual, small-group, and whole-class activities). The teacher who limits him- or herself to either massed or distributed activities is less likely to achieve the same degree of understanding and retention as the teacher who avails him- or herself of both methods.

FTCE

*Florida Teacher Certification Exam—
Professional Education Test*

Chapter 22
Competency 21

Chapter 22

COMPETENCY 21

DEFINITION OF COMPETENCY

A teacher relates to his or her students' verbal communications in a manner that promotes students' participation and is still able to retain academic focus.

EFFECTIVE USE OF LANGUAGE

Effective use of language is one of the major components of learning in classrooms. New visual aids and technology have broadened the range of possibilities for instruction, but without words and their proper use the potential for learning is severely limited. Discourse has many dimensions including verbal, non-verbal, and paralingual features. The verbal part of discourse contains the content; the non-verbal includes body language, posture, facial expressions, etc.; and the paralingual features are found in the choices of words, inflections, and subtleties of speech that portray characteristics of speakers, such as arrogance or humility. All three components communicate to students and contribute to the total message that is received.

RELATIONSHIP BETWEEN TEACHERS AND STUDENTS

Underlying the discourse that occurs in classrooms is the relationship between the teacher and students. The best relationship is one that creates a trusting confidence in each other and an environment in which opinions, information, and dialogue can be exchanged in a non-threatening classroom setting. Productive relationships with students can be built by recognizing that interactions occur within three different schemata: open relationships, closed relationships, and transitional relationships. Open relationships emerge when both participants are honest, accepting, tactful, emphatic, and active listeners. Closed relationships develop when neither participant engages in discourse that can be trusted because it is dishonest, secretive, or tactless. Transitional relationships exist when one participant is open and the other is not. Transitional relationships may become open or closed depending on how each reacts to the other over time. The teacher who behaves toward his or her students as a person does in an open relationship has the potential to establish a classroom in which honesty, trust, acceptance, empathy, and active listening become the norm. It is in such a classroom that learning through effective two-way communication is most likely to occur. Thus, the behavior of the teacher can promote the atmosphere that is most conducive to a healthy learning environment for students. If the teacher does not verbalize openly and effectively, it is not possible for the students and teacher to establish the open relationship that will be most effective in the promotion of learning. In addition to a healthy psychological classroom climate, there are technical aspects of communication that make a significant difference in learning. These aspects will be addressed next.

Knowledge about, and application of, communication principals enable a teacher to engage in successful classroom interactions with students. Successful interactions occur when learning is optimized through a partnership in learning with students. It is this positive environment that provides the best hope for teachers to a) show acceptance and value of student responses; and b) ignore or redirect digressions without devaluing student responses.

FEEDBACK

When teachers respond to student responses, they are providing feedback. Feedback can embody various dimensions, and the following four possibilities provide a framework in which teacher responses can be classified. These four types of responses are defined by recognizing that feedback may be positive or negative and it may also be responsible or irresponsible. Thus feedback may be:

I.   Positive and responsible

II.   Negative and responsible

III.   Positive and irresponsible

IV.   Negative and irresponsible

These four categories help clarify how the teacher can show acceptance of and value for student response, and also how to redirect digressions. Responses in Category I include praise for acceptable student comments which should be provided specifically, immediately, and sincerely. Responses in Category II include teacher comments that correct student errors, describe faulty logic or misinformation, and other student errors that might occur in classroom discussions. Teacher criticism in Category II should be given tactfully and be the basis for improving student learning. Category III responses are exemplified by the teacher who tolerates student errors and even gives praise for sub-standard comments by lowering standards or allowing inaccurate responses to stand without correction. Category IV responses are negative reactions by teachers to students and are delivered in a harsh and derogatory manner. Sarcasm and insults are included in Category IV responses. The two types of responsible categories (I and II) will support student responses that are acceptable and also maintain reasonable standards by correcting student responses that are not acceptable. The teacher who accepts student comments and values their remarks uses language that is responsible and maintains a relationship in which tolerance for positive and negative remarks is based on optimal student learning and mutual respect. The two types of irresponsible categories (III and IV) will either sugarcoat wrong answers and lower standards listed above, or create tension and hostility by using tactless sarcasm or insults to criticize student work. The teacher who fails to correct student errors by accepting sub-standard student responses dilutes the quality of learning and risks the loss of respect from students and colleagues who recognize such behavior. The teacher who corrects with sarcasm, or other demeaning behavior, creates tension and fear in students. A tense classroom atmosphere will reduce student cooperation, ingenuity, creativity, and the quality of classroom discussions.

DIGRESSIONS

One of the difficult challenges teachers face is how to ignore or redirect digressions without devaluing student responses. The best approach to this problem is to make preparations that eliminate or minimize this behavior. The teacher behaviors that promote student attentiveness and reduce digressions include a) connected discourse; b) single questions; c) marker expressions and techniques; d) emphasis; e) task attraction and challenge. Teacher behaviors that do not promote student attentiveness include a) scrambled discourse; b) vagueness; and c) question overload.

CONNECTED DISCOURSE

Connected discourse is discussion based on a given topic or theme, in which the information that is exchanged leads to one or more conclusions or major points. The teacher's role includes clarification of the theme or topic to make certain students know the central focus of the discussion. It is also necessary to structure questions and activities that will enable the class to reach closure on the topic under consideration.

Single questions avoid question overload, give focus for student responses, and provide students with an unambiguous task. Single questions can either stimulate higher order thinking or ask for simple recall, but when they are properly stated they are not confusing. Complex topics can be broken into smaller parts through the use of single questioning, and can be developed gradually, which will ensure that the topic will be understood better; it is best to avoid trying to do too much at once.

MARKER EXPRESSIONS

Marker expressions are the equivalent of italics, underlining, or color marking passages in written documents. They are points of emphasis the teacher uses to help students focus on or retain the most salient information in a discussion. They can be used to give appropriate praise to students by linking a previous remark by a particular student to the emphasis at that time. For example, "You remember that yesterday John noticed how the presence of a river was a factor in the location of cities. Today, we see another example of that factor in the establishment of St. Louis."

Emphasis is a technique to help students identify and retain significant information. Teachers can prepare students for essential topics by stating, "This next topic is crucial; I want you to work extra hard at it. Ask questions about anything you do not understand." Other forms of emphasis include repetition, summarizing, and application of the knowledge. All of these methods should be utilized by actively engaging students in classroom activities.

TASK ATTRACTION AND CHALLENGE

Task attraction and challenge are methods to motivate students, and they include teacher enthusiasm for the task at hand. Teachers engage in this behavior by showing their own excitement for the learning that is about to take place. Often, teachers can alert students to the difficulty of a task and challenge them by saying that something will be hard for them to do. When properly presented, a challenge becomes the motivation for students to prove their ability.

SCRAMBLED DISCOURSE, VAGUENESS, AND QUESTION OVERLOAD

Scrambled discourse, vagueness, and question overload are teacher behaviors that make if difficult for students to stay on task. Scrambled discourse is disconnected to the theme or topic under discussion and often includes garbled verbal behavior. Vagueness is evident by the excessive use of indeterminate language (e.g. something, a little, some, much, few, things, you see, perhaps, or actually). Question overload causes confusion because multiple questions or long and involved questions are asked and the student is uncertain about what is expected.

SUMMARY

Effective teachers establish an open and trusting atmosphere that supports interaction with students. Praise is provided immediately and specifically when warranted and constructive criticism promotes learning. Teachers help students achieve by using connected discourse, single questions, marker expressions and techniques, emphasis, and task attraction and challenge.

FTCE

Florida Teacher Certification Exam—
Professional Education Test

Chapter 23
Competency 22

Chapter 23

COMPETENCY 22

DEFINITION OF COMPETENCY

The teacher uses feedback procedures that give information to students about the appropriateness of their responses.

PROVIDE CLEAR FEEDBACK TO STUDENTS

One of a teacher's important functions is to respond clearly to student responses so that the student knows whether a response was correct or incorrect. In order to advance in learning the subject matter, the student requires clear guidance from the authority, the teacher. If the teacher's response is ambiguous or fuzzy, the student may be left confused, or even worse, in error.

Of course, not every question to which students respond in class has a clearly right or wrong answer. Many times, students will be asked, and should be asked, to express their judgments, opinions, values, and conclusions on topics that have many valid perspectives.

Nevertheless, teachers must frequently test, both orally and in writing, their students' knowledge of facts, objective knowledge that leaves little room for judgments or opinions. In doing so, teachers should leave no doubt in the student's mind whether his or her response was right or wrong.

It is through classroom recitations and discussions that the teacher most often responds directly to a student's answer. Here is one example of a question/student answer/teacher response sequence in which the teacher gives clear, unequivocal feedback to the student (and to the rest of the class):

Ms. Jackson:	Who was the first president of the United States? Shannon?
Shannon:	Benjamin Franklin?
Ms. Jackson:	No, Benjamin Franklin was an important leader but he never became president. Lindsey? Who was our first president?
Lindsey:	George Washington.
Ms. Jackson:	That's right. George Washington was the first president of the United States.

Notice that Ms. Jackson gives a clear "no" to Shannon's answer, while at the same time reminding the class that Benjamin Franklin *is* an important figure in United States history.

Notice also that when the correct answer is given, the teacher repeats the correct answer to the entire class. This repetition helps pupils learn the name of the first president and ensures that anyone in the class who did not hear Lindsey's response now hears the correct answer.

Although the teacher's response in the above example may seem so natural and obvious that it should need no commentary, even experienced teachers might sometimes handle their response less effectively than Ms. Jackson did.

Consider the following question/student answer/teacher response sequence that begins with the same question as in the sequence above:

Mr. Lopez:	Who was the first president of the United States? Roberto?
Roberto:	Abraham Lincoln.
Mr. Lopez:	Well, that's an interesting answer, Roberto. Many people do think that Abraham Lincoln was the greatest president we have ever had, and so in that sense he is sometimes considered "Number 1." But was he the very first president chronologically, timewise? Stacey?
Stacey:	George Washington was the first president.
Mr. Lopez:	So, in a sense, both Roberto and Stacey could be right. Lincoln and Washington were both great presidents. Some people think that Lincoln was the greatest; others say Washington was the greatest. But Washington was the first, at least in order of time.

Here Mr. Lopez, perhaps wishing to avoid embarrassing Roberto by saying flatly that his answer is wrong, fails to give a clear-cut, unambiguous response to an answer that is clearly wrong. Instead, he needlessly complicates the question by allowing a different meaning to the word "first"—a meaning which, most likely, neither Roberto nor anyone else in the class had entertained. What had been a simple question requiring a simple answer has become somewhat confusing. The idea of greatness—a matter of judgment—has been introduced into a matter of historical fact.

If Mr. Lopez wishes to lead the discussion in the direction of the relative greatness of presidents, he should settle clearly and decisively the question he first raised: George Washington was the first president. Once that is made clear to everyone, he could go on to take up the question of greatness.

Notice that even at the end of the exchange Mr. Lopez still does not say unequivocally that Stacey was correct when she answered that George Washington was the first president. Instead, he qualifies his statement with the phrase "at least in order of time," a qualification likely to leave some doubt or perplexity in the minds of some of this pupils.

In considering a fact so familiar to adult Americans—that George Washington was the first president—it is good for teachers, especially teachers of the lower elementary grades, to keep in mind that many such facts may *not* be familiar and obvious to some pupils. The teacher's responsibility is to communicate such information clearly and unambiguously, as Ms. Jackson did. The teacher should not unnecessarily confuse a child, as Mr. Lopez did, by introducing a sophisticated interpretation of his own question.

Another area in which it is crucial to give clear, unambiguous feedback to the student is in making written marks and comments on papers and tests. Before returning a set of papers or tests to the class, the teacher should explain clearly any features of his or her marking system that may not be self-evident. For example, the teacher should explain that a circle around a word indicates that the word is misspelled, or that a curlicue through a word or punctuation mark means that it should be deleted.

In marking objective items on a test, the teacher should clearly indicate (with an X, for example) that an answer is wrong. If the teacher puts a question mark beside an answer, the student will be left in doubt as to what the question mark means. Does it mean that the answer is possibly correct but the teacher him- or herself is unsure? Does it mean that the answer is illegible? If so, is it wrong, or does the student have the opportunity of explaining to the teacher what was written? Some students will ask a teacher for clarification of a question mark, but others are more likely to ignore what they do not understand, and so they will learn nothing from their response or from the teacher's question mark.

When an objective answer on a test is wrong, or a word is misspelled or inappropriate, should the teacher write on the paper the correct answer or word? One's answer to this question may vary according to the grade level, the subject matter, and the individual student. In teaching the early elementary grades, it is especially important that the child be given the correct answer so that he or she would be able to compare that with his or her own answer. In later years, the teacher can shift more responsibility to the child to find out and write down the correct answers. The teacher can review the correct answers orally with the whole class and instruct the students to correct their errors. If the subject matter is relatively easy and the student can readily find the right answer or spelling in a book, then it may be best to let him or her do so. If the matter is difficult, however, and the student is unlikely to discover the correct answer without great effort, then it might be best to provide it for him or her.

MAKE SPECIFIC STATEMENTS ABOUT STUDENTS' RESPONSES

While it is crucial for the teacher to indicate clearly whether a response is correct or incorrect, it is also important to encourage students' participation by praising them for intelligent, reasonable answers. In the previous section, Mr. Lopez erred by not indicating clearly that Roberto's answer was incorrect. We may assume, however, that he erred with a noble motive—the wish to find some merit in his student's response and so to reward the student for his effort. The fact that he did so in an instance where the student's answer was clearly incorrect shows that it is not always possible or appropriate to find something praiseworthy in a student's response—beyond the mere fact that the student did give a serious, pertinent response.

Very frequently, however, teachers rightly pose questions that have no clearly correct or incorrect answers. They ask questions that require students to make value judgments, see implications, interpret events, both fictional and historical, express aesthetic preferences, and estimate probabilities.

In such cases, it is not only possible but highly desirable for the teacher to point out to the responding student and to the rest of the class the merits of the response. To do so is much more difficult than simply indicating that a response is correct or incorrect. It requires the teacher to listen carefully to the student's response, to ask for clarification if necessary, and to see quickly what it is about the response that deserves notice and praise.

The following example of a classroom exchange illustrates this principle. Mr. Pizzo's eighth-grade geography class is discussing the reasons why cities and towns are often founded on the banks of rivers.

Mr. Pizzo: Why do you suppose that Cairo and Rome and London and Paris were all founded on major rivers? Jeffrey?

Jeffrey: Because the people needed to fish to eat?

Mr. Pizzo: Yes, good, that's true—the ready availability of food sources was certainly a prime consideration to early societies. But are fish the only benefit of rivers? What else do rivers offer people? Ilsa?

Ilsa: Transportation? Didn't they need to get up and down the rivers and out to the oceans?

Mr. Pizzo: They certainly did. To trade with faraway places it was a great advantage to be located on a navigable river. Can anyone think of another benefit?

Here Mr. Pizzo responds well to Jeffrey's answer by telling why it is partially correct. Even though Mr. Pizzo was not "looking for" this answer, he recognizes its validity. If an answer is unexpected but at least partially correct, the teacher should give the student credit for it. If the teacher had said, "Well, that's not what I was thinking of," students might get the impression that responding to questions in class is just a matter of trying to guess what is in the teacher's mind.

While recognizing the worth of Jeffrey's answer, though, Mr. Pizzo also moves beyond it by asking for further, probably more important reasons for river settlements. By doing so, he keeps the discussion going and keeps the students trying to think of reasons why so many large cities were founded on rivers.

METHODS OF CORRECTING STUDENTS' ERRORS

As mentioned earlier, a student's progress in learning depends in part on the effectiveness of the teacher's response to the student's error. The teacher should have a repertoire of effective ways to respond to errors and be able to select the most appropriate response for a given situation. Four productive ways of responding are to:

- simply give the correction,

- explain the error,

- provide the student with information to enable him/her to correct the error, and

- ask the student questions to enable him/her to correct the error.

Simply Give the Correction

Under what circumstances might it be best simply to correct the student? In classroom discussions or question-and-answer sessions, it is often preferable to provide a correction in a matter of fact way when the error is simple (e.g., grammar, pronunciation, word choice). In such cases, to provide explanations or ask questions in order to elicit the correction would unnecessarily slow the momentum of discussion and distract the class from the issue at hand. If the teacher provides the correction simply and quickly, the student and the rest of the class are made aware of the right response without losing the thread of the conversation.

Consider the following situation, for example. In a history class, you are discussing the concept of laissez-faire capitalism, and one of the students mispronounces "laissez" as "layzees." It is much more efficient and less distracting from the topic simply to say the word correctly than to explain to him that "laissez" is a French word and that in "ez" endings the "z" is not pronounced. Asking the student whether he/she is sure he/she is pronouncing that correctly and whether he/she would like to reconsider the pronunciation would embarrass the student and derail the conversation.

In responding to students' papers, too, it is sometimes preferable to write in a correction rather than merely to point out that something is amiss in what the student has written. If you judge that the student will not be able to understand the nature of the error and will not be able to correct it on his own, then it is better to write in the correction. For example, a student writes in a paper the words "embarrassed of her braces." If the teacher were only to underline or circle the word "of," the student would probably be unable to detect what is wrong with that word. It is a matter of idiom that we say "embarrassed by" rather than "embarrassed of," and since the student has the idiom wrong, the child is unlikely to provide the correction. It is more efficient and effective for the teacher to underline or cross out "of" and write "by" above it or in the margin.

Explain the Error

Sometimes, though, it is not enough for the teacher to correct an error; he/she should provide an explanation of the error. It is especially important to do so in situations where the error occurs in the very matter that is being taught at the time. In such cases, a mere correction might not help the students understand why the given response was incorrect.

Imagine the following situation. Mr. Bielski is teaching his class how to convert improper fractions to mixed numbers. After explaining that one divides the numerator by the denominator, which results in a whole number and a fraction whose numerator is the remainder of the division operation, he gives some examples. Then, he asks the class to change the improper fraction $\frac{7}{3}$ to a mixed number. After a moment, one student offers the answer $4\frac{1}{3}$. Instead of just dismissing the answer as wrong, Mr. Bielski sees that the student, instead of dividing the numerator by the denominator, has subtracted the denominator from the numerator, resulting in the number 4. Mr. Bielski explains what the student has done and repeats his explanation of the correct procedure.

In writing comments on students' written work, it is sometimes necessary to explain an error or inadequacy so that the student will understand why the teacher has marked the paper. Because explanations can be very time consuming, teachers often use a system of abbreviations. An English teacher, for example, may use marginal abbreviations such as *agr* for subject-verb agreement, *frag* for sentence fragment, and so on. In doing so, the teacher must make sure, however, that all students understand the abbreviations and the principles they represent.

Provide the Student with Information

Rather than telling the student why a response is wrong, it is sometimes better to lead the student to the correct response. This technique has the advantages of prompting the student to think through the problem and of boosting his or her confidence when the student arrives at the right answer on his or her own. The only drawback is that it can be time consuming, and to use it too frequently might unduly slow the pace of the class.

Imagine that you are teaching a unit on the American civil rights movement in the 1950s and 1960s. You have just asked the class what the leaders of the movement were protesting for or against, and one student answers, "Better jobs." While this answer may be partly correct, you want the class to understand that black Americans were motivated by many more grievances than the quality of jobs. Instead of providing the further answer of "segregation in the schools, public restaurants and restrooms, and the right to vote," you might lead the student toward the answer by reminding him/her that in the 1950s and early 1960s, blacks were denied some of the social and political freedoms they enjoy today.

Ask the Student Questions

This is called the Socratic method, for Socrates practices it frequently in Plato's *Dialogues* to lead his pupils toward a deeper understanding of the truth and a rejection of their previous, uncritical responses. Few teachers are as adept as Socrates in the art of questioning, but every teacher should be able, on occasion, to ask a question or two that will help the student see the error and make the correction.

A fairly common classroom occurrence when this technique is useful is a student's misuse of a word. A student may say, for example, "This is an illusion to Shakespeare," when he means "allusion." In response, the teacher might ask the student, "Isn't an illusion a deception, something that seems real but is not? That's not what you mean here, is it?" At this point the student may be reminded that a subtle reference is called an "allusion"; if not, the teacher may have to explain the distinction between the two words.

Questioning the student is most effective, however, when the error is not just in the use of a word or in a matter of fact but in the student's thinking or reasoning. In such cases, a good teacher can help the student see a flaw in her perception of the world and so correct it. If in a discussion of French cuisine, for example, a student remarked, "French waiters are rude," the teacher might respond by asking the student why he or she says that. When the student says that he or she has eaten at two different French restaurants in town, and both times the waiter was very rude, the teacher could ask if the student thinks that two instances of rudeness are enough to make a generalization about French waiters. Isn't it possible that these two are exceptions to the rule, and that most French waiters are quite courteous? Isn't it even possible that one, or even both, of the waiters he or she encountered are usually polite but happened to be in a bad mood for some reason? Would it be fair for a Frenchman to judge Americans as loud and obnoxious after seeing two such Americans in Paris? Such a line of questioning should help the student realize that he or she was prematurely generalizing about French waiters.

The teacher should be familiar with all four ways of responding to student errors and practice using them in appropriate situations.

FTCE

Florida Teacher Certification Exam—
Professional Education Test

Chapter 24
Competency 23

Chapter 24

COMPETENCY 23

DEFINITION OF COMPETENCY

The teacher conducts reviews of the subject matter.

Sandra Morris has spent several weeks on a Native American unit in her seventh-grade social studies class. She begins each class meeting with, "Yesterday we talked about ..." or "What did we discuss yesterday?" Ms. Morris knows that this summary of previous material is an essential step in creating transitions between units or lessons. Students need specific reminders of what had been covered previously in class in order to better understand the present material.

Giving students background to new material is a way to help them add meaning to text and ideas. For example, an instructor who teaches the elements of a short story over a period of time takes time at the introduction of each new short story to review and rehearse ones that were studied earlier. Integrating new material with material presented previously in class helps students make sense of new material and view learning as a series of building blocks, not skills in isolation.

Ms. Morris says to her literature class, "Yesterday we studied the significance of authorial tone and style in Poe's *Tell-Tale Heart*, and today we're looking at characterization. Can you give me an example of how Poe uses tone to describe a character? How would you define tone?" Here the instructor requires students to mesh what they studied previously with the current story element. Each time they receive a new mental image, they have an opportunity to place it into a meaningful context.

It also helps students to review previous material in order to remember it better and for a longer period of time. They take notes and learn items, not just to put them away and look at them only at test time, but in order to remind themselves on a daily basis what has been learned before.

Without such review, students tend to ignore and certainly forget material until the test, and do not appreciate the importance of careful rehearsal.

Reviews can go beyond oral discussion. Students may write index card summaries of previous material, lists of ideas learned, and outlines of key concepts, submitting those to the instructor, who determines if material is being recalled and understood. Students can act as surrogate teachers, taking the lead role in conducting a five-minute review at the beginning of each class, quizzing one another on central concepts and major ideas from former lessons.

Taking time to review material teaches students an important lesson about learning—that it is imperative to master old ideas before tackling new ones. Teachers in a rush to cover content, or students in a hurry to process it, lose sight of the need to have deep understandings about each piece of information as it appears in the course. Delving into the previous lesson helps students gain insights into the material at hand. A student can ask his- or herself, "What have we already learned that applies in this case? and "How do old scenarios fit the ones at hand?"

Every discipline lends itself to review of certain procedures and knowledge. Summarizing ideas helps students to practice convergent thinking and synthesis, requiring them to place their learning into a meaningful context. If the class has just studied the causes of the Civil War, the teacher takes time to ask the class to recount those causes before moving to effects. If the class has just learned binary equations, the instructor takes time to practice with the class before moving to other problems.

The individual members of the class must be involved and engaged in the summary of previous material; the instructor should not just spoon-feed the class a recap of the material. Students learn to take responsibility for their own learning as they move from one piece of the educational puzzle to another. Each step reinforces knowledge given before, and the rehearsal, whether oral or written, assists students in better remembering at test time.

RECAPPING SIGNIFICANT POINTS

As essential as reviewing previous lessons, recapping significant points of a discussion before moving to a new aspect or problem is equally important. As varying perspectives are given in discussions, students may lose sight of the key points. Asking students to summarize what they have just heard is an excellent way to determine if ideas are being understood.

Students may have missed the major concept or tenet, and multiple interpretations become evident in oral sharing.

Here are some questions that can be utilized to recap points in a discussion before moving on, depending on the discipline or subject:

1. Do the author's ideas make sense? Why or why not?

2. If you had to put the main idea into one sentence, what would you say?

3. Where do you note the difference between fact and opinion here?

4. How can you relate this reading or exercise to your own experiences?

5. What information have you gained that will help you perform a new task?

6. What questions does this article raise?

7. Can you find the supporting details for the main argument here?

8. Based on what you know so far, what can you predict about what will happen next?

9. How would you describe the major events of this historical period thus far?

10. What relationships do you find between early information and present information?

11. Can you give examples of the main points discussed here?

12. Who might disagree with the major ideas here, and why?

Asking students to list in writing what they have learned so far, then orally reviewing it is a quick and effective way to determine if ideas are being understood. Students need time to process and integrate information, with instructors emphasizing depth over coverage.

THESIS, ANTITHESIS, AND SYNTHESIS

Thesis, antithesis, and synthesis are effective ways to recap class discussion and material. Thesis refers to the central message, claim, or point, which students can be directed to find. Antithesis addresses the opposing claims and arguments to the central message. Synthesis is a blend of these two ideas, convergent thinking used to find a common ground between thesis and antithesis. How can we bridge the gap between these oppositional viewpoints? Pointing out conflicts and gaps in concepts helps students to reconcile ideas and commit to a perspective of their own.

RECAPPING DISCUSSION AND REVIEWING SUBJECT MATTER

Recapping discussion and reviewing subject matter helps to reinforce retention of ideas and concepts. Students may not realize the importance of stopping to reflect on what they are learning until the skill is taught to them. The desire to cover content often overshadows the importance of mastering major points one at a time. Each piece of information must be placed in perspective, with the instructor's assistance, and related to the material before and after it.

Instructors who help students to recap major points of a discussion may promote these skills:

1. Use examples and illustrations to support ideas

2. Use oral sharing to gain information, explain ideas or experiences, and seek answers

3. Demonstrate proficiency in constructing meaning from text

4. Relate materials to own background and interests

5. Organize and group related ideas

6. Evaluate the validity of information

7. Recognize persuasive text

8. Sequence information

9. Read for information to use in performing a task

10. Read to confirm predictions about text

11. Identify personal preferences in espousing ideas and opinions

12. Participate in group discussions about central and opposing ideas

13. Check for wholeness or clarity of ideas

14. Describe, analyze, and generalize a wide variety of concepts

15. Identify patterns in logic and arguments

16. Make inferences based on available information

17. Collect, organize, and interpret data in midstream

18. Analyze the likelihood of events occurring

19. Apply major points to real-world problems

20. Make decisions on how to proceed

Recapping and reviewing gives students an opportunity to self-correct, retell, question, and predict, based on the information available.

END OF THE LESSON RECAP

Equally essential to student review of main points during discussions is the end-of-lesson recap, or summary of subject matter. Closure should be brought to each lesson as it concludes, and before another is initiated. Putting a frame on the picture is an important part of learning; recalling key concepts and filling in any gaps of information is vital. Instruments such as self-quizzes may help students to discover how much they have remembered and understand what they have learned.

At the end of the lesson, the teacher or the students can develop ten questions related to the material. If students cannot answer these questions, they know that more study and time are required. Questions can be used as a way to discuss and rehearse the material as well. Misunderstandings and misinterpretations become apparent in classroom oral sharing.

JOURNAL WRITING

Journal writing is another way for students to review material at the end of a lesson or unit. What is the most important or meaningful idea learned here? What is the author's central purpose? Journal writing can be shared among class members for responses and read aloud for discussion. This kind of writing helps students to focus on key ideas, while reflecting in prose narrative style on a summary of the lesson.

COOPERATIVE LEARNING

Cooperative learning can play an integral role in providing review opportunities, with each team member assigned a portion of the material on which to give the group a review. Taking different parts of a chapter or dividing the unit into themes, group members are responsible for listing the key points. The entire cooperative group creates a list for the class, and lists are compared across groups for the one that most effectively covers the material. The class draws conclusions concerning the ideas based on cooperative efforts.

Some other skills that can be built by students through careful end-of-lesson review include these:

1. Develop an understanding of terms and definitions

2. Examine one's own value positions in relation to the material

3. Develop the skills and understandings needed to perform tasks related to the material

4. Suggest changes and improvements in ideas and concepts

5. Defend ideas with specific examples and statistics

6. Explain ways in which the material might relate to a real-world context

7. Summarize the philosophical positions inherent in the material

8. Evaluate ways ideas relate to other disciplines or subjects

9. Explore models and applications of the material

10. Relate concepts and issues to the surrounding cultural, historical, philosophical, and political circumstances

11. Compare and contrast major ideas

12. Communicate effectively about interpretations of issues

13. Predict how variables and events will interact and make projections based on current evidence

14. Research case studies as examples of available information

15. Consider the consequences of studied events and behaviors

16. Examine patterns of thoughts

17. Develop questions based on the material that lead to new understandings

18. Determine the difference between theory and fact

19. Analyze written statements for validity

20. Look for discrepancies and conflicting points of view

WEEKLY AND MONTHLY REVIEWS

To ensure retention of material, students should also be engaged in weekly and monthly reviews of subject matter. Like end-of-lesson summaries, weekly reviews must address key points and organize concepts.

For example, if an instructor has taught students about technology terms for a week, before introducing new terms, time should be taken to ensure understanding of the current vocabulary. Similar techniques, such as self-quizzes, graded quizzes given by the instructor, journal writing, cooperative learning activities, and oral review of the material can be used.

A technology instructor might conduct a review by stating, "We have covered several computer terms this week. In the next ten minutes, I want you to write as many of these terms as you recall from memory, with their definition beside each one." Students can then compare their results with class notes and discuss any questions related to material with the instructor and peers. Without such a review, neither instructors nor students would have an opportunity to synthesize knowledge or discover gaps in learning.

Weekly reviews help instructors determine if students are making responsible use of information and knowledge. Can students place isolated facts into a meaningful context? Can they relate them to real-world problems and applications? Are all terms and definitions clear? It is essential that students have clear understandings and mastery, if possible, of current material, before they move on to any new ideas.

Along with weekly reviews of subject matter, effective instructors spend time at the end of each month to look back at what has been learned and accomplished. This monthly review reinforces concepts and gives students assistance in retaining material. Monthly reviews must cover the scope and sequence of all major ideas and give students an overview and sense of completeness. Are there any issues or topics not understood by the class as a whole? Where is understanding weak? The review reveals such gaps in the knowledge base.

Students should take an active role in the monthly summary, bringing all applicable notes and materials. Instructors can ask students to list three or four major themes or concepts they discover in their notes. Emphasis should be placed on unifying concepts: Students should ask themselves which ideas stand at the center of the information, which are central to developing others, and which are missing or unclear?

Another approach to monthly reviews is to require students to write possible test questions that cover the material. Students examine the material in terms of what is fundamental or key. Test questions can be shared with the class, who can attempt to answer them in writing, and then discuss their responses. Writing test questions helps students to sort out and prioritize information, as well as synthesize and analyze ideas. The teacher, the textbook, and experts in the discipline must be brought together at this point to provide an effective overview of material.

SUMMARY

Does any of the new knowledge make other information obsolete? Do any new facts replace previous ones? Reviews provide an opportunity for field testing the worthiness of ideas. Extensive understanding of concepts may not occur until the learner places knowledge in an overview, that is, in an overall perspective. Coherence and interrelatedness of ideas become apparent when one focuses on the process of knowing how to arrive at different forms of knowledge.

Overall, in conducting reviews of subject matter, instructors must pay close attention to a summary of the previous lesson at the beginning of the new one; a recap of the significant points of discussion before moving on to a new topic; and a weekly or monthly review of lessons to ensure long-term retention. In going over what has been learned, teachers need to ensure that knowledge is placed into a meaningful context.

Reviews can be oral, written, and even completed by technological means. Students may use e-mail to answer teacher questions about material, to form study groups around organizing questions, and to communicate about the central point of each lesson. It is the educator's responsibility to reinforce the idea that each idea and skill should be mastered before a new one is integrated into the learning experience.

What is the student's responsibility in review of material? A central obligation of the student is to bring all necessary notes, text, and materials to the review session and to keep current on topics and issues introduced in the course. Through the review experience, students can discover gaps and discrepancies in their comprehension and absorption of ideas, themes, and facts.

Oral and written summaries of what has been learned give shape to the course design and help students differentiate the end from the beginning. They visualize the overall course concept and achieve a global view through synthesis and convergence of major themes. The summary brings a wholeness to the material, taking seemingly isolated bits of information and tying them together with a common thread. What are the similarities and differences in these concepts? How does this issue contrast with that one? Review brings a unity and coherence to the scope and range of ideas presented in the class.

Review also reinforces the notion of organization and sequence, placing ideas into a meaningful time frame and order. As each part of a lesson is introduced during the week or month, students do not always see how the parts make up the whole or fit together. In summarizing items from the course, the learner amasses the wealth of facts and opinions learned and makes sense of them, fitting them into a useful pattern.

From class goals to objectives to assessment, each instructor has certain aims for each course. If time is not given to focusing on main concepts before new ones are introduced, students do not have an opportunity to process and inculcate what they have learned. Learning is looking back as well as looking ahead. Students who rush through material or attempt to process it too quickly miss the dual experiences of reflection and introspection. Material must apply to their real-world, ill-defined problems in such a way that it guides them in effective decision-making.

Involving students in effective review of material is fundamental to learning, comprehension, and retention of ideas.

FTCE

Florida Teacher Certification Exam—
Professional Education Test

Chapter 25
Competency 24

Chapter 25

COMPETENCY 24

DEFINITION OF COMPETENCY

A teacher creates classroom tests and tasks to measure students' accomplishments of the teacher's and the school's objectives.

CLASSROOM TESTS

There are fundamental professional and technical factors that must be taken into account to construct effective classroom tests. One of the first factors to recognize is that test construction is as creative, challenging, and important as any aspect of teaching. The planning and background that contribute to effective teaching are incomplete unless evaluation of student performance provides accurate feedback to the teacher and the student about the learning process. Good tests are the product of careful planning, creative thinking, hard work, and technical knowledge about the different methods of measuring student knowledge and performance. Classroom tests that accomplish their purpose are the result of the development of a pool of items and refinement of those items based on feedback and constant revision. It is through this process that evaluation of students becomes valid and reliable.

Tests serve as a valuable instructional aid because they help determine pupil progress and also provide feedback to teachers regarding their own effectiveness. Student misunderstandings and problems as revealed on tests help the teacher understand areas of special concern in providing instruction. This information also becomes the basis for remediation of students and revision of teaching procedures. For these reasons, the construction, administration, and proper scoring of classroom tests is one of the most important activities in teaching.

PRINCIPLES OF TEST CONSTRUCTION

The discussion in this chapter is based on the following principles of test construction:

1. Tests should be constructed according to a blueprint that reflects the objectives of the content to be learned.

2. Tests should reflect the knowledge and skills intended for students to acquire in proportion to the emphasis given to the various objectives in the unit of learning being tested.

3. The type of test items provided for students to answer should be chosen according to the best testing procedures for the particular knowledge or skill the student is expected to acquire.

When a given unit or theme of instruction is prepared, the effective teacher identifies learning objectives for students. The content is then organized and materials and methods for instruction are planned that will help students achieve those objectives. Prior to the administering of tests, the teacher will have a general idea of how the class is progressing in achieving those objectives, and he or she can usually identify those students who seem to be learning better than others. But, the classroom also has a limited number of students performing at any one time, and the teacher is only sampling the performance of the students in that class. In a testing situation, the teacher has an opportunity to include every student in a common activity that has the potential to assess all students on a common task.

TEST BLUEPRINTS

In order to optimize this opportunity, the classroom test must be carefully constructed by using a plan that reflects objectives and measures student learning. It is the responsibility of the teacher to identify, select, and construct test items that appropriately assess attainment of objectives. This can be accomplished by starting with a test blueprint and then preparing test items according to the blueprint. A test blueprint is a plan for the teacher to assess the relative importance of the objectives to be tested and to identify the type of items or activities to test for those objectives. The following discussion explains how to develop and utilize a test blueprint.

Objectives

If a unit of instruction contains several objectives, it is most likely that some objectives require more emphasis than others. The teacher should make a judgment about the degree of emphasis given to each objective so the test will reflect this proportional emphasis. This judgment is the first step in preparing a test blueprint. For example, a unit with four objectives might include the following distribution:

Objectives

I	II	III	IV
20%	30%	15%	35%

This allocation of percentages to the different objectives is the foundation on which the remainder of the blueprint will be developed. After determining the relative importance of each objective, the teacher should allot class time, provide instruction, and evaluate students according to the proportional importance of each objective. This entire process should be viewed as a cooperative effort between the teacher and the students in which they work in much the same manner as a coach does to make his or her team the best they can be. As the planning for instruction occurs, and as the instruction is provided, the teacher should concurrently prepare test questions that coincide with the planning and instruction. While preparing a lesson, the teacher should be making notes about test items that evaluate the intended learning of the students. By preparing test items while planning lessons, the teacher can make the instruction appropriate and increase the validity of the test at the same time. Another excellent time to prepare test items is immediately after completing the daily instruction. At this time, the learning that took place is fresh in the mind of the teacher and any special events or discussions that should be reinforced through a test can more easily be recalled.

TEST ITEMS

The test items used in an examination will vary according to the content that is being taught. The teacher must choose the type of items that will be most effective for evaluating students according to the content they have learned. Multiple-choice items may be useful to test a wide range of objectives, and an essay question may be a better choice to test for knowledge about a single event. The length and type of tests will also be influenced by factors such as time and frequency for testing. Tests will vary if they are weekly quizzes or semester examinations. Tests that have essay questions require more time than items that call for simple recognition. These are factors that must be taken into account when the test is actually assembled. However, at the time the test questions are being drafted, the most important criterion is to develop test questions that are most appropriate for the content. The questions most commonly prepared are: true/false, essay, multiple-choice, listing, matching, sentence completion, and recall.

As instruction progresses and as test items are constructed, the learning of the students and the development of the test by the teacher coincide. When the instruction and learning of the unit is nearly ended and the teacher prepares to test the students, it is time to complete the test blueprint.

For the next step in preparing the blueprint, the teacher should list the number of test items prepared under each objective according to the type of item. This step in making the blueprint is illustrated with the following example:

Objectives

	I	II	III	IV
Question Type	20%	30%	15%	35%
true/false	6	8	4	11
multiple-choice	3	7	2	9
matching		1		2
essay	1	1		1
recall	4	6	2	8
Totals	14	23	8	31

This blueprint contains 76 test questions and includes five types of questions. Thus, a pool of items has been developed from which the teacher can prepare the test. The teacher must also take into account the relative difficulty and comparative weight of the different questions. Essay questions are more difficult than true/false questions and should carry different weight or value. The item available for the test will limit the number of items that can be included on the examination. The resolution of these issues will determine the final length and selection of items for the test. For example, if the examination period is the length of a typical class period, the final allocation of items for the test could be as follows:

	Objectives				
	I	II	III	IV	Total
Question Type	20%	30%	15%	35%	
true/false	3	4	2	2	11
multiple-choice	3	2	3	4	12
matching	1	2			3
essay				1	1
recall	2	4	2	2	10
Totals	9	12	7	9	37
% of points	20	30	14	36	100

The final test prepared in this example contains 37 of the original 76 items. It includes 11 true/false items, 12 multiple-choice items, three matching items, one essay, and 10 recall items. The weight or value of each item must next be determined to make certain the value given to each objective is proportionally tested on the examination. In this case, the point value assigned to each type of item may be as follows: true/false = one point; multiple choice = two points; matching = five points; essay = 20 points; recall = three points. With these assigned values to each item, the number of points possible on this test is 100. The points to be earned for each objective are as follows: I = 20 points; II = 30 points; III = 14 points; IV = 36 points. Thus, the test reflects the emphasis given to the objectives and includes a variety of test items whose value vary with their difficulty.

Only 37 of the original 76 items were used for this test. The remaining 37 items are still valuable items and should be kept for future use. These additional items can be used to create another form of this test, which will also increase test security. Some of the items on the selected test may prove to be faulty and, therefore, they will need to be replaced by items from those placed in reserve. A filing system or a computerized schedule can be established in which each item can be analyzed and recorded. A history of that item will enable the teacher to refine the pool of items available for future testing of the objectives in each unit of instruction. The next section in this chapter explains recognized criteria for the construction of test items.

CONSTRUCTING TEST QUESTIONS

The most common items teachers construct for testing include essay, true/false, multiple-choice, recall or short answer, and matching. Each of these should be written according to standards that increase the chances of the test being valid, reliable, fair, and serving the unique purpose of that particular test. A brief discussion of the major considerations in constructing these test questions follows.

Constructing Essay Questions

Essay questions are asked to produce a student narrative about an event or to write an explanation that cannot be provided in a better form. Essay items require more time for student responses than other types of items, and the number of essay questions on a test will depend partly on the amount of testing time available and the nature of the questions. Essay questions should be stated clearly, and they should not be overly complex. The teacher should know what an "ideal" answer is and should write a response after the question has been formulated to identify with the question and the student who will be responding. By writing a correct response, the teacher also establishes a standard for grading the student papers. After writing the preferred response, the teacher should evaluate if the question is the most effective stimulus to obtain the answer that will evaluate the objective under consideration. If the teacher determines that a correct answer is one that contains four facts and the narrative is relatively unimportant, then the test might be revised to ask students to list the four facts and save the time of writing the narrative. If the time required is excessive and unrealistic, the teacher may assign students to write an essay as an assignment in order to determine attainment of the objective.

Constructing True/False Items

True/false items are relatively easy to construct, but certain criteria are essential to avoid errors in their construction. A statement should clearly be either true or false. Statements that are conditionally true, or are true or false most of the time, are confusing and do not reliably measure student knowledge. Statements that contain absolutes provide clues that have little to do with the content. Words like never and always are examples of such words. True/false items provide a quick check on student learning and can be used for short quizzes, but their validity is suspect. The chance of guessing correctly is 50 percent and with a little knowledge and a few subtle clues in some of the questions, a student who knows very little may score at the 70 or 80 percent level on a true/false test.

Constructing Multiple-Choice Questions

Multiple-choice items contain an opening statement, which is called the stem, followed by choices, which are called alternatives. The multiple-choice test is popular in standardized testing for a very good reason. A well-constructed, multiple-choice test is the most efficient and most effective way to reliably assess student knowledge.

There are two broad categories of multiple-choice questions. Some multiple-choice questions are based on a short essay or narrative in which an event or situation is described. In these cases, several questions usually are asked about the narrative and alternatives are provided for students to select the correct answer. A single episode may provide information from which four or five test items can be written. Another more common multiple-choice item is free standing and contains all the information necessary within the single item. These are usually items with a brief stem of one or two statements followed by alternatives. In either case, the stem must be written clearly, contain no ambiguities, and direct the student with sufficient information to select the correct response. The stem must avoid clues that are unrelated to the content. For example, an item in which the stem ends with the word "an" should have alternatives that all begin with a vowel so grammatical clues do not point to the correct answer. It is also necessary to be aware of avoiding information in one question that will help a student respond correctly to another question in the test. Another error to avoid is creating a sequence of multiple-choice questions in which the answer to one question is dependent on a correct answer to another question.

Alternatives for Multiple-Choice Questions

The test developer must make a decision about how many alternatives to provide for each multiple-choice item. On a given test, the number of alternatives should be the same for each item. Otherwise, the different items would vary in difficulty for the wrong reasons. The preferred number of alternatives is four and the rationale for this recommendation is based on a balance of limiting the chance of guessing the correct answer and the difficulty of writing plausible alternatives.

If only two alternatives are provided in a multiple-choice item, the guessing factor is the same as in a true/false item (50 percent) and the weaknesses in true/false items exist in this case. However, two plausible alternatives are usually not too difficult to write. If three alternatives are provided, the guessing factor is reduced from 50 percent to 33 percent, which is a gain of 17 percent, but still allows considerable chance or luck to enter into the score. Again, three alternatives can usually be constructed without excessive difficulty. When four alternatives are used, the guessing factor is reduced by another 8 percent and it is usually possible to construct four plausible alternatives, but this number becomes difficult at times. If five alternatives are written instead of four, the guessing factor is only reduced by 5 percent and it is extremely difficult to construct five plausible alternatives for every item. Thus, the guessing factor and the difficulty of constructing plausible alternatives work in tandem to recommend four alternatives as the preferred number. It is also recommended that each alternative should stand alone and avoid those alternatives that say "all of the above," "none of the above," "two of the above," and so forth. The format for the items and the instructions should make it easy for the students to respond. Answer sheets for blackening in correct answers may be chosen if the age of the students and the nature of the test make this feasible. Usually, the teacher will ask students to mark on the test and circle correct answers or write in a space provided.

Constructing Recall Items

Multiple-choice items call for students to recognize the correct answer and are "recognition" items. When the student must remember the correct answer to a question, then the item is a "recall" item. Short answer questions are recall questions and they are usually written in language similar to classroom discussions. Recall items are typically constructed as direct questions or as a "fill in the blank" format. In either case, the student must supply the information rather than recognize it from a list of alternatives. Questions of this type can be difficult to score when students provide answers that are similar to the correct answer but not exactly what the teacher had in mind. Furthermore, some questions can be answered correctly although they do not answer the question. Faulty questions will encourage faulty answers. For example, the following item might be on a test, "Abe Lincoln had a reputation for being very _____." The answer the teacher had in mind is "honest." But the student who writes "tall" can make a strong case for giving a correct response. A list of responses from which the student must choose will eliminate this problem, but it also makes the item a recognition item, even if the list of choices exceeds the number of questions by a large margin. Questions that call for longer answers, such as a sentence or two, also create similar grading problems for the teacher. Careful wording of recall questions and making certain a single question is raised will strengthen the quality of recall questions.

Constructing Matching Items

The final type of question discussed here is the matching item. Matching items contain two lists, and the student is expected to match items on one list with items on another list. For example, a matching item might be the names of states in one list and the names of state capitals in the second list. The student would be asked to match the number of one state, perhaps Indiana, with the capital, Indianapolis, which would be in the second list. These questions should avoid lengthy lists of more than six or eight items. Also, the second list should be longer than the first so that the last answer does not automatically align with the final response. If the matches the teacher wants on the test are lengthy, several items can be constructed. If the capitals of all 50 states were to be matched with their respective state, this might be tested by creating six or seven matching questions to minimize reading time and optimize testing time.

Grading matching items poses special factors. One student may match all of the items correctly while another may miss only one. Does the second student miss the entire question or receive partial credit? What constitutes a wrong answer, and is it possible to be partially correct? Most objective items are either right or wrong, but matching items pose a different situation because there are several questions to answer within the item. The teacher must make the grading decision in advance and inform the students how the matching items will be graded.

SCORING THE TEST

After the test has been constructed, administered, and scored, criteria or standards of performance will be applied. With the exception of tests for total mastery, standards will include some degree of subjectivity. Custom has established a general grading scale that varies slightly in different school districts, but, typically, letter grades are attached to results on a percentage scale. That scale often looks something like this:

A = 94-100

B = 87-93

C = 78-86

D = 70-77

F = below 70.

The teacher needs to exercise professional judgment about the difficulty of the test and must make the necessary adjustments when assigning student grades. If the highest score on the test is a 95, then some recommend that all scores be raised by five points. This adjustment is based on the belief that the best student in the class deserves a score at the top of the scale and other scores should be adjusted accordingly. Under this plan, a student with a score of 68 would not fail, but would receive a 73 which would be a D.

Another grading plan is pass or fail. In this case, the student either does or does not perform the task successfully. In a swimming class, if the requirement is to swim 25 yards, then students could be graded as pass or fail. The purpose of this test may not be to see who can swim the fastest, but to make sure everyone learns to swim at least 25 yards. This latter standard is called criterion testing and can be applied in academic and skill areas of learning. It is most important that the teacher establish acceptable standards, that tests assess student acquisition of the knowledge or skills that meet these standards, and that the evaluation of the test can be done as objectively as possible.

This next section addresses procedures for evaluating and revising tests on the basis of content validity, reliability, and student response.

EVALUATING AND REVISING TESTS

After the test has been administered and scored, the teacher has a wealth of information available for analysis. This discussion will focus on a few of the most useful techniques and procedures for evaluating the test and determining how to improve it. The most obvious analysis is to determine the range and the arithmetic average of the scores of the students. Judgments about this information depend on the purpose of the test and the level of difficulty expected. If the test is designed to assess mastery, then student attainment of high scores is desirable. If the test is designed to discriminate among students according to who knows the most, then a wider distribution of scores should be expected.

Mastery

Mastery is a desirable expectation when certain fundamental knowledge must be learned perfectly to assure correct future learning. Tests of spelling or multiplication facts are examples where perfect scores should be expected. Students who make errors in these fundamentals will be unable to learn more advanced topics, and testing for 100 percent mastery is desirable. Mastery may be operationally defined as less than 100 percent if the knowledge contains some optional areas whose failure to understand perfectly or perform exactly is still acceptable. Advanced knowledge in the sciences, subtle interpretations in literature, or performance of a skill at less than a perfect level (making seven out of ten basketball free throws) are instances where mastery may be defined as less than 100 percent. In order to define "mastery" in this context, a standard or criterion is set as a minimum below which student performance is unacceptable.

Analysis of Tests

When a test is designed to sort students according to their relative knowledge or skill, a different analysis of the test is followed. A test that discriminates students from one another along a knowledge continuum should separate those students who are most knowledgeable from those who are least knowledgeable about the content of the test. There are two kinds of analysis that help determine if the test has succeeded in doing this. One analysis requires a tally of the percent of students who answer each item on the test correctly. Any item that is missed by everyone or is answered correctly by everyone does not distinguish one student from another. If any item is answered correctly or incorrectly by everyone, then the test has determined what students know, or don't know, but it has not helped sort students according to their knowledge. Such items should be reviewed by the teacher and remain if their purpose is either to test for mastery or provide a psychological climate of success while taking the test. Items that are answered correctly or incorrectly by at least some of the students are items that have some discriminatory power. It is almost certain that on a comprehensive test most students will miss some of the questions. The further analysis described next helps determine if the test has ranked or sorted students correctly.

This second analysis is undertaken by dividing the students according to the half of the class that obtained the highest scores and the half who obtained the lowest scores. The percent who answered each question correctly in each half of the class should be compared. This comparison is done to see if any items were answered correctly by more students in the lower half of the distribution than in the upper half. Any item that has a lower percent correct by the best performing students should be reviewed and examined for grammatical or other obvious errors. A slight discrepancy should not be considered an error in the test. If 30 students take a test and the students with the 15 worst scores exceed the percent right on an item by the 15 best students by a small margin, the item is not necessarily faulty. However, a large discrepancy of 15 to 20 percentage points is a good basis for further analysis. The item may be acceptable, but it also may be ambiguous or it may punish some students for "knowing too much." By making this comparison, specific items on the test are identified that may not properly examine students and can be revised according to the weakness in the item. Some items found may be so faulty that they should not even count on the test and may be discarded in order to assign a fair final score. Weaknesses may be in the format, content, or structure. Most test items can be analyzed on this basis, and the problem with the few items that discriminate in the reverse direction are usually not difficult to detect. However, the multiple-choice question is a special case that can be analyzed more thoroughly and refined on the basis of objective data. A discussion of this further analysis of multiple-choice items is provided next.

Analyzing Multiple-Choice Questions

For the purpose of this discussion, we will assume there are four alternatives in each multiple-choice question from which students will make their selection. We will also assume that each item has been compared according to students who have the highest scores with those who have the lowest scores. The item analysis that is described next calls for a more detailed but rather easy way to evaluate multiple-choice items.

Every alternative should function and be chosen by at least someone who takes the test. In a typical class of 30 students, if each alternative is chosen by at least one student, then the item will be answered correctly by no more than 90 percent of the students. This will be true because at least three students would need to provide an incorrect answer for each alternative to be chosen. Such an item meets the standard of less than 100 percent correct and all the alternatives in the item contribute to the purpose of the item. If any alternative is not selected by the students, that item should be rewritten to either include plausible alternatives in each case or to ask for that information with a different kind of question.

In addition to the systematic analysis of test items, all student responses should be read to identify mistaken thought processes, lack of knowledge, inadequate skill, or misunderstandings the students have revealed in their responses. These errors in student thinking can be deduced from an inspection of their responses.

CONCLUSION

After completing the item analysis and the comparative scores of the highest scoring and lowest scoring students, it is helpful to return to the lessons that were taught and revise lesson plans on the basis of student performance. It is also crucial to return the scored tests to the students and use their responses as a basis for further teaching. Correct answers should be praised and errors should be corrected. Re-teaching should occur to help students avoid future mistakes or misconceptions about the content of the test.

FTCE

Florida Teacher Certification Exam—
Professional Education Test

Chapter 26
Competency 25

Chapter 26

COMPETENCY 25

DEFINITION OF COMPETENCY

A teacher should create a testing environment for students in which they can display their knowledge and skills, and obtain sufficient information about the quality of his or her test performance.

Considerable effort is necessary to develop tests and other procedures to evaluate students. However, if the testing environment in which the student is expected to perform is neglected, the evaluative information obtained on students will be suspect. The purpose of this narrative is to describe and explain procedures for establishing a proper testing environment. The discussion in this chapter provides information about administering teacher-made, pencil-paper tests. In the case of standardized testing, the information provided to the proctor should be strictly followed to make certain the conditions under which the test was normed are also the conditions under which the students take the test. Performance tests that measure skill acquisition call for demonstration of proficiency in a given task. Some of the discussion that follows can be generalized to skill testing and standardized tests, but that is not the primary focus of this chapter. Thus, this chapter describes the procedures to follow in the administration of teacher-made, paper-pencil tests.

The three phases of testing described in this chapter are (1) preparation for testing; (2) test administration; and (3) formative feedback.

PREPARATION FOR TESTING

Preparation for testing includes responsibilities for the teacher and consideration for the student. The teacher's responsibility for testing begins prior to the actual testing situation. During the time when instruction and learning take place, the teacher should make certain the class understands what knowledge is especially important for them to learn. It is the responsibility of the teacher to focus learning on the critical elements of the content to be learned and to examine students on their acquisition of this critical knowledge. Tests should not be used to "trick" students by testing for obscure information. The relationship between teaching and testing should be congruent and fair.

When tests are given to students, the teacher must pay attention to the logistics and details of administering the test. The test material should be prepared sufficiently in advance to make certain it is clearly printed and void of spelling or grammatical errors. There must be enough copies for every student and some extras in case a faulty test is given out. The best possible room environment should be provided, which includes proper lighting, ventilation, temperature, and reduction of noise. The test should be scheduled to avoid conflicts with events such as fire drills or public address announcements. Confer with the principal to avoid conflicts with school activities that may interfere with a desirable testing environment. Bring extra supplies of paper and pencils for those who forget them or break their pencils during the test. Place a notice on the door that notifies others that "testing is in progress—do not disturb." Such a notice should prevent interruptions, except for emergencies. The seating in the room should allow each student to work independently and provide for adequate proctoring. These logistical matters are not entirely in control of the teacher, but any of these procedures that can be followed should be completed to assure the fairest possible test administration.

Prior to the administration of the test, the teacher should orient the students to the testing situation. The teacher should also provide assurances to the students with positive remarks that encourage them to do their best. The purpose of the test should be explained, including information about how the test results will be used and how the results are relevant to them personally. Students should be informed about when the results of the test will be reported to them and how this feedback will be provided. In some cases it is appropriate for an entire class to discuss the test results, and in other cases it is best to keep test results personal and confidential. Students should know how the results will be reported to ease their minds about this procedure, and to give them one less factor that may contribute to their test anxiety.

If the test contains any special considerations about taking the test or scoring procedures, the students should be told what they are. For example, if a test includes essay questions, they should be given reasonable parameters to help them pace their time. A single essay question can consume their entire time; if there are several questions, the students might be told to limit their writing time on each question to assure coverage of the entire examination. If certain types of questions carry more weight than others, the students should be told the point value of the different questions. True/false items might be worth one point and multiple-choice items might be worth two points. The test itself should also contain information. The time allotted for the test should be sufficient to enable all students who are reasonably well-prepared to be able to demonstrate their knowledge.

TEST ADMINISTRATION

Students should be kept informed about the time remaining as they progress through the examination. If a clock is in the room in a conspicuous location, this may be sufficient. It may be helpful to provide information about the time remaining by writing it on the board. The proctor might write times on the board in minutes such as ten, five, three, and one. As these remaining times arrive, the proctor can draw a line through the appropriate number. Thus, students can tell at a glance how much time is remaining. The proctor might suggest a pace for a long test that is divided into several sections. If students should complete the first section by a certain time, the proctor should announce, "You should have completed section one by now. If you have not done so, move on to section two." Students should be told in advance if the proctor is going to provide this information.

The Proctor

The proctor must be sensitive to the importance of time during a testing situation. The time spent before the actual testing begins should be minimal. Most students come to a testing situation ready to answer questions and do not want a long delay in getting started. In some cases, the pre-test information may even be provided in a previous session, and test materials may already be on student desks in a folder or upside down so everyone can start promptly when told to begin. Delays by the teacher prior to the testing reduces the time available for students to respond and increases test anxiety. The time provided for the test itself should be the same for everyone. Everyone should be expected to "run the same race" in order to determine the comparative knowledge each student has on the content being tested.

Proctoring the examination calls for close attention to students without "hovering" over the class in a way that may be a distraction. The proctor should not be preoccupied with other tasks during the test. Students should be instructed to remove all materials from their desks and to have an extra supply of pencils and paper. Students whose pencils break during an examination should not be allowed to go to a pencil sharpener and disturb others. The proctor can quietly supply a pencil after receiving a signal from the student. Proctors should not engage in conversation with any student during the examination. Some students may request information, such as the definition of a word. If the proctor responds, it may appear to other students that the proctor is providing unfair assistance. If all the preliminary details have been provided, if the test contains the required information, and if every student has listened and has come prepared, no student should have any questions during the examination.

The proctor must assure that all students do their own work. Crib notes, conversation between students, and signals that students may have created to help each other should all be monitored. In most cases, if the proctor is in the back of the room, the temptation for students to cheat is minimized. When students cannot see where the proctor is looking, they tend to keep their own eyes from wandering. If the room is small and desks are close, making it easy for students to look on other desks, it may be necessary to create different forms of the same test. This can be done by reversing the order of the questions or any other reorganization of the test that will protect its integrity.

FORMATIVE FEEDBACK

After the test has been completed and collected, the teacher should score the test and give feedback to students as promptly as possible. In a discussion of the test results, it is essential to identify correct responses and express approval to the students for doing well on those items. It is important to provide overall information, such as the range of scores, the average, and the grade distribution. It is helpful to identify common errors made by students and to take time to explain the correct responses. Students may challenge answers, and a discussion of these inquiries should be provided without getting into arguments. The teacher and the students can both benefit from a discussion of items where there is a difference of opinion.

SUMMARY

An acceptable testing environment requires teachers to: (1) prepare students by emphasizing the critical knowledge for students to learn; (2) establish a setting with clear instructions and fair tests for students to complete; and (3) give feedback that praises correct responses and corrects errors and misunderstandings.

FTCE

Florida Teacher Certification Exam—
Professional Education Test

Chapter 27
Competency 26

Chapter 27

COMPETENCY 26

DEFINITION OF COMPETENCY

The teacher establishes an effective system for maintaining student records.

Teachers will develop a sense of what progress their class has made based on their many hours of interaction with the students. It is very important, however, to keep accurate records of student achievement in addition to the more business-related tasks of attendance and inventory. Reviewing these records provides the teacher with the opportunity for self-evaluation: Is the class performing better in some areas than in others? Are the students being graded on a variety of tasks? Am I meeting the requirements of the curriculum? Careful recording will allow for detailed report cards and a more reliable assessment of the individual students and the class as a whole. This knowledge will facilitate meaningful and specific conferences with students and parents.

This chapter will review different forms of recordkeeping, grade reporting, and the laws surrounding the maintenance of permanent student records.

RECORDING STUDENT AND CLASS PROGRESS

Grade Books

The most traditional method of student records, the grade book, is also considered to be the official document of class progress. Grade books contain information such as:

- Date of assignment;
- Type of assignment (test, open-ended assignment, essay, homework);

- Student grade for assignment;

- Total grade points possible for assignment;

- Class participation; and

- Comments/notes.

In addition to storing information, the grade book should be organized to reflect the system that will be used to calculate grades. Will tests count more than homework assignments? Will any assignments be merely for credit rather than a grade? Similarly, use of the grade book should be flexible, to account for additions and retractions from the teaching schedule. Grade books should be updated frequently to accurately track the growth of the class.

Examination of an organized grade book should provide the teacher with a look at the status of any particular student in a given area at any time. The information stored in a grade book can then be placed into a graph or a chart for an easy visual representation of class progress.

Checklists and Scales

To follow student development in a particular subject area, teachers can also work with checklists. The skills and concepts being taught in a particular content area can be listed for each student, and then checked off when the student has reached mastery. Notes can be written next to a skill if a student is experiencing difficulty or ease with a specific skill or concept. The teacher can then assess the strengths and weaknesses of the class in each skill area and plan lessons accordingly.

Similar to checklists, teachers can also use a rating scale to record the level of ability that a student demonstrates in a particular area.

Portfolios

Teachers can also record a student's overall growth in a particular area or over the whole syllabus by using portfolio assessments. Portfolios are folders that contain various samples of a student's work that are date-stamped and then archived. Portfolios can show the scope of what a student has studied and the growth that has occurred as a result, while providing a very special and personalized look at the child. Additionally, the portfolio gives the teacher an overview of a student's abilities so that the teacher can determine an appropriate level of instruction. Portfolio assessment is flexible, and any combination of the methods described here can be used. It is important to note, however, that portfolios should only be used to assess each student individually, or to evaluate the work of the teacher. They should not be used to compare one student to another.

All types of work can be contained in a folder, and there can be folders for different topic areas, such as distinct portfolios for math, reading, and science. Teachers may select the pieces to include in the portfolio, or teachers can ask the students what they would like to include. Examples of work samples that can be kept in a portfolio include creative writing samples, artwork, journal writings, science reports, and math problems. Students or the teacher can include record logs that detail such facts as books read, math concepts mastered, or science experiments completed. Each sample placed in the student's portfolio can contain a description of the assignment and what the student and teacher felt about the finished product, in addition to the date. Personal notes from students, teachers, and parents may be included as well.

At any point in the year, the student and teacher will have a rich resource from which to review. When examining a portfolio, the teacher should be looking for student strengths, weaknesses, abilities, and achievements. The teacher may wish to review the portfolio, and both student and teacher can discuss what they think about the samples and determine what they both wish to accomplish in the future. Portfolios can also be used in parent conferences to provide insight into the student's growth in the class.

Teachers may also develop class portfolios containing samples from all of the students in the class for a similar type of review of the classroom and its experiences as a whole.

Anecdotal Records

Even with all these methods of recordkeeping, there may still be other information that the teacher would like to record. Anecdotal records are information comments, about either the class in its entirety or about individuals, that are dated and maintained in one place. Remarks about behavior, social development and skills, attitudes about school, learning styles, or any other important thoughts or day-to-day observations should be noted in the anecedotal record. Anecdotal records may also contain information about parent phone calls and conferences by including the date, time, and topic of discussion.

These tools should provide a teacher with the methods to integrate a complete system for evaluating student and class progress and achievement.

REPORTING STUDENT AND CLASS PROGRESS

Report Cards

The information that a teacher has recorded about students and their progress is reported to parents and school administration, generally in the form of a report card. Most report cards reflect the grade-point averages for each subject of study, student attendance, and student tardiness. Some report cards provide an area for comments about student behavior and attitudes. Report cards are valued by parents because they are similar to what parents themselves received when in school, and because they convey a student's academic standing in an easy-to-understand manner.

Parent-Teacher Conferences

Parent-teacher conferences are another means of communicating student progress to parents. Typically, a school will have formal, school-wide parent-teacher conferences over a specific period of time. Conferences may also be initiated at any time of the year if the teacher or if the parents feel they are necessary. These meetings provide the teacher and the parents (or guardians) with an opportunity to discuss their views of the student's feelings toward learning. Specific work samples, such as in a portfolio, may be reviewed and future goals and expectations for the student should be discussed. The parents and the teachers can also determine a plan for how the parents can become actively involved in the student's education. Any concerns from either side can be addressed. At times, the students themselves may be involved in the conference.

Narrative Reports

If a parent is unable to attend a conference due to scheduling difficulties, the teacher can provide a narrative report, which is a written assessment detailing the student's strengths, weaknesses, and future goals. Narrative reports can also be used if a student is experiencing an unusual situation that is making his/her grades inconsistent or inaccurate. The narrative report is a more informal but more detailed record than a report card.

MAINTAINING PERMANENT STUDENT RECORDS

Schools consistently maintain records for students throughout their academic experience. The permanent school record is overseen by the school administration and minimally contains the following information:

- Personal:
  - Parents'/guardians' names and contact information;
  - Attendance/tardiness;
  - Immunization records;
  - Pertinent health information and health needs;
- Academic
  - Past teachers;
  - Grade-point averages/transcripts;
  - Standardized test scores; and
  - Any other specialized test results.

Additionally, the record contains any narrative comments from school professionals who have worked with the child about his or her progress, physical and mental well-being, and behavior. Any other information that is important to the history and to the understanding of the child or the child's particular situation is also maintained in the permanent student record. When necessary, information relating to the custody of children with divorced parents is also noted. These data are strictly confidential, and should only be discussed with the parents, school administration, and relevant teachers.

The permanent student records are filed in a specific and locked fireproof location and cannot be removed unless they are signed out by a teacher or administrator; at this point, the records are the responsibility of that person. They are considered to be legal documents.

Attendance, grade, and health information are generally updated annually. Any other important data are updated as they occur. The current teacher is also responsible for updating any anecdotal information or specialized testing results that are deemed necessary to record. Just as the record is updated by each new teacher, the student record will follow the student to the new school if the student leaves the current one.

UNDERSTANDING THE RESPONSIBILITIES OF STUDENT RECORDS

Teachers frequently review the student records of incoming students at the beginning of a school year. Therefore, it is important to keep in mind that what is included in a student record can influence the opinions of a student's future instructors and administrators. The teacher's comments should be as objective and informative as possible, avoiding any potentially harmful remarks. The responsibility of the student record should not be taken lightly; teachers must take care to focus only on professional, rather than personal, opinions of the student's strengths and weaknesses.

Just as the permanent school record is a confidential and legal document, teachers should similarly be cautious with other student records. Student's grades, progress, tests, homework, and information about personal situations should only be discussed with the student, the student's parents, and the school administration.

FTCE

Florida Teacher Certification Exam—
Professional Education Test

Chapter 28
Competency 27

Chapter 28

COMPETENCY 27

DEFINITION OF COMPETENCY

The teacher uses computers in education.

EDUCATIONAL TECHNOLOGY IN THE PRIMARY CLASSROOM

Technology is an important part of the world and, therefore, must be an important part of the educational environment. Students should be exposed as early as possible to computer literacy so that they will be prepared for a technologically advanced society. Appropriate software can be used to meet content standards and curriculum goals. Teachers must be able to integrate their existing curriculum to meet these standards. Students must be versed in computer curriculum to prepare them for their future.

Classroom Management

There are a variety of classroom settings that can be utilized with regard to computers. Some classes may have only one computer, while others may have a computer lab. The majority of teachers and students have access to at least one computer in the class.

The teacher must use a variety of innovative methods to allow the students to have quality computer time whenever possible. The computer can be used as an audiovisual tool, with new lessons presented by the teacher to the students, using the computer as an electronic blackboard. It can also be used as a technology center, where students can research subjects, take tutorial lessons, and learn word-processing skills. The students, as well, can use the computer for visual and oral presentations when multimedia projects are presented to the class.

Because of limited computer time, most work has to be completed before arriving at the computer. The school version of most software includes excellent ideas for setting up a station and gives seatwork activities for that specific program. Students can print out the graphics and keep them in a folder to be used while working at their desk. They can prepare their entire project before working at the computer.

If a teacher is working with a bank of computers (three or more), assigning small groups is the best method of classroom management. Many primary classrooms already use centers and small group activities as part of the classroom management system. The computer center can be used as one of these learning centers. Themes can be used for the students to research science topics, for example. Reference books, multimedia encyclopedias, and posters can be placed in the center. The students can then exhibit their work on a bulletin board that is part of the computer center. Name checklists can be used so the students are aware of their turn to work at the computer. While a group of students is at the computer, the other students are also at work at other workstations in the class. Students can then rotate with the rest of the class after a certain time allotment.

In some schools, a media center is used so that there is a place for teachers, as well as students, to access computers. In most cases teachers bring their classes into the center at a scheduled time every week. Some administrators prefer this type of arrangement because every student is assured of computer time and it is less costly than supplying computers in every classroom. Each child is given a disk to save his or her work. The disk is then placed in a specific classroom file so that the child has easy access to his or her disk each time he or she enters the center. Usually a computer technician or computer teacher, an assistant, and the classroom teacher are in the center. When the child needs assistance, one suggestion is for the student to place a red cube on top of the computer. The teacher can then scan the room for those children requiring aid. Children can use a green cube to indicate that they have completed their project and are now ready to explore selected computer programs on their own.

Integrating Computers in Instruction

In any classroom environment, one of the major teaching problems is student motivation. Students have a natural motivation to use computers. The more they are exposed to computers, the more they want to learn. A teacher must also exhibit a sense of excitement toward computers. Computers in the class offer a direct integration with classroom curriculum.

Planning for a computer-based lesson is similar to planning for a traditional lesson. The traditional format generally includes: topic, materials, goals and objectives, procedures, and assessment. Once a topic and objective are chosen, then it is necessary to find the materials and resources available to help meet these objectives. Technology is not always the best resource. Sometimes the traditional book, pencil, and paper is the best mode. Many times a marriage of the two (tradition and technology) is needed.

EDUCATIONAL TECHNOLOGY IN THE SECONDARY CLASSROOM

Computer Software Tools

There are several software tools which are extremely useful for teachers and students. Word processing allows teachers and students to write, edit, and polish assignments and reports. Most programs have a spelling-checker or even a grammar-checker to enhance written products. Students in all subjects can use word processors to write term papers or reports of their research. Many word processors allow writers to put the text into columns so that students can produce newsletters with headlines of varying sizes. For example, an English class could write a series of reviews of Shakespeare's plays or sonnets, add information about Shakespeare and his times, then collect everything into a newsletter as a class project. There are also desktop publishing programs which allow text and graphics to be integrated to produce publications, such as a class newsletter and school newspapers and yearbooks.

Databases are like electronic file cards; they allow students to input data, then retrieve it in various ways and arrangements. History students can input data about various countries, e.g., population, population growth rate, infant mortality rate, average income, and average education levels. They then manipulate the database to call out information in a variety of ways. The most important step in learning about databases is dealing with huge quantities of information. Students need to learn how to analyze and interpret the data they see in order to discover connections between isolated facts and figures and how to eliminate inappropriate information.

On-line databases are essential tools for research. Students can access databases related to English, history, science—any number of subject areas. Most programs allow electronic mail (e-mail) so that students can communicate over the computer with people from around the world. There are also massive bibliographic databases which help students and teachers to find the resources they need. Many of the print materials can then be borrowed through interlibrary loan. The use of electronic systems can geometrically increase the materials available to students.

Spreadsheets are similar to teacher grade books. Rows and columns of numbers can be linked to produce totals and averages. Formulas can connect information in one cell (the intersection of a row and column) to another cell. Teachers often keep grade books on a spreadsheet because of the ease in updating information. Once formulas are in place, teachers can enter grades and have completely up-to-date averages for all students. Students can use spreadsheets to collect and analyze numerical data which can be sorted in various orders. Some spreadsheet programs also include a chart function so that teachers can display class averages on a bar chart to provide a visual comparison of the classes' performance. Students can enter population figures from various countries, then draw various types of graphs, bars, columns, scatters, histograms, and pies to convey information. This type of graphic information can also be used in multimedia presentations. There are also various stand-alone graph and chart software packages.

Graphics or paint programs allow users to draw freehand to produce any type of picture or use tools to produce boxes, circles, or other shapes. These programs can illustrate classroom presentations or individual research projects. Many word processing programs have some graphic elements.

Computer-Assisted Instruction

Many early uses of computers tended to be drill-and-practice, where students practiced simple skills such as mathematics operations. Many elaborate systems of practice and testing were developed with management systems so that teachers could keep track of how well the students were achieving. This type of software is useful for skills that students need to practice. An advantage is immediate feedback so students know if they chose the correct answer. Many of these programs have a game format to make the practice more interesting. A disadvantage is their generally low-level nature.

Tutorials are a step above drill-and-practice programs because they also include explanations and information. A student is asked to make a response, then the program branches to the most appropriate section based on the student's answer. Tutorials are often used for remedial work, but are also useful for instruction in English as a second language. Improved graphics and sound allow nonspeakers of English to listen to correct pronunciation while viewing pictures of words. Tutorials are used to supplement, not supplant, teacher instruction.

Simulations or problem-solving programs provide opportunities for students to have experiences which would take too long to experience in real-time, would be too costly or difficult to experience, or would be impossible to experience. For example, one of the most popular early simulations allowed students to see if they could survive the Oregon Trail. Users made several choices about food, ammunition, and supplies, then the computer moved them along the trail until they reached their goal or died along the way. There are several simulations which allow students to "dissect" animals. This saves time and materials, is less messy, and allows students who might be reluctant to dissect real animals to learn about them. Other software might explore the effects of weightlessness on plant growth, a situation which would be impossible to set up in the classroom lab. There are several social studies simulations which allow students to do things like invent a country, then see the effects of their political and economic decisions on the country.

Selection and Evaluation Criteria

The effective teacher uses criteria to evaluate audiovisual, multimedia, and computer resources. The first thing to look for is congruence with lesson goals. If the software doesn't reinforce student outcomes, then it shouldn't be used, no matter how flashy or well-done it is. A checklist for instructional computer software could include appropriate sequence of instruction, meaningful student interaction with the software, learner control of screens and pacing, and motivation. Other factors should be considered, such as the ability to control sound and save progress, effective use of color, clarity of text and graphics on the screen, and potential as an individual or group assignment.

In addition to congruence with curriculum goals, the teacher considers his/her students' strengths and needs, their learning styles or preferred modalities, and their interests. Students' needs can be determined through formal or informal assessment. Most standardized tests include an indication of which objectives the student did not master. Mastering these objectives can be assisted with computer or multimedia aids.

Learning styles may be assessed with a variety of instruments and models, including those developed by Rita Dunn and Anthony Gregorc. Students with highly visual learning modes will benefit from audiovisuals.

Student interests may be revealed by a questionnaire, either purchased or developed by the district or teacher. A knowledge of student interests will help the teacher provide resources to suit individual needs. The effective teacher can design activity choices which relate to class goals but also to student interests.

Evaluation of resources should be accomplished in advance by the teacher, before purchase whenever possible. Evaluation is also conducted during student use of materials. Assessment after student use may be by considering achievement level of the students and/or by surveys which ask for students' responses.

COPYRIGHT LAWS FOR COMPUTER PROGRAMS

Computer technology is becoming a larger focus of the classroom. In addition to being part of the curriculum, computers are frequently used by educators as aids in storing information and developing lesson materials.

Computer software programs fall under the domain of copyright law. Computer programs, such as a word processing program or a graphic design program, are defined as "a set of statements or instructions to be used directly in a computer in order to bring about a certain result" (P.L. 96-517, Section 117).

Backups, or copies of a computer program, are frequently created in case the original disk containing the computer program becomes damaged. Such copies are not considered infringements of the copyright law as long as the following is true:

a. The new copy or adaptation must be created in order to be able to use the program in conjunction with the machine and is used in no other manner.

b. The new copy or adaptation must be for archival purpose only and all archival copies must be destroyed in the event that continued possession of the computer program should cease to be rightful.

c. Any copies prepared or adapted may not be leased, sold, or otherwise transferred without the authorization of the copyright owner.

Copies of a computer program cannot be shared or borrowed. The same original disk should not be used to install a program on more than one machine unless the owner has a license to do so from the computer software company. If unsure about the licensing status of a computer program, the teacher can check with the media specialist or school administrator.

Teachers are role models for their community; it is important that all educators be aware of these laws and be in complete compliance.

FTCE

Florida Teacher Certification Exam—
Professional Education Test

Practice Test 1

PRACTICE TEST 1

Professional Education Test

(Answer sheets appear in the back of this book.)

TIME: 2.5 Hours
         140 Questions

**DIRECTIONS: Read each question carefully and select the best an-
swer. Mark your responses on the answer sheet provided.**

---

1. Rules for computer use in a classroom should be determined and
   explained

   (A) before any student reaches a computer.

   (B) as students show their skill levels.

   (C) to each student individually.

   (D) six weeks after things have settled down.

2. How can computer software be used in a classroom?

   (A) To explore the Internet

   (B) To record class computer skill growth

   (C) For the class newspaper

   (D) All of the choices listed are ways computer software can be used
       in a classroom.

3. If only one computer is available to a class, students should be able to
   use the computer

   (A) singly or in small groups.

   (B) if they are familiar with computers.

    (C) only during full class instruction.

    (D) to record class progress.

4. A student portfolio

    (A) contains artwork by a student.

    (B) is used to compare student work.

    (C) is graded on a scale.

    (D) contains documents and/or products to show student progress.

5. What is the narrative report approach?

    (A) Students describe how they feel they are doing.

    (B) A formal report card

    (C) Teachers provide parents with a written assessment of a student's progress.

    (D) Parents and teacher discuss a student's attitudes about learning.

6. A student's permanent school record should be discussed with the

    (A) student's parents/legal guardians, current teachers, and school administrators.

    (B) parents only.

    (C) school administrators only.

    (D) school administrators and parents only.

7. When are students more likely to score higher on a test?

    (A) When the questions are multiple choice

    (B) When they are not coached by a teacher

    (C) When they are familiar with the test format and content

    (D) When the format is always changing

8. Teachers can provide a positive testing environment by

    (A) encouraging students to be anxious about a test.

(B) providing a comfortable physical setting.

(C) surprising students with disruptions and distractions.

(D) emphasizing the consequences for poor performance.

9. Feedback sessions for a test are most effective

(A) when they are immediate.

(B) when they are delayed by a day or so.

(C) when they are delayed for a few weeks.

(D) when the feedback is written on paper only.

10. If mastery level for a skill is set at 75%, what does the student need to accomplish to exhibit mastery?

(A) A grade of C or higher

(B) A grade of B or higher

(C) Answer 75% of all of the particular skill questions correctly

(D) Answer 75% of all of the skills correctly

11. Good and Gouws found that effective teachers reviewed

(A) verbally.

(B) at the end of a lesson.

(C) as students showed weaknesses in specific areas.

(D) daily, weekly, and monthly.

12. A teacher says, "We have just finished looking at *Sense and Sensibility.* Let's go through our notes and review the traits of each character in the novel." This is an example of

(A) lesson-end review.

(B) lesson-initiating review.

(C) month-end review.

(D) topic summary.

13. Kallison Jr. found that subject retention increased when lessons included

    (A) reviews.

    (B) comprehension checks.

    (C) outlines at the beginning and a summary at the end.

    (D) lesson-initiating reviews.

14. A student describes an analysis of a recent Presidential address for the class. The teacher replies, "You have provided us with a most interesting way of looking at this issue!" The teacher is using

    (A) simple positive response.

    (B) negative response.

    (C) redirect.

    (D) academic praise.

15. When a teacher asks the class if they agree or disagree with a student's response, the teacher is using

    (A) redirect.

    (B) corrective.

    (C) positive feedback.

    (D) direct response.

16. Effective praise should be

    (A) authentic and low-key.

    (B) used sparingly.

    (C) comprised of simple, positive responses.

    (D) used to encourage high-achieving students.

17. While waiting for students to formulate their responses to a question, a student blurts out an answer. The teacher should

    (A) ignore the answer entirely.

(B) respond immediately to the student's answer.

(C) silently acknowledge the student's response, and then address the response after the question has been answered by someone else.

(D) move on to another question without comment.

18. What is one way of incorporating non-performers into a discussion?

(A) Ask a student to respond to a previous student's statement.

(B) Name a student to answer a question.

(C) Only call on students with their hands raised.

(D) Allow off-topic conversations.

19. In the middle of a discussion, a student asks to sharpen a pencil in response to an academic question. The teacher should

(A) see if the pencil needs to be sharpened.

(B) allow the student to sharpen the pencil.

(C) signal no, and then ask someone else the question.

(D) repeat the question to the student.

20. What is one benefit of practice activities?

(A) The teacher can observe where students need additional instruction.

(B) The students can develop their creative writing skills.

(C) Students can revisit previously learned skills.

(D) Students can learn new concepts.

21. When a teacher leads choral chants, the teacher is

(A) practicing aural skills.

(B) practicing vocal exercises.

(C) having students repeat basic skills orally.

(D) repeating what the students answer.

22. One use of homework is to

    (A) introduce new concepts.

    (B) provide structure to the classroom.

    (C) develop short-term retention.

    (D) revisit learned skills and concepts.

23. The question, "What was the name of Hamlet's father?" is

    (A) a high-order question of evaluation.

    (B) a low-order question that can be used to begin a discussion.

    (C) a transition.

    (D) questioning a skill.

24. "After you finish reading the passage, get out your history books and read the next section" is a

    (A) teacher redirect.

    (B) high-order activity.

    (C) transition statement.

    (D) test of complex skills.

25. One benefit of using transition statements is that

    (A) students are oriented to the classroom pace.

    (B) non-performers are being tested.

    (C) it enables high-order questioning.

    (D) it determines if students understand the directions.

26. When assigning a specific writing exercise, it is best to

    (A) assign a clear due date.

    (B) describe what should be included and how it will be graded.

    (C) allow students to write what they wish.

    (D) describe how the paper was graded when it is returned.

27. Bulletin boards, letters home, and a test with point values given for questions are examples of

    (A) standardized test preparations.

    (B) methods conveying performance standards.

    (C) engaging all students in an exercise.

    (D) evaluating the success of a lesson.

28. If a teacher asks, "Does everyone understand where to place their answers?" the teacher is probably

    (A) using a transition between lessons.

    (B) determining if the class understands the directions.

    (C) assuming that the students were off-task.

    (D) introducing a new skill.

29. If a teacher introduces a concept using examples and non-examples and asks the class to provide a definition of the concept, the teacher is considered to be teaching

    (A) deductively.

    (B) inductively.

    (C) using definitions.

    (D) using examples.

30. When teaching a concept, the teacher should provide

    (A) examples and non-examples.

    (B) several examples.

    (C) only interesting examples.

    (D) definitions.

31. Teachers should present scientific laws

    (A) in scientific terms.

    (B) by having the students repeat them.

(C) by analyzing causal conditions and their effects.

(D) to younger students.

32. What is the most important factor in a student's academic success?

(A) Prior knowledge

(B) Parental influence

(C) His or her attitudes and perceptions about learning

(D) The student's permanent records

33. Student learning is most successful when

(A) objectives are clearly outlined.

(B) colorful graphs and maps are used.

(C) the same examples are used.

(D) the classroom size is small.

34. Changing to an interactive approach, switching to a cooperative group activity, and incorporating manipulatives during the course of a lesson are examples of

(A) alternate behavior.

(B) getting students back on-task.

(C) management transition.

(D) skill practice.

35. Written academic feedback is most productive when it

(A) is delayed by a day.

(B) is uniform.

(C) includes at least one positive remark.

(D) is not specific.

36. Using student ideas and interests in a lesson

(A) takes students off-task.

(B) detracts from the subject content.

(C) does not allow for evaluation of students' prior knowledge.

(D) increases learning and student motivation.

37. Which of the following is a useful way of bringing a daydreaming student back on-task?

(A) Call on the student.

(B) Walk over and stand near the student.

(C) Question the class.

(D) Stop and stare at the student.

38. Piaget's theory of cognitive development states that

(A) children should be able to understand complex directions.

(B) younger children are unable to understand complex language.

(C) younger children will be unable to understand directions, even in simple language.

(D) directions should not be given to young children.

39. Teachers convey emotion through

(A) body language, eye contact, and verbal cues.

(B) verbal contact and cues.

(C) voice levels.

(D) the way they listen.

40. Controlled interruptions

(A) can be positively directed with procedures already in place.

(B) should be monitored on a by-case basis.

(C) are inevitable in a classroom.

(D) do not disrupt the classroom.

41. When introducing academic laws, the teacher should

    (A) teach related rules at the same time.

    (B) state the rule and have the class repeat it.

    (C) provide several examples.

    (D) state the rule, provide examples, and provide exercises.

42. A teacher tells a class that when a task is completed, book exercises should be worked on. This teacher is using

    (A) a transition.

    (B) wait-time avoidance.

    (C) taking students off-task.

    (D) wait time.

43. In a study, Fischer found that in an effective classroom, how many minutes per hour were spent on off-task behavior?

    (A) Four minutes

    (B) Ten minutes

    (C) No time

    (D) As long as necessary when passing out papers

44. Children under the age of eight

    (A) are unable to answer questions.

    (B) process information more slowly than older children.

    (C) can answer the same questions as slightly older children.

    (D) cannot learn in a cooperative environment.

45. How should learning activities be designed?

    (A) They should be selected by the students.

    (B) The activities should be based on specific objectives.

(C) They should test for knowledge.

(D) They should be on a daily basis.

46. Marshall Rosenberg categorized learners as

(A) rigid-inhibited, undisciplined, acceptance-anxious, and creative.

(B) undisciplined and high-achieving.

(C) undisciplined, disciplined, and high-achieving.

(D) fearful, undisciplined, and disciplined.

47. Before working with mathematical word problems, a teacher needs to determine that

(A) the student can complete the math unit.

(B) the student is at a high enough reading level to understand the problems.

(C) the math textbook mirrors the skills used in the word problems.

(D) the class will be on-task for the problems.

48. Objectives given to a class for student mastery

(A) should be tailored to students at all levels.

(B) should only be expected of certain students.

(C) should be ignored.

(D) are unnecessary.

49. Goals for individual students

(A) should be based upon the student's academic record.

(B) should be the same for all students.

(C) are created from individual observations only.

(D) are developed after considering the student's history and motivation.

50. When a teacher conducts an entry survey, he or she is

    (A) reviewing the skill mastery of a student.

    (B) cataloging what a student has learned over the year.

    (C) recording student background information.

    (D) testing for knowledge.

51. When developing evaluation methods for a test project, which factors should be considered?

    (A) General learning needs

    (B) Developmental stage for younger children

    (C) Class averages

    (D) The student's developmental stage and the information to be tested

52. When maintaining a running reading record, a teacher is

    (A) tape recording while a student reads aloud.

    (B) writing what a student reads aloud.

    (C) testing for comprehension.

    (D) noting what books have been read.

53. If a student incorrectly answers a question during a discussion, the teacher can guide the student to the correct answer by

    (A) asking another student.

    (B) providing the correct answer.

    (C) asking the student a series of questions to guide him or her to the correct answer.

    (D) assigning the question as homework.

54. When evaluating a child's writing ability in an assignment, it is useful to

    (A) view all of the drafts.

(B) evaluate the final copy.

(C) see that a lot of words were crossed off.

(D) have the student read the final copy aloud.

55. What can be determined by behavioral observation?

(A) Concept comprehension

(B) Ability to organize concepts

(C) Amount of time spent on-task

(D) Verbal skills

56. In the beginning of the year, David was a quiet child. However, in the middle of the year he is starting to frequently shout out and cause disruptions. What should an effective teacher do first?

(A) Send David to the office.

(B) Talk to the school administration.

(C) Use verbal and nonverbal cues to try to modify the behavior.

(D) Contact David's parents.

57. When reprimanding a class, which is most effective?

(A) Loud shouting

(B) The threat of harsh consequences

(C) Using a soft voice

(D) Angry outbursts

58. If a teacher is considered to be "with it," that teacher

(A) is always aware of what is going on in the classroom.

(B) wears modern clothes.

(C) understands student trends.

(D) uses language that the students relate to.

59. Canter and Canter's assertive discipline asserts that positive behavior should be

    (A) the standard.

    (B) positively reinforced.

    (C) part of the classroom rules.

    (D) not met with consequences.

60. While the teacher is reading aloud to the class, Caroline is telling jokes to get the students to laugh. According to Gordon's Teacher Effectiveness Training, who "owns" the problem?

    (A) The teacher

    (B) Caroline

    (C) The students in the class

    (D) The teacher, Caroline, and the students in the class

61. "You seem to feel that you aren't doing well in this subject" is an example of a(n)

    (A) evaluative statement.

    (B) directive statement.

    (C) nondirective statement.

    (D) judgment.

62. Using the operant behavior model, what is negative reinforcement?

    (A) Operant behavior

    (B) Stimulus for operant behavior

    (C) Unknowingly strengthening negative behavior

    (D) Removing something unpleasant after the asserted or expected behavior has occurred

63. Robert always calls out answers to questions without raising his hand. The teacher always ignores his answers. The teacher is trying to use

    (A) negative reinforcement.

    (B) extinction.

    (C) noninterventionism.

    (D) punishment.

64. According to Rath's values clarification, most student misbehavior is the result of

    (A) a student's cognitive deficits.

    (B) the student's inability to view alternatives.

    (C) students not knowing or thinking about their values.

    (D) a lack of indicators.

65. A student is misbehaving in class, so the teacher institutes an exclusion time-out. What will happen?

    (A) The student will sit out in the hallway for a period of ten minutes.

    (B) The student will observe the class, but without any reinforcement.

    (C) The student will ask to be alone.

    (D) The student will be unsure of what the reinforcement will be.

66. The purpose of Glasser's reality therapy is to

    (A) guide students toward realistic behavior by using reinforcements.

    (B) incorporate psychoanalytical and educational techniques.

    (C) clarify value systems.

    (D) aid the student in behaving responsibly.

67. A female student comes up to a teacher and says that a relative has been touching her in a way that makes her uncomfortable. What do you do?

    (A) Contact the school administration.

    (B) Talk to her and call her parents.

    (C) Nothing

    (D) Talk to another teacher.

68. Students start using drugs and alcohol

    (A) due to curiosity, desire for pleasure, peer pressure, and/or problem avoidance.

    (B) to deal with stress from school.

    (C) due to parental influences.

    (D) depending on social groups.

69. Social isolation, unwarranted nausea, headaches, and irrational fears or obsessions are symptoms of

    (A) nerves.

    (B) nothing.

    (C) tall tales.

    (D) neurotic disorders.

70. If a child in your class suffers from serious emotional disturbances, it is important to

    (A) maintain open communication with the parents.

    (B) keep the child separate from the other students.

    (C) only discuss the student with other teachers.

    (D) keep an eye on attendance.

71. You suspect that one of your students suffers from some form of psychotic disorder. You should first

    (A) talk to the student.

    (B) contact your school administration.

    (C) get a second opinion from another teacher.

    (D) set up a meeting with the parents and the student.

72. If there is a tornado warning, your class should be

    (A) evacuated from the building.

    (B) on the top level of the building.

    (C) in your classroom.

    (D) in a first-floor room away from windows.

73. A teacher ran out of copies of a worksheet before handing them out to the entire class, thus interrupting

    (A) materials.

    (B) class interest.

    (C) instructional momentum.

    (D) passing out the papers.

74. "Invitational learning" is the result of

    (A) a well-built classroom space.

    (B) use of a good teaching voice.

    (C) fun classroom exercises.

    (D) good lighting.

75. A student's positive self-concept

    (A) is the result of feelings of superiority.

    (B) is an important factor in the student's ability to learn.

    (C) is a reflection of the parent's opinion.

    (D) will be the same for everyone in an entire class.

76. Which of the following are the components of the process approach model?

    (A) Transform and teach

    (B) Sensing and acting

    (C) Reach, touch, and teach

    (D) Reaching and teaching

77. What is one skill demonstrated by invitational teachers?

    (A) They are separate from the students.

    (B) They ignore student feelings.

    (C) They use the behavioral method approach.

    (D) They are active listeners.

78. When teaching cooperative learning skills, the teacher should

    (A) foster student independence.

    (B) set up practice situations for skill mastery.

    (C) allow the students to foster the skill on their own.

    (D) form groups of students with various backgrounds.

79. Cooperative groups help to develop the students' abilities to

    (A) avoid misbehavior.

    (B) develop logic skills.

    (C) interact with their peers.

    (D) stay on-task.

80. A record of a student's general behavior and activities over a period of time is called a

    (A) portfolio.

    (B) behavioral observation.

    (C) global assessment.

    (D) formal observation.

81. Class activities should be graded on the basis of

    (A) student participation.

    (B) cooperative groupings.

    (C) criteria explained to the class.

    (D) the students' seatwork following the activity.

82. Inductive thinking can be fostered through which activity?

    (A) Choral chanting of skill tables

    (B) Computer experience

    (C) Multiple-choice questions

    (D) Personal-discovery activities

83. True-false questions on tests are considered

    (A) to promote guessing.

    (B) to promote inductive learning.

    (C) difficult for younger children.

    (D) very reliable.

84. Which is an environmental factor in operant conditioning?

    (A) A reflex action

    (B) A sticker incentive

    (C) Sounds

    (D) Teacher "with it"-ness

85. Which of the following is based on the theories of Piaget?

    (A) Children cannot learn until they are cognitively ready.

    (B) Judgments are made on the basis of physical consequences.

    (C) The classroom should be arranged to facilitate learning.

    (D) Negative behavior should be ignored.

86. How can a teacher elicit a high-order response from a student who provides simple responses?

    (A) Ask follow-up questions.

    (B) Repeat the questions.

    (C) Ask the same questions of a different student.

    (D) Ask another student to elaborate on the original response.

87. In a classroom discussion, when should a teacher delay speaking?

    (A) After asking a question

    (B) After a student response

    (C) Never

    (D) After questions and after responses

88. Bloom divided educational objectives into which of the following domains?

    (A) Knowledge, affective, and evaluation

    (B) Cognitive, affective, and psychomotor

    (C) Affective, value judgments, and psychomotor

    (D) Knowledge, comprehension, and application

89. During which of Piaget's stages of cognitive development will a child be able to solve concrete problems in a logical fashion?

    (A) Preoperational

    (B) Concrete operational

    (C) Sensorimotor

    (D) Formal operational

90. According to Erikson, when does a developmental crisis occur?

    (A) When a child is unable to keep up with his/her peers

    (B) When a child can accomplish some, but not all, age-related tasks

(C) When the resolution of a conflict will have later repercussions

(D) During early childhood

91. At what approximate age will one be at Erikson's industry versus inferiority stage of development?

(A) Elementary-middle school

(B) Early childhood

(C) Early adulthood

(D) At all ages

92. What is the range of the score that approximately 68% of the general population will receive on an intelligence quotient test?

(A) 100-120

(B) Below 50

(C) Above 100

(D) 85-115

93. A lesson where students are given a tankful of water and various objects and are asked to order the objects by weight would be considered a(n)

(A) science lesson.

(B) discovery-learning lesson.

(C) inductive-reasoning lesson.

(D) eg-rule lesson.

94. Kohlberg's developmental levels of preconventional, conventional, and postconventional aid a teacher in understanding a student's

(A) cognitive development.

(B) language acquisition.

(C) moral development.

(D) inductive reasoning.

95. Elaine suffers from brief losses of contact with the outside world and misses what is happening in class for periods of one to thirty seconds. Elaine may have

    (A) epilepsy.

    (B) problems at home.

    (C) a hearing impairment.

    (D) an articulation disorder.

96. The experiences of children outside of the classroom may result in

    (A) school phobia.

    (B) after-school activities.

    (C) lowered self-esteem.

    (D) cooperative learning.

97. What is one important feature of classroom management?

    (A) Speaking in a loud voice

    (B) Developing a conduct code during the first half of the year

    (C) Carefully stating expectations at the beginning of the year

    (D) Ignoring minor infractions

98. In the beginning of the school year, the teacher notices that a student speaks in a monotone as compared to the rest of the class. There is no note of this in the student's record. What should the teacher do?

    (A) Contact the parents.

    (B) Include singing in the lessons.

    (C) Contact the speech therapist.

    (D) Contact the school administration.

99. A student has started to come to class late, only to either sleep in class or to slur his words. You suspect that he may be drinking alcohol. What should you do?

    (A) Discuss this change in behavior with him personally.

    (B) Arrange for a meeting with his parents.

    (C) See if his friends have noticed this behavior in other classes.

    (D) Contact the school administration.

100. According to Piaget, at what age will students be able to develop scientific reasoning?

    (A) 2–7 years

    (B) 11–15 years

    (C) 7–11 years

    (D) 15–17 years

101. A teacher is working in the back of the room with a group of students while, in the front of the classroom, students are working on individual math problems. The teacher is able to tell when a student in the front of the room is going off-task. What is the teacher demonstrating?

    (A) "with it"-ness

    (B) Overlapping

    (C) Group focusing

    (D) Immersion

102. In a ninth-grade English class during an essay test, the teacher notices that two students are working off each other's papers. Which of the following would be an assertive discipline response?

    (A) Remind the class that cheating is against the rules of the classroom.

    (B) Ask the students to the teacher's desk and quietly inform them that they will not get credit for the exam due to their cheating.

(C) Walk around the room, pausing at the cheating students' desks.

(D) Announce to the entire class that the two students will not be getting credit for this exam.

103. Which of the following contribute to the development of student responsibility?

(A) Clear requirements, specific assignments, progress monitoring, and feedback

(B) Frequent feedback, continual assessment, and student-developed assignments

(C) Student portfolios and frequent feedback

(D) Student self-management, monitored progress, and frequent feedback

104. What should be avoided when intervening in student misbehavior?

(A) Speaking calmly and quietly

(B) Addressing more serious infractions first

(C) Waiting for a period of time before addressing the disruption

(D) Encouraging alternate behavior

105. A teacher wants to systematically observe how frequently a student is disruptive in class. What is one important thing that the teacher should do first?

(A) Arrange for someone not involved to observe the student.

(B) Carefully define the disruptive behavior.

(C) Wait until the class is doing seatwork.

(D) Record the behavior in intervals of 10 to 30 seconds.

106. A student was causing disruptions, but only during the middle of the day. When the teacher changed the student's seat to one closer to the door and away from the window, the disruptions ceased. What could have caused the change?

(A) The teacher did not appear to be as loud.

(B) The student grew out of a phase.

(C) The student was distracted by the recess activities he/she observed outside.

(D) The student did not like the subject being taught.

107. Which is an example of specific praise?

(A) "I really like the way that Alice is doing her work!"

(B) "Good for you! That is the top grade in the class!"

(C) "I am very pleased to say that everyone did a great job on the test!"

(D) "Your careful work made this special, especially in your art-work!"

108. How can a teacher reprimand a student while maintaining the academic focus of a class?

(A) Respond with a punitive or angry desist.

(B) Respond with a simple reprimand.

(C) Ignore the behavior.

(D) Take the student out of the room.

109. What is the self-fulfilling prophecy?

(A) Students produce work that matches their personal expectations.

(B) Teachers can predict student progress.

(C) Incorrect assumptions or beliefs become true because they are expected.

(D) Students are unable to understand teacher expectations.

110. A teacher begins a lesson with the following: "Today I want to briefly go over yesterday's problems before we introduce a few new algebraic laws. You will then have the opportunity to work with your partner on proving these laws." What is this teacher doing?

(A) Cooperative learning

(B) Giving a pep-talk

(C) Informing the students of what the objectives for the day will be

(D) Reviewing yesterday's work

111. Preformationism is the view that children

(A) grow developmentally.

(B) are miniature adults.

(C) have different cognitive abilities at different ages.

(D) are shaped by their experiences growing up.

112. When assigning seatwork exercises, an effective teacher always

(A) provides corrective feedback.

(B) includes review questions.

(C) allows students to grade their neighbors' papers.

(D) introduces new concepts.

113. What teacher behavior can decrease class disruptions and increase class participation?

(A) Reprimanding the class as a whole

(B) Frequent review

(C) Showing genuine enthusiasm for the task at hand

(D) Intermittent reprimands

114. A systematic and continuing evaluation that can lead to changes in the curriculum or class design is known as

(A) formative evaluation.

(B) summative evaluation.

(C) thematic units.

(D) ongoing evaluation.

115. If a teacher wanted to organize a lesson using the jigsaw cooperative learning method, he or she would

   (A) provide a lecture of direct instruction, followed by seat work.

   (B) divide the students into heterogeneous groups, each student in a group assigned to be an expert in a particular area, all experts to meet to learn about their assignments, and then go back to their original groups to teach their knowledge area.

   (C) allow students to determine the topic to study; in groups, the students and the teacher plan learning tasks and goals, implement the plan, analyze their results, and then present their findings to the class.

   (D) allow the students to work at different learning centers until it is time to rotate to the next one.

116. Which example of feedback is the most effective?

   (A) "Your paper's argument should be stronger."

   (B) "That was a good shot!"

   (C) "When you gave your class presentation, you were speaking so softly that we could not hear you in the back of the room."

   (D) "You gave a nice talk."

117. When does language develop in children?

   (A) When they are one year old.

   (B) When they are two years old.

   (C) When they are five years old.

   (D) It varies.

118. What is the developmental task at Erikson's early childhood psychosocial stage?

   (A) Trust versus mistrust

   (B) Intimacy versus isolation

   (C) Initiative versus guilt

   (D) Autonomy versus doubt

119. A student reads aloud correctly when working with small groups, but has difficulty reading aloud to the class from the board. What could be the problem?

(A) The student is nervous about reading aloud to the full class.

(B) The student is having difficulty seeing the board.

(C) The work on the board contains more difficult passages.

(D) The student is actually performing the same in both situations.

120. Devices used to aid memorization using rhymes, acronyms, songs, or stories are called

(A) choral responses.

(B) repetitions.

(C) codings.

(D) mnemonics.

121. Which of the following is an operant?

(A) A stimulus

(B) A consequence

(C) A reinforcement

(D) A deliberate action

122. What does an achievement test measure?

(A) How much a student has learned in a particular subject area

(B) How a student compares to a set performance standard

(C) Specific learning problems

(D) What career a student may be interested in

123. Children who have been abused

(A) are at great risk of being abused again.

(B) always ask for help.

(C) will not be hurt again.

(D) are easily spotted.

124. When working with ESL students, the teacher should be aware that

(A) students should only speak English in class.

(B) an accepting classroom and encouraging lessons will foster learning.

(C) the student should be referred to a specialist.

(D) limiting the number of resources available is beneficial to the students.

125. Student Teams-Achievement Divisions (STAD) uses

(A) homogeneous groups, elements of competition, and rewards.

(B) preparation, presentation, practice, and evaluation.

(C) heterogeneous groups, elements of competition, and rewards.

(D) description, content, practice, review, and follow-up.

126. In selecting materials for a class, the effective teacher will look at

(A) the ratio of pictures to text.

(B) the size of the font used.

(C) if the material can hold the attention of learners of all types.

(D) the size of the material.

127. Students are having problems with a passage of text. What could be done to help these students?

(A) Incorporate visuals.

(B) Use a different book.

(C) Have other students read the passage aloud.

(D) Have the students read the passage aloud.

128. Which of the following is an effective system of study skills?

    (A) A word processing program

    (B) Previewing, questioning, reading, reflecting, reciting, and reviewing

    (C) Re-copying vocabulary and spelling words

    (D) Reading picture captions

129. According to Gardner, there are how many different kinds of intelligence?

    (A) Seven

    (B) Three

    (C) Six

    (D) One

130. What are the essential components of cooperative learning tasks?

    (A) Reward systems and prizes

    (B) Individual students selecting teammates

    (C) Pairs of students teaching each other

    (D) Heterogeneous teams working toward goals

131. When dealing with classroom management, the effective teacher

    (A) responds to deviant and compliant behavior.

    (B) reprimands every other disruption.

    (C) only acknowledges major disruptions.

    (D) formulates a new plan daily.

132. Long-term memory

    (A) will disappear in approximately 20 seconds unless rehearsed.

    (B) is very limited.

    (C) is permanent and appears unlimited.

    (D) will exist for a few months unless rehearsed.

133. Sequential language acquisition occurs when students

    (A) learn a second language after mastery of the first.

    (B) learn a second language at the same time as the first.

    (C) learn two languages in parts.

    (D) develop language skills.

134. Pat was given a test which consisted of being asked to repeat several digits forward and backward. Additionally, Pat was given some vocabulary questions. What kind of test was Pat given?

    (A) A vocabulary test

    (B) An achievement test

    (C) An intelligence test

    (D) An arithmetic placement test

135. Teachers should provide a variety of experiences and concrete examples for children with reading difficulties since some children

    (A) come from environments with limited language exposure.

    (B) have poor learning habits.

    (C) have trouble distinguishing letters.

    (D) can speak well, but have difficulty reading.

136. Effective teachers can build the self-esteem of students by

    (A) posting all failing grades on a bulletin board.

    (B) using negative reinforcement.

    (C) providing successful experiences for each student.

    (D) amplifying responses.

137. Behaviorism is interested in which of the following?

    (A) Cognitive abilities

    (B) Rewarding peer interaction

(C) Teacher-initiated learning

(D) Full discovery learning

138. A student frequently leaves his seat during lessons and causes disruptions. The teacher can try to get the student to cooperate by

(A) ignoring the student.

(B) yelling at the student.

(C) trying to determine why the student is misbehaving.

(D) assigning more seat work.

139. The raw score in the results of a test indicates

(A) the percentage of questions answered correctly.

(B) the number of items answered correctly.

(C) how a student compares to other students.

(D) the overall grade.

140. A teacher wants to test the computational skills of the students. The best type of questions to use would be

(A) word problems.

(B) true-false questions.

(C) problems with few words.

(D) vocabulary questions.

STOP
If time still remains, you may go back and check your work.

PRACTICE TEST 1

ANSWER KEY

1.	(A)	29.	(B)	57.	(C)	85.	(A)	113.	(C)
2.	(D)	30.	(A)	58.	(A)	86.	(A)	114.	(A)
3.	(A)	31.	(C)	59.	(B)	87.	(D)	115.	(B)
4.	(D)	32.	(C)	60.	(A)	88.	(B)	116.	(C)
5.	(C)	33.	(A)	61.	(C)	89.	(B)	117.	(B)
6.	(A)	34.	(B)	62.	(D)	90.	(C)	118.	(C)
7.	(C)	35.	(C)	63.	(B)	91.	(A)	119.	(B)
8.	(B)	36.	(D)	64.	(C)	92.	(D)	120.	(D)
9.	(B)	37.	(B)	65.	(B)	93.	(B)	121.	(D)
10.	(C)	38.	(B)	66.	(D)	94.	(C)	122.	(A)
11.	(D)	39.	(A)	67.	(A)	95.	(A)	123.	(A)
12.	(A)	40.	(A)	68.	(A)	96.	(C)	124.	(B)
13.	(C)	41.	(D)	69.	(D)	97.	(C)	125.	(C)
14.	(D)	42.	(A)	70.	(A)	98.	(C)	126.	(C)
15.	(A)	43.	(A)	71.	(B)	99.	(D)	127.	(A)
16.	(A)	44.	(B)	72.	(D)	100.	(B)	128.	(B)
17.	(C)	45.	(B)	73.	(C)	101.	(A)	129.	(A)
18.	(A)	46.	(A)	74.	(A)	102.	(B)	130.	(D)
19.	(C)	47.	(B)	75.	(B)	103.	(A)	131.	(A)
20.	(A)	48.	(A)	76.	(C)	104.	(C)	132.	(C)
21.	(C)	49.	(D)	77.	(D)	105.	(B)	133.	(A)
22.	(D)	50.	(C)	78.	(D)	106.	(C)	134.	(C)
23.	(B)	51.	(D)	79.	(C)	107.	(D)	135.	(A)
24.	(C)	52.	(B)	80.	(B)	108.	(C)	136.	(C)
25.	(A)	53.	(C)	81.	(C)	109.	(C)	137.	(C)
26.	(B)	54.	(A)	82.	(D)	110.	(C)	138.	(C)
27.	(B)	55.	(C)	83.	(A)	111.	(B)	139.	(B)
28.	(B)	56.	(C)	84.	(B)	112.	(A)	140.	(C)

DETAILED EXPLANATIONS
OF ANSWERS

Practice Test 1

1. **(A)** Whether in a classroom dedicated to computers or in a room with a computer center away from the main group, computer rules should be emphasized and then posted in the classroom to avoid any confusion or any experimentation with the machines. Therefore, answers (B), (C), and (D) are incorrect.

2. **(D)** The Internet can be accessed using a browser program, such as Netscape® or Internet Explorer® (A). Class records can be maintained in a recordkeeping program, such as Excel (B). Class newspapers can be created using desktop publishing programs (C).

3. **(A)** As long as students are well-informed about procedures ahead of time, it is possible to rotate computer use among single students or small groups so that the class can optimize their experience with computers. Therefore, answers (B), (C), and (D) are not the best choices.

4. **(D)** A portfolio keeps a collection of dated samples of a student's work over time. There can be a single portfolio for all subjects, or portfolios for specific subjects. The work contained in a portfolio then becomes an accurate representation of a student's progress. It may contain artwork by a student, but is not limited to artwork (A). It is not used to draw comparisons between students (B), nor is the project graded on a scale (C).

5. **(C)** Teachers compose narrative reports which describe a student's strengths, weaknesses, behaviors, progress, and any other information to supplement the information that is conveyed in a report card. They can be used if a parent cannot attend a parent-teacher conference, for example. Answer (A) is incorrect because it is the teacher, not the student, who describes how the student is performing. It is not a formal report card (B), but is used to supplement the information on the report card. Answer (D) is also incorrect because narrative reports can be used as an alternative to parent-teacher conferences.

6. **(A)** A student's permanent record, which is a file containing all aspects of a student's background, should only be discussed with the student's parents, legal guardians, teachers, and school administrators. It is a highly personal and comprehensive student record. It may be discussed with the student's parents (B), or the school administrators (C), but is not only limited to school administrators and parents (D). Teachers also have the right to discuss the student's record. Therefore, answers (B), (C), and (D) are incorrect.

7. **(C)** Research has shown that students perform better on tests when they are familiar with the test content and test format. It does not matter if the test contains a particular type of question (A), as long as the students know what to expect. Students have greater success in testing situations when their teacher is enthusiastic about their results (B). Students perform poorly when the test format changes frequently (D).

8. **(B)** Students are able to perform better on tests when their physical setting, which includes lighting, temperature, and seating, is favorable. When students feel anxious over a test (A), or when teachers threaten against poor performances (D), students do not perform as well. Outside disruptions (C) can break a student's concentration, most specifically in younger children.

9. **(B)** Research has shown that it is favorable to provide feedback in test situations when the feedback is delayed by a day or so, rather than giving immediate feedback (A). Delaying the feedback session for a few weeks is not beneficial to the students because too much time has elapsed (C). A class review of the test has been shown to be more beneficial in clearing up misunderstandings than handwritten notations (D).

10. **(C)** When a teacher sets a mastery level at a certain percentage and the student reaches that percentage, he or she is considered to have mastered that skill and receives a grade of "A" for his or her efforts. Therefore, answers (A) and (B) are incorrect. Answering 75% of all of the skills correctly (D) is also incorrect because in order to master a particular skill, the student does not need to master all of the skills.

11. **(D)** Good and Gouws found that effective teachers conducted reviews as part of their daily, weekly, and monthly routines. Therefore, answers (A), (B), and (C) are incorrect because they were not findings in their study.

12. **(A)** The language that the teacher uses indicates that this is a lesson-end review that draws upon what the students have noted during

the lesson. It cannot be answer (B) because the lesson has already been taught and, therefore, the teacher is not initiating the lesson. Answer (C) is also incorrect because the teacher is not reviewing at the end of the month, but at the end of the lesson. Answer (D) is incorrect because the students are not summarizing the novel, but are reviewing character traits.

13. **(C)** Kallison Jr. found that subject matter retention was increased when the teacher provided an outline detailing what would be discussed during a lesson and a summary of the lesson at the end. Therefore, answers (A), (B), and (D) are incorrect because they were not part of the findings.

14. **(D)** Academic praise is comprised of specific statements that give information about the value of the object or about its implications. A simple positive response (A) does not provide any information other than the praise, such as the example, "That's a good answer!" There is nothing negative (B) about the teacher's response. A redirect (C) occurs when a teacher asks a student to react to the response of another student.

15. **(A)** A redirect (A) occurs when a teacher asks one student to react to the response of another student. A corrective (B) occurs when a teacher responds to a student error by explaining why it is an error and then provides a correct answer. When teachers are redirecting, they are not giving any feedback (C), nor are they directly responding to the student comments (D).

16. **(A)** Praise has been shown to be the most effective when it is authentic and low-key (A). It should be used frequently; therefore (B) is incorrect. It should consist of complex responses that provide information about the reasons for the quality of the student response (C); therefore (C) is incorrect. It should be used to provide all students with positive experiences (D); therefore (D) is incorrect.

17. **(C)** If the teacher ignores the answer entirely (A) or moves on to another question (D), it devalues the student response. If the teacher responds immediately to the digression (B), the disruptive behavior has been rewarded. The correct answer is (C).

18. **(A)** Non-performers are students who are not involved in the class discussion at that particular moment. Asking students to respond to student statements (A) is one way of incorporating non-performers into a class discussion. Therefore, answers (B), (C), and (D) are incorrect.

19. **(C)** Body language is an effective way of avoiding digressions in class. This answer choice provides the best method of dealing with the

disruptive behavior while maintaining the class momentum. Checking to see if the pencil needs to be sharpened (A) and repeating the question to the students (D) disturb the class momentum. Allowing the student to sharpen the pencil (B) rewards the student's disruptive behavior.

20. **(A)** Practice activities provide an opportunity for teachers to monitor students to see if additional instruction is needed after a lesson (A). Practice activities are used for any subject matter just featured in the class lesson; therefore, (B) is incorrect. Practice activities reinforce skills that the students have just learned, rather than reviewing old material (C) or introducing new concepts (D).

21. **(C)** When students repeat basic facts, spellings, and laws, it is called a choral chant.

22. **(D)** Homework should be used to reinforce the learning done in the classroom (D), rather than to start new lessons (A). This will help to place the skills learned in long-term memory (C). Effective classroom management is needed to form structure in a classroom (B).

23. **(B)** A high-order question (A) tests the student's ability to apply information, evaluate information, create new information, etc., rather than to recall simple content. Transitions (C) are used to connect different ideas and tasks. The information that the question is looking for is one of content, not skill. The question presented here is a low-order question that ensures that a student is focused on the task at hand and can be used to develop into higher questioning.

24. **(C)** This transition statement is used to inform the student of what the expected tasks are as the class moves from one subject to another. A redirect (A) occurs when a teacher asks one student to react to the response of another student. A high-order activity (B) tests the student's ability to apply information, evaluate information, create new information, etc., rather than simple content or simple skills. Transitions (C) are used to connect different ideas and tasks. Answer (D) is incorrect because this is a statement and is not intended to test the students.

25. **(A)** Transitions allow students to be aware of future events, topics, and expectations (A). Transitions are not class discussions, so students cannot be classified as either performers or non-performers (B). Transitions set up events rather than questions (C) and are generally supplemented by formalized instructions for each topic or event (D).

26. **(B)** It is very important to outline what is expected from students, especially in writing assignments where the grading can be more subjec-

tive. This overshadows announcing a due date (A), and while it is important to give feedback on how something was graded (D), this information should be outlined at the beginning. Students will be able to find a balance between writing what they want (C) and meeting their writing objectives.

27. **(B)** Bulletin boards, letters home, and clearly marked point values given on a test are ways to communicate with students and their parents about grading expectations. This could include conveying information about standardized testing (A), but does not apply to engaging students in an exercise (C). The success of a lesson can only be based on student responses and achievement (D).

28. **(B)** It is important to make sure that students understand directions so as to limit any factors that may prevent a successful lesson. This question is not a transition between tasks (A) and does not assume that the students were not paying attention (C). It is a way of monitoring something that has already been explained. Answer (D) is incorrect because the teacher is not introducing a new skill.

29. **(B)** In inductive teaching, the students are provided with examples and non-examples and are expected to derive the definition from this information. In deductive teaching (A), the teacher defines a concept and provides a few examples and non-examples. Definitions (C) and examples (D) are important parts of inductive and deductive teaching.

30. **(A)** It has been found that it is most effective to provide a few examples and non-examples in teaching a concept. The actual number of examples (B) does not make a difference, nor do the examples all have to be interesting (C). From the examples and non-examples, students can inductively determine the definition (D) of the concept.

31. **(C)** It is important that students understand the "why" and "because" that are behind a scientific law. Research has shown that the use of linking words helps students to see relationships between cause and effect. Discussing these laws in scientific terms (A) may only cause confusion for the students. Merely being able to repeat a law (B) does not show that the students understand the concept. Children between the ages of four and seven are not able to understand or order cause-and-effect relationships (D).

32. **(C)** It has been shown that the most important factor in academic success has been the student's attitudes about learning. This is more influential than parental influences (B), academic history (D), or prior knowledge (A).

33. **(A)** Students are able to learn the most when they are aware of and

understand exactly what is expected of them. This overshadows the use of special materials (B), repetition of examples (C), or classroom size (D).

34. **(B)** Changing to an interactive approach, switching to a cooperative group, and using manipulatives are all methods of getting students more actively involved in a lesson because it forces them to be occupied with the task at hand.

35. **(C)** Written academic feedback should contain specific comments on errors and how to improve them. It should also contain a positive remark that notes an aspect of the assignment that was done well. Therefore, delaying feedback by a day (A), specifying uniform guidelines (B), and presenting feedback in a vague manner (D) are not the correct answer choices.

36. **(D)** Students are likely to be more enthusiastic when things that they enjoy are the subject or focus of a lesson, which in turn helps to build the academic success of the lesson.

37. **(B)** If a teacher notices that a student is daydreaming, walking over to the student or placing a hand on his or her shoulder are ways of bringing the student back on-task without disrupting the flow and the momentum of the lesson. Calling on the student (A), who will probably be unable to answer, or stopping and staring at the student (D) will result in lost momentum. Asking questions of the class (C) may not bring the student back on-task.

38. **(B)** Piaget developed four stages of cognitive development. As a child goes through each stage new abilities will have been developed, but they will be unable to have this ability until they reach that particular stage. Children under the age of eight do not have the understanding of language that grasps complexities (A). Accordingly, teachers should use simple language when working with these children (C, D).

39. **(A)** Even without saying a word, teachers can communicate a variety of emotions with their body language, eye contact, and verbal cues. Smiles, movement, posture, and eye contact with students can all convey the enthusiasm of an effective teacher. Body language can even convey that teachers are actively listening to their students by maintaining eye contact and leaning into the conversation.

40. **(A)** Controlled interruptions include students missing supplies, students late to class, students returning after an absence—minor disruptions that can be minimized with procedures that are already in place. For example, if a student is missing a supply needed for a class, he or she would

know to sign out for a replacement from the supply shelf. These types of disruptions are inevitable, but can be managed.

41. **(D)**   When introducing an academic law, the teacher should use the multistep process of stating the rule, providing examples, and then providing exercises. Thus, students are introduced to the concept, can see how it relates to the examples given, and can then try to apply the law on their own. It is a process that requires higher-level thought, rather than just repetition (B). The teacher should not teach related rules (A) until the students are familiar with the initial concept. Only providing examples (C), without stating the rule and providing exercises, is not an effective way to introduce the law.

42. **(A)**   The teacher is using a transition to keep the momentum of the class going. Students now know what is expected of them, and those that finish the first task early will be able to move onto the next easily.

43. **(A)**   Off-task behavior includes taking attendance, passing out papers and books, and any other administrative duties. Fischer found that in the average classroom, eight minutes per hour were spent on off-task behavior. In an effective classroom, however, four minutes were spent on off-task behavior, due to the use of established procedures in the classroom.

44. **(B)**   When designing learning activities, teachers should be aware that younger students process information more slowly than their older counterparts. Activities for younger children should be simple and short in duration.

45. **(B)**   The learning activities in class should be based on specific objectives, preferably ones that are closely related to the recent objectives of the class.

46. **(A)**   Teachers need to stimulate all types of students and be aware of their needs. Marshall Rosenberg has categorized them as rigid-inhibited, undisciplined, acceptance-anxious, and creative.

47. **(B)**   It is important to ensure that the word problems given to students are at their reading level, otherwise, a teacher will be unable to evaluate their successes with these problems accurately. Answers (A), (C), and (D) are not the best answers to the question.

48. **(A)**   The objectives given to a class should be applicable for all of the levels within the class to be fair and effective. It is necessary to detail these objectives to the class so that they are aware of what is expected of

them. Objectives should not only be expected of certain students (B), but should be expected of the entire class. They also should not be ignored (C) and are important for the class and should not be deemed unnecessary (D).

49. **(D)**   Individual goals for a student should be developed after reviewing both the student's history and assessing the student's motivation. This will ensure that the goals can be met by the student. Goals should not be based solely on the student's academic record (A) or created from individual observations only (C). They should also not be the same for all students (B) since students learn at different levels and aim for different goals.

50. **(C)**   At the beginning of the year, the teacher may complete an entry survey of the students in the class to collect background information such as age, family members, health, special interests, strengths, weaknesses, languages spoken at home, etc. This will allow the teacher to get to know the students and provides a basis for future growth. An entry survey does not review the skill mastery of a student (A), catalog what a student has learned over the year (B), or test for knowledge (D).

51. **(D)**   When evaluating a test or project, it is important to consider the developmental stage of the student and its relation to the task. Additionally, the evaluator should consider what objectives should have been met by the task. The general learning needs (A) of the student are not considered because the teacher is evaluating a specific project where specific learning objectives are to be met. The developmental stage is not to be considered only when teaching younger children (B). Class averages (C) are also not an effective method of evaluating a test or project.

52. **(B)**   A teacher keeps a running reading record by writing down what the student actually reads aloud. This helps the teacher in identifying and addressing what the student may need to increase reading skills.

53. **(C)**   If a student answers a question incorrectly, it is possible to guide him or her to the correct answer by asking a series of questions. If a student is unsure of a particular historical figure, for example, and gives an incorrect name in response, the teacher can ask questions that are associated with the correct name.

54. **(A)**   If a teacher is able to view all of the drafts that led to the final product, the teacher will have insight into how the content and form of the assignment were developed, thus giving a look into the student's writing process. This is not reflected in the final copy (B), and is not possible with just crossed-out words (C). Having the student read the paper aloud (D)

lets the teacher evaluate the student's reading ability more than his/her writing ability.

55. **(C)** Behavioral observation is the examination of what the student does during class time. A teacher should be interested in how much time a student spends on-task and how much time is spent off-task. Teachers generally observe a student for a limited period of time and mark the activities in which the student is engaged. If a particular activity, such as talking, appears frequently, it is noted.

56. **(C)** A teacher should first try to modify the behavior in the classroom with management techniques. However, if the behavior continues to persist, the teacher should discuss the matter with the student's parents (D).

57. **(C)** Studies have shown that reprimands are more effective when they are made in a soft, controlled manner. Loud shouting (A), threats (B), and angry outbursts (D) cause more anxiety in a classroom rather than effectively modify behavior.

58. **(A)** A teacher's "with it"-ness relates to the ability to observe and manage disruptions quickly, quietly, and at all times. For example, a "with it" teacher that is helping a student with deskwork would be able to detect and distinguish any disruptive behavior in a different part of the room.

59. **(B)** Canter and Canter's assertive discipline is a system for teachers to maintain a positive classroom while managing misbehavior situations constructively. One of the fundamental ideas is that proper behavior in a classroom should result in positive consequences, which in turn promote a positive classroom environment.

60. **(A)** According to Gordon, ownership of the problem belongs to either the student, the teacher, or there is no problem if the behavior is not affecting anyone negatively. Caroline's jokes are keeping the teacher from effectively reading to the class. Therefore, the teacher owns the problem, and can tailor a response based on methods that Gordon supplies.

61. **(C)** Nondirective statements are a way of showing a student that the teacher is listening, but do not make a judgment or point the conversation into a specific direction. Directive statements (B) do just the opposite. The statement is also not evaluating (A) or judging (D), so these answers are incorrect.

62. **(D)** A negative reinforcement occurs when an adverse stimulus is removed after the desired behavior has occurred.

63. **(B)**   The teacher is not providing any sort of reinforcement for Robert's behavior in the hope that, without reinforcement, Robert will lose interest, and the behavior will die out.

64. **(C)**   According to Rath, student misbehavior is the result of a student not knowing or thinking about his or her values. Rath considers this to be due to mental or physical abilities, emotional experiences, or a lack of values.

65. **(B)**   In an exclusion time-out, which is generally used for less severe misbehaviors, the student will be placed where the class can be observed, but will not receive any reinforcement. Exclusion time-out usually lasts for five to ten minutes.

66. **(D)**   Reality therapy is used to help the student to face reality and be responsible for his or her own actions. If a student misbehaves, the teacher should 1) help the student identify the problem; 2) aid the development of a value judgment about the behavior; and 3) assist the student in developing a plan to change the behavior.

67. **(A)**   The teacher should contact the school administration, who will then arrange for a trained professional to talk to the student. Answers (B), (C), and (D) are not the correct actions to take.

68. **(A)**   All types of students start using drugs and alcohol out of curiosity, desire for pleasure, pressure from peers, and/or to avoid problems (A).

69. **(D)**   These are symptoms of a neurotic disorder. A neurotic disorder is an emotional disorder that endangers a child's well-being and should be taken very seriously.

70. **(A)**   It is important to keep strong communication lines open with the parents so that the child can get the best possible care and understanding from both the parents and the teacher.

71. **(B)**   Psychotic disorders are rare in children, but if you do suspect that something is wrong you should contact your school administration.

72. **(D)**   In case of a tornado, you should evacuate everyone to the first floor of a building and then place students near walls that are away from windows. Everyone should crouch on the floor and then cover their heads with their hands. The teacher should evacuate students to the first floor of the building, but not outside the building (A). Students should also not be on the top level of the building (B) or in a classroom (C) unless the classroom is on the first floor and students are away from windows.

73. **(C)** To keep students on-task, it is very important to keep any distractions to a minimum, or else the instructional momentum will be lost. Always be sure to have enough copies of materials, and check to see if audio-visual equipment is working properly.

74. **(A)** Invitational learning takes place in a classroom that is welcoming; that is, one that is adequately sized, well-built, and properly equipped. The physical setting of a classroom can greatly influence learning. Special attention should also be paid to lighting, ventilation, and proper exit and entry locations.

75. **(B)** How a student views him- or herself is a very important factor in how well he or she will learn. Students with low self-esteem or who do not accept themselves will not perform as well as students with a positive self-concept.

76. **(C)** The process approach can be used in a variety of fields. It uses a sensing function (reach), a transforming function (touch), and an acting function (teach). Students take in information, abstract and add value to this information, and then act on an alternative that is based upon the information.

77. **(D)** Invitational teachers display behaviors and attitudes that are inviting, rather than disinviting, to students. Some of these behaviors include reaching out to each student, listening with care, and being "real" with students and with themselves. Invitational teachers do not separate themselves from the students (A), ignore student feelings (B), or use the behavioral method approach (C).

78. **(D)** Cooperative learning requires that students work with their peers in heterogeneous groups, with each student adopting a strong role. This requires that the students first learn how to work with one another using cooperative skills. The students should see the need for these skills, should be able to understand and practice these skills, and should be able to practice these skills until they appear natural to the students. Since cooperative learning requires students to be in groups, it does not foster student independence (A) or allow the students to foster the skill on their own (C). Cooperative learning also does not set up practice situations for skill mastery (B).

79. **(C)** One of the main goals of cooperative learning is to have students work together and teach one another for improved peer interaction.

80. **(B)** A behavioral observation is a written record of a child's behavior and activities for a given time period, and notes the start and end times

of observation and the specific activities of the student. A portfolio (A) is a collection of date-stamped samples of a student's work. A global assessment (C) informally details a student's interaction with peers, general attitudes, typical behaviors, and relations with school work. Formal observations are assessments with a specific focus on a particular behavior during a specific class time.

81. **(C)** All class activities should only be graded according to the criteria that the teacher specifically outlines to the class before the activity has started. Student participation (A), cooperative groupings (B), and seatwork (D) can all be graded, but only if the students are informed of the grading criteria.

82. **(D)** In inductive thinking, students derive concepts and definitions based upon the information provided to them, which can be fostered through personal-discovery activities (D) where students try to determine the relationships between the objects given to them. Choral chanting (A) practices skills; multiple-choice questions (C) test objective knowledge; general computer experience (B) fosters computer knowledge.

83. **(A)** Due to their 50-50 chance nature, true-false questions are considered to promote guessing and should not be used as the sole source of evaluation. They do not promote inductive learning (B) and are not a reliable method used to evaluate a student (D). There is also no reason to believe that true-false questions are more difficult for younger children than older children (C).

84. **(B)** In operant conditioning, behavior occurs after an environmental factor (its antecedent) and before an environmental factor (its consequence). Teachers can guide desired behavior by changing the antecedent, the consequence, or both. Using a sticker incentive is a way of strengthening, or reinforcing, the desired behavior.

85. **(A)** Piaget believed that children developed in sequential cognitive stages and that they would be unable to understand a concept that was in a stage higher than the one that they were in. For example, children are unable to understand the concept of reversibility until they reach Piaget's concrete operational stage (around ages 7–11). Answers (B), (C), and (D) are not based on the theories of Piaget.

86. **(A)** A teacher can guide a student to a higher-level answer through questioning. Repeating the question (B) would probably elicit the same response, and asking a different student (C, D) would not help the original student who provided the simple response.

87. **(D)** Delaying calling on a specific student after posing a question allows the entire class to compose an answer to a question; waiting to speak after a student gives a response allows the class to think of a reply. Both methods are ways of keeping students on-task.

88. **(B)** Bloom classified educational objectives into a classification system that was divided into three domains—cognitive (memory and reasoning), affective (emotions), and psychomotor (physical abilities).

89. **(B)** In Piaget's concrete operational stage, children will be able to solve concrete problems, and understand laws of conservation, classification, seriation, and reversibility.

90. **(C)** Erikson developed a psychosocial theory of development, and believed that at each stage of development a person is faced with a conflict whose resolution prepares the person for the next stage. For example, an infant's conflict is trust versus mistrust.

91. **(A)** Erikson believed that elementary through middle-school-aged children (ages 6–12 years) were faced with the conflict of industry versus inferiority.

92. **(D)** Sixty-eight percent of the population will receive IQ scores ranging from 85–115.

93. **(B)** A discovery-learning lesson is one where the class is organized to learn through their own active involvement in the lesson. In inductive-reasoning lessons (C), the students are provided with the examples and non-examples and are expected to derive definitions from this information. The eg-rule method (D) moves from specific examples to general rules or definitions. The lesson may take place in a science class (A), but is still a discovery-learning lesson.

94. **(C)** Kohlberg created sequenced stages of moral reasoning. The stages are: preconventional moral reasoning, conventional moral reasoning, and postconventional moral reasoning.

95. **(A)** Epilepsy is a nervous disease characterized by seizures resulting from uncontrolled firing of brain neurons. *Petit mal* epilepsy results in brief episodes where the person seems to be in another place. *Grand mal* epilepsy seizures are periods of two to five minutes of uncontrolled jerking movements.

96. **(C)** Teachers will have a classroom full of students with a variety of backgrounds. Some outside school experiences, family or otherwise, will result in lowered self-esteem for some students.

97. **(C)**   It has been shown that it is very important for a teacher to carefully explain the objectives and procedures of the classroom from the beginning. These objectives and procedures should then be consistently enforced throughout the year. Speaking in a loud voice (A) may intimidate the students and is not an effective method of classroom management. Developing a conduct code during the first half of the year (B) is not effective because students need to know what is expected of them from the beginning. Ignoring minor infractions (D) is not a feature of classroom management.

98. **(C)**   The student may have a speech impediment. The school speech therapist should be contacted for further consultation.

99. **(D)**   If you suspect that a student has a substance abuse problem, it is important that you contact the school administration to deal with the situation properly.

100. **(B)**   According to Piaget's stages of cognitive development, children develop their scientific thinking in the formal operations stage (11–15 years).

101. **(A)**   A teacher's "with it"-ness relates to the ability to observe and manage disruptions quickly, quietly, and at all times. For example, a "with it" teacher that is writing on the blackboard would be able to detect and distinguish any disruptive behavior in the back of the room.

102. **(B)**   The assertive discipline response would be for the teacher to ask the students to come to his/her desk and quietly inform them that they will not receive any credit on their exams because they were cheating. According to Canter and Canter, answers (A) and (C) are passive, while answer (D) is hostile.

103. **(A)**   Students will be able to develop their responsibility in classrooms that provide clear objectives and assignments, are monitored for progress, and where students are given frequent feedback on their actions.

104. **(C)**   It is important to immediately address disruptions to associate the disruption with the reprimand. When students are misbehaving, answers (A), (B), and (D) are effective actions that the teacher should perform.

105. **(B)**   In completing an observation, it is important to define what it is exactly that you are looking for. The teacher can complete the observation personally (A), and does not have to wait until the class is involved in seatwork (C). Recording the behavior at intervals of 10 to 30 seconds (D) is much too frequent.

106. **(C)** The classroom can have an effect on the behavior of the students, and should be taken into consideration as an important factor when managing student behavior.

107. **(D)** Specific praise should compliment the specific behavior that is being rewarded, and comment on how the specific behavior resulted in good work. Answers (A), (B), and (C) are examples of praise, but they are not specific.

108. **(C)** Ignoring the behavior will deny the student the attention that is probably desired and will not interrupt the flow of the classroom. Misbehavior, however, should only be ignored when it is not affecting anyone in the class.

109. **(C)** It has been shown that students can internalize what a teacher expects of them and will perform at that level, whether it is positive or negative.

110. **(C)** The teacher is outlining the plans for the day so that the students will be aware of what is expected of them.

111. **(B)** Preformationism was the medieval view that children were actually little and already-formed adults.

112. **(A)** Teachers should always provide corrective feedback to student work. Seatwork may or may not consist of review material (B), can be graded by other students if the teacher reviews the results (C), and should not introduce new concepts (D).

113. **(C)** Studies have shown that a teacher's genuine enthusiasm for learning is a powerful influence in helping children to learn.

114. **(A)** Formative evaluations are comprised of the information collected before or during instruction to assess students' prior knowledge for planning purposes. Formative evaluations are not assessments of student work or behavior, but, rather, are used to design lesson and unit plans or student arrangements. Summative evaluations (B) are comprised of the information about how well a student or teacher has performed after instruction. Thematic units (C) are a series of lessons that cover a variety of subjects where the lessons are all connected by a particular theme. Most methods of evaluation can be ongoing (D).

115. **(B)** Jigsaw is a cooperative learning technique where students are separated into mixed groups; each student then becomes an expert in a particular area and teaches the group about this area. Choice (A) describes

formal instruction, choice (C) describes the group investigation approach, and choice (D) briefly describes the use of learning centers.

116. **(C)** Effective feedback should be specific about the student's work and explain how the teacher's comments relate to the work. (C) is the best example of this.

117. **(B)** Language begins to develop when children are around two years old.

118. **(C)** The conflict of initiative versus guilt occurs in Erikson's early childhood psychosocial stage (ages 6–12).

119. **(B)** If a student can read from a book without difficulty, but is having difficulty with the board, there may be a vision problem. The student should be moved to the front of the class to see if there is an improvement.

120. **(D)** Mnemonics are devices used to aid memorization, such as using ROY G. BIV to remember the colors of the rainbow (Red, Orange, Yellow, Green, Blue, Indigo, and Violet). Choral response (A) is the oral repetition (B) of skills or words, and coding (C) is making marks or taking shorthand.

121. **(D)** An operant is a behavior that is influenced by the event prior and after its occurrence. For example, if a child is told that he or she will receive an ice cream cone if he or she cleans his/her room, the operant is the child cleaning his/her room. The behavior is influenced by the promise of an ice cream cone.

122. **(A)** An achievement test measures how well a student has performed in a particular area. A criterion test measures how the student performs compared to a set performance standard (B). A diagnostic test measures any specific learning problems (C). Vocational tests try to indicate what careers may be of interest to students (D).

123. **(A)** Children who have been victims of child abuse are at great risk of being abused again. This is why it is very important for teachers to contact their school administrators if they suspect that a child is being abused. The law requires teachers to do this. Children who have been abused will not always ask for help (B) and are not always easily spotted (D). More often than not, the child will be abused again (C).

124. **(B)** It is very important that all students feel welcome, but it is especially effective for ESL students to feel comfortable and welcomed in their classrooms.

125. **(C)**   The Student Teams-Achievement Divisions (STAD) is a cooperative learning approach that places students in teams of mixed abilities and has rewards for individual and group effort.

126. **(C)**   Since a teacher will be working with students of all levels and abilities, it is important to select texts that can be useful to all students.

127. **(A)**   If a student is having difficulty understanding a particular passage, it may be helpful to use visual interpretations of what is being described. If a child is unsure of what a white picket fence is, for example, then he or she should see either a white picket fence or a picture of a white picket fence.

128. **(B)**   Previewing, questioning, reading, reflecting, reciting, and reviewing (remember PQ4R) has been shown to be an effective way of studying.

129. **(A)**   Gardner believed that there are seven kinds of intelligence, including bodily, knowledge of self, logical-mathematical, musical, spatial, understanding of others, and verbal intelligence.

130. **(D)**   Cooperative learning techniques all have in common the use of heterogeneous groups working toward goals.

131. **(A)**   In an effective classroom, a teacher will reprimand misbehavior and provide positive feedback for appropriate behavior.

132. **(C)**   Long-term memory is thought to be unlimited and permanent. Short-term memory is limited in capacity (B). Answers (A) and (D) are not characteristics of long-term memory.

133. **(A)**   Students speaking two languages learn in one of two ways: sequentially, in which one language is mastered before the study of the second language has begun (A), and simultaneously, in which both languages are learned concurrently (B). Sequential language acquisition does not mean a student learns two languages in parts (C) or develops language skills (D).

134. **(C)**   Pat was given an intelligence test. A vocabulary test (A) would not ask for the repetition of digits; an achievement test (B) would evaluate what the student had learned about a particular subject; math questions were not included on the test (D).

135. **(A)**   Some students may not speak English at home, or may have limited exposure to the vocabulary of the classroom. It is important to be aware of these factors and provide the materials appropriate to help guide mastery.

136. **(C)** A student's enthusiasm for learning and overall self-esteem will increase if she or he has positive and successful experiences in the classroom. Posting grades (A) is a violation of a student's right to privacy. Using negative reinforcement (B) and amplifying responses (D) are not methods of building a student's self-esteem.

137. **(C)** Behaviorism is teachers modifying the behavior of students through the use of reinforcements.

138. **(C)** Student misbehavior generally occurs for a reason. Instead of ignoring (A), yelling (B), or giving more work to the student (D), it is beneficial to try to determine the actual causes behind the behavior.

139. **(B)** A raw score is the number of items answered correctly. The percentile rank is a measurement of how the student's results compare to others taking the test (C). The raw score is not the percentage of questions answered correctly (A) or the overall grade (D).

140. **(C)** If a teacher just wants to look at the computational skills of a class, then the problems should have very few words, since reading comprehension is a different skill. Therefore, answers (A), (B), and (D) are incorrect.

FTCE

**Florida Teacher Certification Exam—
Professional Education Test**

Practice Test 2

PRACTICE TEST 2

Professional Education Test

(Answer sheets appear in the back of this book.)

TIME: 2.5 Hours
         140 Questions

DIRECTIONS: Read each question carefully and select the best answer. Mark your responses on the answer sheet provided.

---

1. "I" messages are a means of communicating effectively, especially in situations where confrontation is necessary or conflict is possible. "I" messages

    (A) require eye contact.

    (B) are statements beginning with the word "I" where the speaker states his or her thoughts and feelings.

    (C) are statements beginning with the word "I," where the speaker states his or her goals and expectations.

    (D) are incomplete messages where the speaker states, "I want..." and lets the other party complete the sentence.

2. A teacher asks her class, "What do you think should happen if a student is caught cheating on a test?" By asking her students to participate in the process of establishing this rule, the teacher

    (A) assures that few students in her class will attempt to cheat.

    (B) uses consensus to help build classroom support for the rule about cheating.

(C) is certain that everyone in class understands that cheating is a serious offense.

(D) has identified the students who will be most likely to cheat.

3. A very bright student, scoring in the top 10 percentile on standardized achievement tests for children his age is already well-known throughout the school for causing trouble because of behavior problems. To help this student, the teacher should suggest that

(A) the student receives a prescription for Ritalin or another drug to control hyperactivity.

(B) the student is diagnosed for attention deficit disorder (ADD).

(C) the student would be served best in a private school or home schooled.

(D) the student's parents come to school to meet and discuss his behavior at home.

4. A student asks, "Why do we have to write so many papers in this class?" A good response from the teacher would be to say

(A) "You ask too many questions instead of doing your work."

(B) "Next year you will have to write twice as many papers as you have written this year, and we have a big test coming up in two weeks. I want you all to be ready."

(C) "The reason you have to write papers is because I've told you to and I'm the teacher."

(D) "There is no reason. It's just something that all students have to do in school."

5. At the end of class, the teacher asks the students to write a one-sentence summary. She writes on the board, "Who, What, When, Where, How, and Why," and tells the students to write one sentence answering those questions from the day's class. This is an effective way for the teacher to

(A) teach sentence structure.

(B) help students summarize the lesson.

(C) engage her students in journal writing.

(D) get feedback about how students feel about her class.

6. A teacher could expect to find all of the following in the student's permanent record EXCEPT

(A) standardized achievement test scores (such as the CAT).

(B) a record of disciplinary actions taken against the student during his or her enrollment.

(C) any intelligence or psychological tests documenting learning disabilities.

(D) samples of the student's written work.

7. To encourage students to read more books on their own time, a teacher develops a reward system to give students tokens for the books they read depending on the difficulty and the length of the book. At the end of the semester, students will be able to use their tokens to purchase "rewards" from the school store (pens, pencils, erasers, notebooks, and so forth). This reward system appeals to students who are

(A) intrinsically motivated.

(B) extrinsically motivated.

(C) reading below grade level.

(D) able to purchase their own school supplies.

8. A teacher writes on the board "All men are created equal" and asks each student to explain the meaning of the statement. One student says that it means that all people are equal, but another student says that it just applies to men, and a third student says that it is a lie because not all people are equally good at all things; for example, some people can run faster than others and some can sing better than others. The teacher's instructional aim is to

(A) see if students can reach consensus on the meaning of the statement.

(B) see how well students can defend their beliefs.

(C) provoke the students to disagree with the statement.

(D) engage the students in critical thinking and to allow them to express their opinions.

9. Until recently, a very quiet, reserved student had completed all her work on time and was making satisfactory progress. Lately, however, she has been erratic in her class attendance, and when she comes to class, she appears distracted. She is having trouble staying on-task and finishing her work. She has failed to turn in several recent assignments. On the last writing assignment, she wrote a very graphic poem about a girl who is sexually assaulted. The level of details used in the poem was shocking to the teacher who should

(A) ignore the topic of the poem, grade it on its poetic merit only, and return it to the student, waiting to see what will happen with the next assignment.

(B) grade the poem on its poetic merit and return it to the student with a written comment that she would like to talk to her about the poem.

(C) ask the student to stay after class, return the poem, and ask the student about it.

(D) make a copy of the poem and distribute it to other teachers to solicit their opinions about the poem.

10. A communication tool or language device which teachers use to motivate, evaluate, practice, guide, and even invite students to the learning experience is the

(A) declarative sentence.

(B) exclamation of "Eureka!"

(C) question.

(D) common verb.

11. A teacher observes that a student is falling asleep during class. The teacher gets up from his chair at the front of the room and stands beside the student's chair for a moment. He bends down and asks the student if she is feeling okay. The student wakes up and begins paying attention. This is an example of a teacher's

(A) evaluation of a student's mental health.

(B) use of verbal and nonverbal signals to direct a student's attention.

(C) intrusion on a student's privacy.

(D) failure to deal assertively with a student's behavioral problem in class.

12. A teacher, aware of Jean Piaget's theory of cognitive development, brought a pizza to class before teaching her students about fractions. She showed the whole pizza pie to the class and then cut it in half. The students were shown the two pieces. She then cut the pizza again, showing the class the four pieces. She proceeded until she had cut the pizza into 16 pieces and gave each student in her class one piece of the pie. The instructional rationale for the teacher's behavior was to

(A) demonstrate to her class when sharing a pizza with 15 other people, each person only gets a small slice of pizza.

(B) demonstrate to her class that a part of a pizza is less than the whole pizza.

(C) provide a concrete example to her class of an abstract concept of number fraction.

(D) meet the physiological (hunger) needs of her students before teaching them a math lesson.

13. An instructionally effective way for a teacher to maximize student recall is to begin class by

(A) engaging the students in singing a song to make them feel more comfortable.

(B) conducting a review of previously studied material.

(C) giving a "pop" test or quiz to see how much the students remember from the last class.

(D) asking students if they have any questions about their homework assignment.

14. Which of the following teacher responses corrects a student response by giving correct information?

   (A) "Okay, Stacey, can you think of anything else you'd like to say?"

   (B) "Buster, your answer is wrong; *believe* is spelled '*b-e-l-i-e-v-e*' not 'e before i.' "

   (C) "Jill, that answer is incorrect; what made you think that was the way to spell *neighbor*?"

   (D) "Elliot, that answer is wrong; does anyone know what the correct answer is?"

15. Research supports all of the following statements about the use of computers in education EXCEPT:

   (A) Computers in the classroom have a motivational effect on many students.

   (B) Students who use computers to write papers in class write longer papers.

   (C) Computerized tests cannot measure higher-order thinking skills.

   (D) When utilizing technology (such as computers), the teacher needs a back-up plan in case the technology fails.

16. A teacher encourages students to use a spell checker when they write papers. If the teacher allows students to write and prepare typed papers at home, the first thing to consider is

   (A) whether or not students have access to a computer and/or word processor at home.

   (B) whether or not students' parents would end up writing the paper.

   (C) whether or not the students can be trusted to do their own work.

   (D) whether or not the students will have time to do extra work at home.

17. If a student is diagnosed with a learning disability

   (A) there is little a classroom teacher can do to affect a difference in achievement for that student.

(B) the student can usually acquire accommodation strategies to support his or her achievement with proper intervention and appropriate instruction.

(C) the parent is almost always to blame for failing to provide adequate support for the student's achievement.

(D) the student cannot realistically expect to achieve academic skills necessary to attain a college education.

18. Effective teachers understand that student performance on subject-matter tests indicate

(A) how innately intelligent or smart a student is.

(B) the student's general aptitude.

(C) how likely a student will be successful on future tests.

(D) a student's particular skills or knowledge at a particular point in time.

19. The belief that corporal punishment is the best way to respond to student misconduct

(A) is outdated and obsolete.

(B) does not have widespread support in the educational community.

(C) leads to a decrease in school delinquency problems.

(D) correctly identifies the approach to take with students who misbehave.

20. A teacher usually stops her high school history class about five minutes before class time is over and asks the students to write a one-sentence summary of what they have learned in the class. When class is over, the students must turn in their summaries, which their teacher reads. By doing this, the teacher is

(A) gathering data on students' writing skills.

(B) using a classroom assessment technique to determine what her students are learning.

(C) giving students a chance to unwind from classroom activities.

(D) losing valuable and productive class time.

21. According to Benjamin Bloom's taxonomy of learning, which of the following would be most difficult or require more specialized processes?

    (A) Evaluation

    (B) Analysis

    (C) Recall

    (D) Synthesis

22. An effective way to check students' understanding of directions or an assignment is to

    (A) ask, "Does everyone understand?"

    (B) ask, "Are there any questions?"

    (C) say, "Student Name, do you know what you're supposed to do?"

    (D) move around the room and check to make sure that everyone has started the assignment and is doing it correctly.

23. The problem: "Bill is taller than Ann, but Ann is taller than Grace. Is Ann the tallest child or is Bill the tallest?" This question requires students to use

    (A) inductive reasoning.

    (B) deductive reasoning.

    (C) hypothesis formation.

    (D) pattern identification.

24. When a teacher uses a student's response as a springboard to ask additional, more detailed questions, the teacher is

    (A) correcting student answers.

    (B) elaborating on student answers.

    (C) accepting student answers.

    (D) affirming student answers.

25. A good student who is usually polite and well-behaved is going on a weekend vacation with his family. On Wednesday, the student is so

talkative that his teacher has to tell him twice to stop talking and listen. On Thursday, he and another student get into a big argument about who is going to erase the chalkboard. The teacher reasonably concludes that

(A) the student should go to the school nurse to see if he is coming down with something.

(B) the student is exhibiting disturbing characteristics which may require professional intervention.

(C) the student is in a heightened emotional state because he is anticipating an outing with his family.

(D) the student is a spoiled child who needs to learn better self-control.

26. If the other students laugh when a first-grade girl says, "I want to be a truck driver when I grow up" and tell her that "Girls can't drive big trucks," what should the teacher do?

(A) Tell the class to quiet down, that the student can be whatever she wants to be when she grows up.

(B) Tell the class that most truck drivers are men.

(C) Tell the class that women and men can both be truck drivers, depending on their skills.

(D) Ask the class to vote on whether women should be truck drivers.

27. A teacher asks her eighth-grade English students to select a career they would enjoy when they grow up and then find three sources on the World Wide Web with information about that career. She tells the students that they must find out how much education is required for this career. If the career requires post-secondary education, then the student must find a school or college that provides this education and find out how long it will take to be educated or trained for this career. Through this assignment, the teacher is helping her students to

(A) explore short-term personal and academic goals.

(B) explore long-term personal and academic goals.

(C) evaluate short-term personal and academic goals.

(D) synthesize long-term personal and academic goals.

28. A teacher consistently returns graded papers to her students within three days of their turning their work in. She writes very complete comments on each paper to help students understand what they have done correctly or incorrectly on their assignments. Doing this is important to the teacher's instructional goals because

(A) it is easy to fall behind in grading if a teacher doesn't keep up with the workload.

(B) grading papers is an important part of a teacher's job performance.

(C) students have a responsibility to keep track of their graded work.

(D) providing students with information about their performance is one way to help them improve their performance.

29. An effective way for teachers to establish standards for student behavior in the classroom is to

(A) adopt the same rules and regulations that were enforced in school when they were students.

(B) survey the literature to develop a comprehensive list of standards.

(C) consider the characteristics and socially-accepted norms of the school community.

(D) borrow ideas from the major religions of the world.

30. Classroom control is integral to successful instruction because

(A) the teacher cannot dispense knowledge in a chaotic environment.

(B) students cannot learn in a noisy classroom.

(C) the teacher has to establish that he or she is the "boss" or leader, and the class has to follow the leader.

(D) the teacher and the students must work in tandem, each having certain rules and protocols to follow.

31. If academic assessment reveals that a female student has a low range IQ (70 - 80), and the student (although in the sixth grade) has reading

skills at the second-grade level and math skills at the first-grade level, the teacher should

(A) continue with class as before, including the student in class activities but doing nothing special to draw attention to the student and her skill deficiencies.

(B) investigate the possibility of sending the student to a lower-grade class where she can repeat some of the subjects she has had before.

(C) meet with the student and her parents to discuss the best way to proceed with class instruction and make sure that their questions about their student's achievement are addressed.

(D) encourage the student to try harder because if she really tries hard she can do better.

32. In order to provide appropriate motivation for everyone in class, an English teacher assigns the class to write a 300-word essay and specifies that

(A) there are two different topics from which students may choose to write.

(B) there are two different topics from which students may choose to write, and if a student wants to write about another topic, then he or she should get approval from the teacher for that topic.

(C) every student will write about the same topic.

(D) each student must find a topic to write about and get it approved in advance.

33. A teacher showed her class a 12-inch ruler. She and her students have talked about how to use the ruler to measure one-foot lengths. The students have measured several items in the room. Through this activity, the teacher has

(A) taught her class the principle of cause-and-effect.

(B) provided her class with a stated principle or law.

(C) taught her class about comparison and contrast.

(D) provided applications of a law.

34. Drill and practice exercises, such as the use of flashcards, are appropriate activities for

   (A) task analysis.

   (B) divergent thinking.

   (C) memory work.

   (D) critical thinking.

35. When a teacher asks a student, "When you were studying for your spelling test, did you remember a mnemonic we talked about in class for spelling principal that 'a principal is your pal'?," the teacher is

   (A) leading the student in a divergent thinking exercise.

   (B) teaching the student mnemonics or memory devices.

   (C) asking questions to guide the student in correcting an error.

   (D) modeling inductive reasoning skills for the student.

36. Which of the following activities will promote long-term retention?

   (A) Engage students in weekly and monthly reviews.

   (B) Give students a unit outline at the beginning of each new unit of study.

   (C) Provide students with worksheets to supplement each lesson.

   (D) Assign daily homework based on the day's lesson.

37. Mastery testing means that

   (A) students can retake tests until they have achieved a specified standard.

   (B) all students achieve a 90 percent or higher on a test on their initial attempt.

   (C) students are allowed to use their books and other materials to help them when they take tests.

   (D) students with special needs are given accommodations or alternatives for testing.

38. The teacher's grade book is all of the following EXCEPT

   (A) a record of student attendance and performance on assignments and tests.

   (B) a confidential record of student and class performance.

   (C) a record of assignments, tasks, and tests given throughout the school year.

   (D) an open record of public information.

39. The most important factor to consider when determining if a student possibly has a learning disability is

   (A) the circumstances surrounding the mother's pregnancy and the student's birth.

   (B) the discrepancy between the student's tested aptitude and performance on a standardized achievement.

   (C) the amount and type of learning stimuli provided in the student's home.

   (D) whether or not the parents have read to the student on a regular basis.

40. A student making top grades in class has received a percentile score of 63 on a nationally standardized math test. The best explanation of the student's score is

   (A) a percentile score of 63 means that on a scale of 1–100, the student is 37 points from the top.

   (B) a percentile score of 63 means that out of a group of 100 students, 37 would score higher and 62 would score lower, meaning that the student has done well by scoring in the top half of all students taking the test.

   (C) a percentile score of 63 is just like a grade of 63 on a test; it means that the student made a low D on the test.

   (D) a percentile score of 63 means that out of a group of 100 students, 37 would score higher and 62 would score lower, showing a big difference between the student's performance on the standardized test and in class.

41. Which of the following teacher responses more clearly provides student feedback that a response is incorrect?

    (A) "No, that is not the answer."

    (B) "Well, let's think about this further. Mary, do you want to add anything?"

    (C) "Good try, but ... Kurt, what would you say?"

    (D) "Well, that's a good point you've made, but that's not the answer I was looking for."

42. When a test is described as being stable, dependable, and predictable, the test has

    (A) content validity.

    (B) construct validity.

    (C) reliability.

    (D) statistical variance.

43. Essay tests are

    (A) graded on a purely subjective basis.

    (B) generally more difficult than objective-type tests (such as multiple-choice).

    (C) adaptable for assessing lower- or higher-order thinking.

    (D) favored by teachers over other kinds of tests.

44. A letter grade system (assigning A, B, C, D, and so forth) to indicate student performance is an example of

    (A) a nominal measurement scale.

    (B) an ordinal measurement scale.

    (C) an interval measurement scale.

    (D) a ratio measurement scale.

45. A good way for a teacher to use reinforcement techniques to promote on-task behaviors and promote student motivation is to

(A) praise each student for his or her answer, whether the answer is right or wrong.

(B) avoid calling on students who do not raise their hands.

(C) provide affirmation for correct answers and to thank students for their effort when their answers are wrong or incomplete.

(D) be sure to call on each student at least once in class.

46. Doing a test in a music appreciation class, the teacher plays several short compositions for the students. The students must listen to the music and decide if the piece is an example from the Baroque period or the Rococco period. By assigning her students this task, the teacher is teaching her students to

(A) evaluate musical compositions from two distinct periods.

(B) distinguish musical compositions from two related periods.

(C) define the two schools of music.

(D) appreciate different musical forms.

47. A biology teacher is teaching his high school class about brain waves. He tells the class that one kind of wave, alpha waves, occurs at a frequency of 8–13 cycles per second. He then describes the other kinds of brain waves and gives their frequency. A good test of his students' ability to apply this knowledge would be to

(A) give them four photographs of brain scans with the different brain waves charted and ask them to identify each type.

(B) ask them to write from memory the descriptions of the four different types of brain waves.

(C) give them a multiple-choice test where they have to answer questions about all four types of brain waves.

(D) All of the above.

48. A teacher tells her class that 1 meter equals 39.37 inches or 3.28 feet or 1.09 yard. The teacher has

    (A) taught her class the principle of cause-and-effect.

    (B) provided her class with a stated principle or law.

    (C) connected cause-and-effect principles.

    (D) provided applications of a law.

49. A quiet classroom is

    (A) a good classroom.

    (B) a negative learning environment.

    (C) inappropriate for some learning activities.

    (D) the classroom of a teacher who has appropriate control of his/her students.

50. One reason it is worthwhile for parents to be involved in their children's schooling is that

    (A) children whose parents are involved in school activities perform better in school.

    (B) parents who are involved in school activities are stricter than parents who are not involved.

    (C) parents who are involved in school activities are easier to get along with than parents who are not involved.

    (D) teachers have more influence over the parents who are involved in school than those who are not involved in school.

51. Two students always finish their assigned work before their classmates. Consequently, they are usually disruptive to the rest of the class, who are still working. An effective way to help the two students learn time-management skills and to keep them out of trouble would be for the teacher to

    (A) send them to the principal's office for their horseplay.

    (B) point out the careless errors they make on their assignments for not taking their time and for not giving more thought to their work.

(C) plan activities for students who finish their classwork early.

(D) count 10 points off their assignment for each time he has to tell them to quiet down.

52. A teacher decides to show his class a video of *The Crucible* after the class has read the play in class. All of the following are reasonable assumptions EXCEPT

(A) he does this to help the students who are struggling reading the play to understand the book.

(B) he does this to reward his students by giving them a "day off."

(C) he does this to help his students appreciate the visual presentation of the written word.

(D) he does this to allow his students to critique the differences between the book and the video.

53. A bright and cheerful student with a flair for the dramatic is confined to a wheelchair as a result of a birth defect. Her junior high speech teacher would like to recommend that this student try out for the school play. The teacher should

(A) tell the student about the play and let the student decide whether or not to try out for a part.

(B) encourage the student to try out for the play, assuring her that she can win a part.

(C) be sure that the student knows all about the behind-the-scenes roles to be played, so if she doesn't get a stage role she can still be part of the crew.

(D) wait to see if the student shows any interest in being in the play.

54. When a teacher observes a significant difference between a student's usual classroom performance and the student's performance on standardized tests over a period of time, the teacher might reasonably suspect that

(A) the student suffers from test anxiety and just doesn't perform well on standardized tests.

(B) the student is an overachiever, working hard to achieve in spite of not really understanding the mathematical concepts he or she should know.

(C) a number of factors might be contributing to the student's poor performance on standardized tests and much better performance in daily assignments and routine tests.

(D) the student might be cheating on her daily assignments and regular tests and thus, is unable to do well on the standardized tests on which it is harder to cheat.

55. A teacher asks his students to name great Americans who have made significant contributions to American culture. As students start calling out names of people, the teacher notices that all the names are those of white men. The teacher then

(A) chastises the students for their bigotry.

(B) adds the names of some men and women of color to the list.

(C) asks the students to think of some women and people of color to add to the list.

(D) asks the students if they have ever heard of Dr. Martin Luther King, Jr.

56. A teacher makes sure that the aisles between the desks in her high school classroom are at least three feet wide in order to

(A) make sure that desks are accessible to all students in her class, including those using crutches or wheelchairs.

(B) promote a feeling of interdependence among students.

(C) provide individual attention to each student.

(D) discourage collaborative learning.

57. When a teacher observes a very talented student involved in many high school activities with a history of making top grades keeping to himself, never socializing with others, losing weight, looking pale, and seeming weak and mentally listless in class, the teacher should

(A) ask the P.E. teacher to talk to the student and other boys in class about sex and dating.

(B) ask the student to keep a journal where he can record his thoughts and feelings.

(C) call the student's parents to see if there is anything wrong at home.

(D) tell the student about his or her concern and ask if he/she can make an appointment for the student to see a counselor.

58. When a teacher suspects that a student is using drugs, the teacher, as a conscientious professional, should

(A) contact the appropriate school authorities in order to protect other students and secure help for the student in question.

(B) contact the student's parents to let them know that their son or daughter is in trouble.

(C) alert other teachers to the situation so they can be watching for unusual behaviors.

(D) keep quiet about her suspicions until she has collected enough evidence to prove that the student has a drug problem.

59. A proven technique for effective communication involves listening carefully to the speaker and then paraphrasing, in the listener's words, what the listener heard the speaker say. For example, if the speaker says, "I am absolutely beside myself over what X said," then the listener might reply, "It sounds like you are really angry at X." This technique is called

(A) reflection.

(B) mirroring.

(C) neurolinguistic programming.

(D) message deconstruction.

60. A junior high science teacher was encouraged to relate instructional objectives and activities to the interests, feelings, and experiences of her students. One way that she was able to do this was by

(A) giving her students an interest survey to determine their interests, preferences, likes and dislikes, and experiences.

(B) allowing students to select the assignments they would complete.

(C) encouraging students to do their best.

(D) creating a progress chart to allow each student to graph his or her class performance.

61. As a teacher explains to his class the biological concept of feedback systems (loops) involving the control center (which receives information and processes information), the receptor (which sends information), and the effector (which receives information and produces a response), he finds that using a metaphor (a comparison) is helpful. He decides that the best metaphor is

(A) a computer with a monitor and a printer.

(B) a computer with a floppy disk drive and a hard drive.

(C) a telephone system, a person making a call, and the phone.

(D) two audio speakers attached to a compact disc player.

62. As the teacher distributes a test to the class, the best statement to make is

(A) "Students, I believe that you all are well-prepared for the test. I am confident that you will do your best."

(B) "Students, this is the hardest test I've ever given my students, so you must really work hard."

(C) "The last time I gave this test, no one passed. I'll be surprised if this class can do better."

(D) "Students, I doubt if anyone will be able to complete this test in the time allowed."

63. When a teacher assigns an algebra class 20 problems to solve every day for two weeks as practice before the unit test, this is an example of

(A) massed practice.

(B) distributed practice.

(C) timed practice.

(D) concept mapping.

64. The most effective time for students to retain information is for them to review or study

(A) within 8 hours of the material first being presented.

(B) 24 hours after the material is presented.

(C) more than 24 hours after the material is first presented but just before being tested.

(D) None of the above.

65. An example of a question or task requiring synthesis (from Bloom's taxonomy) would be which of the following?

(A) Here are five words. Write a sentence using these five words and adding any other words you might need.

(B) Describe how Columbus, in his search for the New World, ended his journey in the Caribbean Islands.

(C) Compare Freud's theory of psychosexual development to Erikson's theory of psychosocial development.

(D) Diagram the sentence written on the board.

66. School policy states that, "All students will be treated with dignity and respect." Which of the following would be an exception to this policy?

(A) The teacher requests that students reply "Yes, sir" or "No, sir" when answering questions.

(B) The teacher requests that students reply simply "Yes" or "No" when answering questions.

(C) The teacher addresses students as "Mr. last name" or "Ms. last name."

(D) The teacher addresses the male students as "Mr. last name" and the female students by their first names.

67. Learning experts such as Madeline Hunter and David Kolb talk about the learning/teaching cycle. The term *cycle* is used because

   (A) the learning process is based on a series of steps or sequences.

   (B) the learning process is recursive and constantly recycling itself.

   (C) learning focuses on the developmental stages of the student.

   (D) the teacher controls the process.

68. A teacher plays a piece of music for her music appreciation class, telling the students that it is an example from the Romantic period. She plays the piece again and asks the students to describe the piece. After students describe the music, she asks them to define "romance." The teacher is engaging her students in

   (A) inductive reasoning.

   (B) deductive reasoning.

   (C) oral interpretation.

   (D) evaluation.

69. Which of the following is not an example of a closed question?

   (A) Which bear's bed was too soft?

   (B) What was the name of the girl who went to the three bears' house?

   (C) Why did the girl go to the three bears' house?

   (D) What happened when the girl sat in little bear's chair?

70. A common and effective method of assessing students' prior knowledge of a topic or skills in a particular subject area is to

   (A) administer a subject-specific or task-specific pre-test.

   (B) ask students about what they have learned or studied before.

   (C) examine a student's academic records to see what grades the student made before.

   (D) administer a general achievement test.

71. If a teacher notices that one of his or her best students, one who usually performs very well on class assignments and routine tests, appears worried about an upcoming standardized test, asking many questions about the test, the teacher might suspect that

    (A) the student is already starting to think about how to cheat on the test.

    (B) the student is unduly worried about the test.

    (C) the student really doesn't care about the test but wants the teacher's attention.

    (D) the student needs psychological assessment and counseling to help with anxiety.

72. In order to help a student who has very creative and sophisticated ideas improve his or her spelling (and, thus, his or her grades in English class), a teacher might suggest that

    (A) the student try typing his next paper on a word processor, using a spell checker.

    (B) the student use simpler words that are easier to spell.

    (C) the student write each misspelled word on the last paper 20 times.

    (D) spelling errors not count against the student on papers.

73. A teacher observes two kindergarten students on the playground who are having a disagreement. The conflict appears to be escalating. Just as the teacher approaches the two students, they are beginning to hit and shove each other. The teacher should

    (A) yell at the students to "Stop!" and grab each by the arm, pulling them apart.

    (B) yell at the students to "Stop!" and send them to the principal's office.

    (C) step between the students to separate them and then ask each one, in turn, to tell what has happened, encouraging them to use their words to express their feelings instead of hitting each other.

    (D) continue to watch the students closely, hoping that they will be able to work out their differences.

74. A teacher overhears a group of students discussing their favorite foods. One student says, "I can't believe that people in China eat dogs." Another student of Indian heritage and Hindu religious training says, "That's the way I feel when I see people eating steak." The teacher, in an effort to show an appreciation of cultural and religious differences, says

    (A) "Some people have difficulty understanding why Americans eat so much meat in their diets."

    (B) "Different people in different cultures and religious backgrounds have different customs when it comes to eating and drinking certain foods and beverages."

    (C) "Everyone knows that a dog is man's best friend."

    (D) "Research shows that it is healthier to not eat meat, but to have a vegetarian diet."

75. Two weeks after a student writes a poem about a rape, she comes to the teacher and confides that she was the girl in the poem. She tells the teacher that her mother's new boyfriend raped her (the student) and that she is afraid her mother will be mad if she tells her what happened. The teacher should

    (A) tell the student to go ahead and tell her mother what happened.

    (B) call the student's mother on the phone and tell her what the student said.

    (C) report the student's sexual assault to the appropriate authorities.

    (D) tell the student that she needs to talk to a school counselor.

76. A teacher wants to start the semester by providing students with complete and explicit guidelines to follow regarding their behavior in class. He decides that the most effective way to communicate this information to his students is to

    (A) make a big poster with all the rules listed, display the poster in class, and discuss each rule with the students.

    (B) ask the students what they think would help everyone in class get along with each other.

(C) survey what the other teachers are doing with regard to class-room management.

(D) present a few of the rules on the first day of each week and then reinforce those rules throughout the week.

77. An effective way to deal with student misconduct is to

(A) make the student an example for peer censure.

(B) let the student choose his or her own punishment.

(C) make the student wait to find out what his or her punishment will be.

(D) provide quick, fair, and consistent correction.

78. A teacher's usual testing procedure is to give students a written exam. However, this semester, the teacher has a vision-impaired student in her class who cannot read small print. Which of the following would be the most effective, efficient, and fair way to test this student?

(A) Use the office copier to enlarge the print on the same tests that the other students will take.

(B) Make an audio tape of the test questions and let the student take the tape to the library to listen and then record his or her answers.

(C) Ask the student to come early or stay later and give him or her a shorter, oral test.

(D) Send the student to the resource room to let the resource teacher or the counselor read the test to him or her.

79. As part of the school's new reading program, students will have the opportunity to read books and take tests on a computer to improve their grades in reading. This is a program supplementing the regular curriculum. The second-grade teacher is worried about how she will find time during the day to listen to the children read these "extra" books and to supervise their computer tests. The most effective and efficient way for her to handle this is to

(A) allow the students to read to each other and test themselves.

(B) allow the students to read to each other and test each other.

(C) arrange for parent volunteers to come to school at select times to listen to the children read and test the children.

(D) require that students come to school early (before class) or that they stay late (after class) to read to her and be tested.

80. A teacher has a routine for distributing papers to the class, for having students get their books, and for writing on the board. The routine is one way the teacher demonstrates that he or she

(A) uses class time efficiently.

(B) has good problem-solving skills.

(C) is a rigid and unreasonable teacher.

(D) expects his/her students to do their best.

81. Content validity for a test refers to

(A) how well the statistical data for the test support replicability.

(B) the mean, median, and mode for the test.

(C) whether the test measures what it purports to measure.

(D) how well students as a group perform on the test.

82. A teacher tells the class, "Tomorrow you will have a test on chapters 5 and 6. There will be 50 matching questions and 10 short answer questions. You will have 45 minutes to take the test." What other important information about the test should the teacher tell the students?

(A) "You should bring two number 2 lead pencils with you. I will provide the answer sheets."

(B) "Don't forget to study! This will be a very hard test!"

(C) "This will be your third test this term."

(D) All of the above.

83. A student expresses concern to the teacher about his grade on his last test. The student is accustomed to making As and is displeased that he earned a C on his last test. One way for the teacher to help the student understand his grade is to

    (A) show the student the grade book so the student can see that few students made As or Bs on the test.

    (B) go over the answer key with the student, explaining why he missed questions.

    (C) tell the student that the grades in class ranged from C to F, that the median grade was an F and the top grade was a C.

    (D) assure the student that the test was very hard and encourage him to study harder for the next exam.

84. Throughout her teaching career, a teacher has noticed that students who sit in the back of the classroom are often quiet, more reserved, and less outgoing. Because of this, the teacher should

    (A) call on them first to help them develop more self-confidence.

    (B) hesitate to call on them since they are shy.

    (C) be certain to include them in class activities so they will become more comfortable.

    (D) keep an eye on them to make sure they are paying attention and not goofing off.

85. Holistic scoring procedures for assessments, particularly writing samples, refer to all of the following EXCEPT

    (A) evaluation on the basis of how effectively a whole message is conveyed to a specified audience for a given purpose.

    (B) the number of misspelled words on the whole paper or sample.

    (C) a qualitative analysis of the entire paper or sample.

    (D) evaluation of the overall effectiveness of the paper or sample.

86. An effective way of starting to construct and sequence short-range objectives for a given subject area is to

    (A) identify the learning goal(s) based on the skills, knowledge, and attitudes to be learned.

    (B) survey the textbook.

    (C) brainstorm with students in the class.

    (D) review the research literature.

87. If a teacher asks a question, calls on a student, and the student doesn't immediately answer, what should the teacher do?

    (A) Say nothing, but give the student more time to think of an answer.

    (B) Say, "We're waiting for an answer."

    (C) Call on another student.

    (D) Restate the question.

88. When teachers are developing lesson plans for students to do assignments using the Internet, which of the following should be the most pressing concern?

    (A) Students might accidentally access an adult-topic or pornographic site as they are doing the assignment the teacher has planned.

    (B) Teachers have no way of knowing which web sites the students access as they work on the computer.

    (C) Web addresses or URLs are constantly changing, and a site may not still be where it was when the teacher developed the lesson plan.

    (D) Students may not be able to find enough information on the Internet to accomplish the assignment.

89. Many standardized tests are criterion-referenced. Criterion-referenced tests are scored according to

    (A) how well a student's performance compares with that of others who take the test.

(B) how well a student's performance compares with those of students in the sample upon which the test was standardized.

(C) how well a student's performance meets an established set of knowledge or skills standards.

(D) the percentage of questions the student answers correctly.

90. An English teacher wants to challenge his students to think critically. He has been teaching about the parts of speech. He writes the following sentence on the board, "The man ran down the street." He asks a student to identify the part of speech of the word "down." The student says that "down" is an adverb telling where the man ran. The teacher should respond

   (A) "No, *down* is not an adverb."

   (B) "Yes, *down* does tell where the man ran."

   (C) "*Down* is a preposition, and *down the street* is a prepositional phrase."

   (D) "Well, *down* does tell where the man ran which is what adverbs do. But in this case, *down* is part of the phrase *down the street*. Do you want to change your answer?"

91. A school has a policy that the Internet will be used only for academic research and that students will not access adult-oriented/pornographic web sites while in the school computer lab. The computer teacher installs a web-filtering device that allows her to specify certain sites and certain kinds of sites as being "off-limits" to users of the computers in the lab. This procedure helps safeguard

   (A) the First Amendment Freedom of Speech rights for the students.

   (B) that no one will access information offensive to others.

   (C) that students will not accidentally or intentionally access certain restricted web sites.

   (D) that students will learn the proper use of the Internet as a research tool.

92. If a student is usually quick to attempt answers to questions, but often blurts out wrong responses, the teacher's best response to the student is to

    (A) say, "Wrong answer, but better luck next time."

    (B) say, "Well, not exactly. But, you're close."

    (C) say nothing, but smile and call on someone else.

    (D) say, "Why don't I give you another minute to think about that answer?"

93. At random and without announcement, students are required to pass through metal detectors as they enter the school. This procedure is used to

    (A) alert students to the possibility that classmates are carrying weapons to class.

    (B) make sure students are not carrying weapons to class.

    (C) remind students that someone is watching them.

    (D) promote school safety.

94. When utilizing "triad teaching," the teacher divides the students in the class, forming teams of people. Each student in the team of three has a specific job: one may be the reader, one may be the recorder, and one may be the reporter. The teacher gives each team a passage to read and interpret or a problem to solve within a certain time limit. "Triad teaching" is an example of

    (A) guided practice.

    (B) reciprocal questioning strategies.

    (C) collaborative learning.

    (D) thematic strategy.

95. Which of the following teacher responses more clearly provides student feedback that a response is correct?

    (A) "Well, Adam that's something no one has thought of before."

    (B) "Yes, Jennifer that is the correct answer."

(C) "Okay, Melissa. Next student?"

(D) "That's a very interesting idea, Billy."

96. A good reason for teachers to use grades is that grades

(A) encourage students to take more difficult classes.

(B) from easier classes carry more weight than grades from more difficult courses.

(C) accurately reflect student performance.

(D) are a traditional system of reporting student performance and have widespread acceptance.

97. When a quiet, polite, and conscientious student never volunteers to participate in class discussions or to respond when called on in class, except to say, "I don't know," and starts to turn in assignments which are incomplete or incorrect—usually both, the teacher has reason to suspect that the student is

(A) using drugs which affect her reasoning ability.

(B) lacking motivation to succeed in class.

(C) lacking the necessary reading, writing, and thinking skills to be successful in class.

(D) succumbing to peer pressure not to excel in class.

98. In meeting with a student's parents, his teacher determines that he is a middle-child in a family with an academically high-achieving older sibling and a younger sibling. There are six years difference in each of the children in the family. The teacher also learns that the student's parents divorced when he was two years old and that he now lives with his mother, stepfather, and his younger sibling, a stepsister. From this information, the teacher can reasonably conclude that

(A) the student faces some competition at home for parental attention.

(B) the student is probably jealous of his siblings.

(C) the student probably has problems with his stepfather.

(D) the student did not acquire the trust he should have developed in an earlier developmental stage.

99. A high school reading teacher finds all of his students reading below grade level. One skill he must teach his students is to determine the meaning of words and phrases in sentences. Which of the following would best constitute a short-range objective for this skill?

(A) Students will complete an exercise using a dictionary to define 50 new vocabulary words.

(B) Students will write a paper using 10 vocabulary words written on the board.

(C) Students will identify the meaning of 10 vocabulary words as used in sentences from a passage in their textbooks.

(D) Students will draw a picture to depict a passage read to them by the teacher.

100. A teacher writes this question on the board, "How do you know if someone is intelligent or not?" The class then is assigned to research the question and develop a list of all the traits and characteristics that define or describe someone who is intelligent. Through this exercise, the teacher has

(A) led her students through an activity of developing criteria against which a judgment can be made.

(B) led her students through an activity of gathering examples.

(C) led her students through an activity of testing if someone is intelligent or not.

(D) engaged her students in a creative-thinking activity.

101. Which of the following is an example of a question or task requiring application thinking skills according to Bloom's taxonomy of learning?

(A) Demonstrate how to fill the printer tray with paper.

(B) What kind of paper is needed to fill the printer tray?

(C) Describe how to load the printer tray with paper.

(D) If the printer does not print after loading the paper tray, what could be the problem?

102. The first thing that a teacher must decide in constructing or assembling a test for a class is

(A) the objective(s) of the test or what the students must be able to do.

(B) how many points the test will be worth.

(C) how long the test should be.

(D) what kind of test should be given (i.e., multiple-choice, essay, fill-in-the-blank, etc.).

103. In order to discourage cheating among students, a teacher could

(A) space the students' desks and chairs around the room so that students are not crowded together in a small space.

(B) prepare different forms of the test so that not all students have the questions in the same order.

(C) proctor the test, staying alert to monitor student behaviors as they take the test.

(D) All of the above.

104. According to theories of learning styles, the most effective way to teach is to

(A) give students a picture or visual image of what they must learn.

(B) tell students explicitly what they must learn.

(C) demonstrate to students what they must learn.

(D) tell students, show them pictures or images, and let them demonstrate to each other what they must learn.

105. Based on the general principles of cognitive psychology and learning theory, receiving rewards for behavior

(A) promotes the occurrence of the behavior.

(B) causes the behavior to diminish.

    (C) allows the learner to discriminate between positive and negative behaviors.

    (D) enables the learner to selectively engage in the behavior.

106. Teachers ask questions to

    (A) engage the students' attention.

    (B) evaluate students' knowledge.

    (C) invite students to learn.

    (D) All of the above.

107. A good example of using existing and easily-available resources to teach a class about the nutritional value of certain foods is for a teacher to

    (A) ask students to research the illnesses resulting from vitamin deficiencies using the Internet.

    (B) have the students do library research to determine the fat content of fast foods.

    (C) bring food packages to class and ask the students to interpret the nutritional labels.

    (D) assign students to keep a five-day food diary, writing down everything they eat for consecutive days.

108. Two teachers have different views of what their students accomplish in the computer lab. One teacher who has had little experience in the computer lab and does not like using the lab, does not feel that students are making progress. On the other hand, the other teacher who has had extensive experience in the computer lab and who enjoys using the lab with students, feels that students are making good progress. To understand the difference in the teachers' perceptions, it is important to know that

    (A) teacher experience with technology has an impact on the effective use of technology.

    (B) the students in both classes enjoy working in the computer lab.

(C) the students in both classes do not enjoy working in the computer lab.

(D) some of the students in both classes enjoy working in the computer lab, and some of the students do not like it.

109. When a teacher includes short stories by authors from various ethnic groups for the class to read, the teacher is demonstrating to her students that

(A) some cultures produce better writers than others.

(B) the short story, as a genre, has certain basic characteristics.

(C) people of different nationalities have vastly different concerns when it comes to human values.

(D) Russian writers are more difficult to understand than Mexican or Japanese authors.

110. As a teacher prepares to distribute copies of a test to the class, someone from the school's grounds crew starts mowing the lawn right outside the classroom windows. The teacher should

(A) administer the test as planned, without any special warnings or allowances.

(B) postpone the test until the mowing is finished.

(C) administer the test with a warning that students should not allow the mowing to distract them.

(D) go the principal's office to complain about the noisy disruption to his planned activities for his class.

111. Authentic assessments refer to

(A) paper and pen tests.

(B) tests where students have done their own work.

(C) projects, portfolios, records, observations, and so forth.

(D) essay-type tests.

112. A teacher begins class by checking attendance. She tells the students that while she is checking attendance, they should get out their books

and review what they had studied during the last class meeting. All of the following are instructional benefits to this practice EXCEPT:

(A) It keeps students from talking while the teacher takes attendance.

(B) It provides students with time to review before the class "officially" begins.

(C) It helps the students to focus their attention.

(D) It helps prepare the student to connect new material with previously learned information.

113. Leading students in the Pledge of Allegiance to the American flag every school morning is an example of

(A) reinforcing student retention through group recitation.

(B) checking student comprehension.

(C) behavior modification.

(D) language development.

114. A student says, "We're having a big test in two weeks! What kind of test?" The best answer is

(A) "Let's not start worrying about the test. We have plenty of time to get ready."

(B) "You're asking questions when you should be writing. Get back to work."

(C) "The test will be to write a five-paragraph theme just like you've been writing in class the last four weeks. It will be graded the same way, and you will have the same amount of time as you have for all the papers you've practiced writing."

(D) "It's going to be a writing test."

115. A teacher teaches his students the difference between systolic and diastolic blood pressure. He then lets his students use a sphygmomanometer to take each other's blood pressure. By doing this, the teacher is

(A) giving his students a hands-on learning experience.

(B) providing an opportunity for students to apply their learning.

(C) appealing to the tactile-kinesthetic strengths of the learners in his class.

(D) All of the above.

116. A teacher demonstrates for the class two different strategies for finding the unknown in an equation. He then asks the class to discuss the two ways of solving the problem. The teacher is teaching a concept through

(A) contrast and comparison techniques.

(B) definition strategies.

(C) abstract application.

(D) causal analysis.

117. As a rule, when confronting a student who has behavioral problems, it is good practice to

(A) get straight to the heart of the matter and give the student your honest appraisal of the situation and your demands for immediately correcting the problem.

(B) start out by listening to all the mistakes the student has made in the past in order to build your case and establish your perspective and then focus on the current problem.

(C) say something nice to the student and make some positive comments to disarm the student so your correction will have greater impact.

(D) gauge your approach to the student by considering the student's characteristics, history, and current problem so as to best meet the needs of the individual.

118. Which of the following is the best example of a long-range goal appropriate to student needs?

(A) By the end of the year, the student will have 90 percent mastery on a test of language usage.

(B) By the end of the semester, the student will have read 10 books.

(C) By the end of the semester, the student will be able to recite the Pledge of Allegiance.

(D) By the end of the grading period, the student will be able to correctly spell ten new vocabulary words.

119. In order to present students with accurate information about alcohol and drug abuse, a teacher should

(A) show her students a recent, major motion picture, depicting the effects of cocaine abuse among white-collar workers in a large American city.

(B) show her students a documentary video made in 1970 about the dangers of marijuana and LSD.

(C) invite a former student who has been in recovery for the last two years to come and talk to her students about how he or she became involved in drugs and how he or she got help.

(D) assign her students to write a five-page research paper about drug abuse.

120. To help kindergarten students stay calm and feel safe and secure during the first bad weather safety drill, their teacher must first

(A) make sure that her students understand that "bad weather" could mean a thunderstorm or a tornado.

(B) establish an environment of trust and safety in her classroom so that the students know they will be safe with her.

(C) lay down the ground rules so that students will know that they may not talk while they are in the hall.

(D) allow her students to practice the procedure of moving to the hallway.

121. A teacher wants to explain a reading score of 2.3 on a standardized reading test to a student's parents. The teacher teaches second grade, and it is March of the school year. The teacher's best explanation of a score 2.3 is

(A) on the second-grade level and means that a student has strong reading skills for the grade.

(B) on the second-grade level, but slightly behind what is expected for the class.

(C) on the second-grade level, third month, and that since school started in August and the student was tested in March, the eighth month, it would be a good idea for the student to get extra help to improve reading skills.

(D) on the second-grade level, third month.

122. Some testing instruments report percentile scores. Percentile scores refer to

(A) how a student's performance compares out of a group of 100 students taking the test.

(B) the percentage of questions the student answers correctly on the test.

(C) a percentage score which has been standardized using a statistical formula.

(D) the percentage of questions the student answers incorrectly on the test.

123. When a test is described as being biased, that means that the test

(A) discriminates between the students who are smart and the students who are not as smart.

(B) discriminates between the students who studied and the students who didn't study.

(C) discriminates among students of diverse population backgrounds (socio-economic status, ethnicity, religion, and so forth).

(D) discriminates among students who have different content-mastery levels.

124. Why is it a good idea for a teacher to give students options and allow them to make choices?

(A) Some teachers dislike telling students what to do.

(B) Some teachers like to give students different options so they can exercise their decision-making skills.

(C) Teachers know different students are motivated and stimulated by different tasks.

(D) Students deserve a break from all the rules and regulations in most classes.

125. Which of the following requires the higher-order thinking skill according to Bloom's taxonomy of learning?

(A) Demonstrate how to change the printer cartridge.

(B) What kind of cartridge does the printer need?

(C) Describe how to change the printer cartridge.

(D) If the printer does not print after the cartridge has been changed, what could be the problem?

126. A high school Spanish teacher is leading the class through a conversational exercise. A student in the class asks, "Do they eat pizza in Mexico?" The teacher's best response is to

(A) ask (in Spanish), "Are you nuts? We're not talking about pizza!"

(B) ask the student (in Spanish) to repeat the question in Spanish.

(C) ask another student in class (in English), "What do you think?"

(D) say (in English or Spanish), "That question is irrelevant to the discussion."

127. An effective way for a teacher to review subject matter is to

(A) tell the class what they will study at the next class meeting.

(B) give students an opportunity to get started on their homework in the last 15 minutes of class time.

(C) ask students to formulate hypotheses (or make predictions) based on what was covered in class.

(D) recap significant points of a discussion before moving to new material.

128. Which of the following is a system for recording the progress of individual students?

   (A) A line graph showing the grades of a student over the course of the semester

   (B) A pie chart showing the distribution of class grades over the course of the semester

   (C) A scatter chart showing the distribution of student grades on a particular assignment or test

   (D) A bar graph showing the range, median, and mode of student grades

129. Sharon and Stan are sitting in the back of the room, giggling, while Mr. Black is attempting to read instructions to the class. The best way for Mr. Black to gain Sharon's and Stan's attention without disrupting the class is to

   (A) shout emphatically at them to "Shut up or else!" to indicate the seriousness of the situation.

   (B) throw an eraser at them as a nonverbal communicator.

   (C) stop reading and glare at them until the whole class is staring at them, utilizing peer pressure to correct their misbehavior.

   (D) walk to the back of the room and stand by their desks while he finishes the instructions.

130. When a teacher has to select between using standardized or nonstandardized (teacher-made) tests, an important first consideration is

   (A) the purpose for administering the test.

   (B) the cost of the test.

   (C) the time allotted for the test.

   (D) the test setting.

131. When a student writes about attempting suicide in a journal, the best way for the teacher to deal with the situation is to

    (A) write encouraging notes to the student in the margins of the journal.

    (B) ask the student to come over to his or her house after school to spend some time together.

    (C) suggest that the student read some inspirational and motivational books.

    (D) take the student's threats of suicide seriously and report the situation to the appropriate school authorities.

132. A teacher wants the students to realize that actions can produce reactions and that decisions have consequences. In order to communicate this message effectively to the students, the teacher should avoid

    (A) making classroom rules that he/she does not want to enforce.

    (B) having strict standards.

    (C) being too friendly with his/her students.

    (D) a democratic style of classroom management.

133. According to current copyright laws, a teacher

    (A) may show a commercially-produced video to a class as long as there is no charge to the student for viewing the video.

    (B) may sell copies of a videotaped televised program aired on commercial television to students as long as it is for educational purposes.

    (C) may freely use in the classroom a videotaped copy of a televised program aired on a commercial news station without limitations.

    (D) may freely use trademarked images from web sites on the Internet.

134. A teacher's body language communicates messages to students just as a teacher's words do. If a teacher tends to stand with arms crossed across the chest or always stands behind the desk or lectern when talking to students, his or her body language sends the message that the teacher is a

(A) warm and caring individual.

(B) very physical and aggressive individual.

(C) very open and independent individual.

(D) distant and aloof individual.

135. "Imagine that you are on the first space shuttle to Mars. What do you think you will see and do when you arrive on Mars?" This is an example of question requiring

(A) critical thinking.

(B) creative thinking.

(C) convergent thinking.

(D) cause and effect thinking.

136. A teacher is concerned that one of her first-grade students is not paying attention to letters and words, although most of the other children in the class already have developed word attack skills and are building vocabularies. The student is bright and does well on math tasks and other skills. The best thing for the teacher to do is

(A) talk to the student's parents and lecture them to start reading to him 30 minutes each day.

(B) follow appropriate channels and see if the student can participate in a tutoring program for slow readers.

(C) continue providing the student with opportunities to acquire reading skills, but let him learn at his own pace when he is ready.

(D) refer the student to the school diagnostician to determine if he has a learning disability.

137. Which of the following teacher responses is a more specific response to a student who has given the correct answer?

(A) "Patty, that answer shows that you have been doing your homework. You have mastered the conversion of fractions into percents!"

(B) "Kelly, what a fantastic answer! Congratulations on your hard work!"

(C) "That is a most ingenuous response, Alexis. I had never thought of that before."

(D) "How did you ever come up with that answer, Maria? That's good work!"

138. The first standard for math class is, "The student understands how to use math to solve problems in the real world." Which of the following would be the best way to test students' performance on this standard?

(A) Give the students ten addition and ten subtraction problems to solve.

(B) Give the students ten addition and ten subtraction problems to solve using a calculator.

(C) Give students a matching test where they must match the standard numeral with its Roman numeral equivalent.

(D) Give students a newspaper ad, and ask them to calculate the cost of several items if those items were on sale for 20 percent off.

139. A very outgoing and friendly student seems insecure at times, and "fitting in" with her clique is very important to her. She doesn't like for people to disagree, and she has shown that she is willing to give in to others to avoid a conflict. The teacher becomes very concerned when she sees the student spending time with students who appear to be involved in gang-related activities. The teacher is

(A) jumping to conclusions by assuming that the student will also become involved in gangs.

(B) justified in worrying that the student will be influenced by her friends.

(C) involving herself in something that is really none of her concern.

(D) underestimating the student's ability to make decisions for herself.

140. A teacher can take information from the student's permanent record to

    (A) discuss with the student.

    (B) make photocopies.

    (C) discuss with the student's parents.

    (D) None of the above.

STOP
If time still remains, you may go back and check your work.

PRACTICE TEST 2

ANSWER KEY

1.	(B)	29.	(C)	57.	(D)	85.	(B)	113.	(A)
2.	(B)	30.	(D)	58.	(A)	86.	(A)	114.	(C)
3.	(D)	31.	(C)	59.	(B)	87.	(A)	115.	(D)
4.	(B)	32.	(B)	60.	(A)	88.	(C)	116.	(A)
5.	(B)	33.	(D)	61.	(C)	89.	(C)	117.	(D)
6.	(D)	34.	(C)	62.	(A)	90.	(D)	118.	(A)
7.	(B)	35.	(C)	63.	(B)	91.	(C)	119.	(C)
8.	(D)	36.	(A)	64.	(A)	92.	(D)	120.	(B)
9.	(C)	37.	(A)	65.	(A)	93.	(D)	121.	(C)
10.	(C)	38.	(D)	66.	(D)	94.	(C)	122.	(A)
11.	(B)	39.	(B)	67.	(B)	95.	(B)	123.	(C)
12.	(C)	40.	(D)	68.	(A)	96.	(D)	124.	(C)
13.	(B)	41.	(A)	69.	(C)	97.	(C)	125.	(D)
14.	(B)	42.	(C)	70.	(A)	98.	(A)	126.	(B)
15.	(C)	43.	(C)	71.	(B)	99.	(C)	127.	(D)
16.	(A)	44.	(B)	72.	(A)	100.	(A)	128.	(A)
17.	(B)	45.	(C)	73.	(C)	101.	(A)	129.	(D)
18.	(D)	46.	(B)	74.	(B)	102.	(A)	130.	(A)
19.	(B)	47.	(A)	75.	(C)	103.	(D)	131.	(D)
20.	(B)	48.	(B)	76.	(A)	104.	(D)	132.	(A)
21.	(A)	49.	(C)	77.	(D)	105.	(A)	133.	(A)
22.	(D)	50.	(A)	78.	(A)	106.	(D)	134.	(D)
23.	(B)	51.	(C)	79.	(C)	107.	(C)	135.	(B)
24.	(B)	52.	(B)	80.	(A)	108.	(A)	136.	(C)
25.	(C)	53.	(A)	81.	(C)	109.	(B)	137.	(A)
26.	(C)	54.	(C)	82.	(A)	110.	(B)	138.	(D)
27.	(B)	55.	(C)	83.	(C)	111.	(C)	139.	(B)
28.	(D)	56.	(A)	84.	(C)	112.	(A)	140.	(D)

DETAILED EXPLANATIONS
OF ANSWERS

Practice Test 2

1. **(B)** "I" statements begin with the word "I" and express the individual's thoughts or feelings. They are not statements of goals and/or expectations (C). "I" statements are not incomplete statements (D), nor are they called "I" statements because eye contact is involved (A).

2. **(B)** This is an example of consensus building. There is no evidence in the scenario described that supports answers (A), (C), or (D).

3. **(D)** The teacher should determine if the student's behavior is consistent in different settings, asking about his behavior at home and in other environments. Although the other options (A, (B), C) might be viable possibilities for future action, the first step is to explore his present behavior.

4. **(B)** An honest and complete rationale for writing papers is the answer the student deserves. Answers (A), (C), and (D) ignore the student's need to know why he has to write papers and, thus, fail to provide the motivational rationale the student may require in order to do his best work. Answers (C) and (D), furthermore, are insulting, failing to show the student respect for his inquiry.

5. **(B)** One-sentence summaries are effective tools for students to use in summarizing a lesson. Answering the questions the teacher wrote on the board is not necessarily a good way to teach students about sentence structure (A) as their writing may or may not be complete, grammatical sentences; the point is for the students to summarize the main ideas or main points. Journal writing is a more personal activity (versus factual recall) and the sentence, if the students have followed the directions, will not provide the teacher any information about how students feel about the class (C, D).

6. **(D)**   The student's permanent record does not include samples of the student's written work. It should, however, contain achievement test results (A), disciplinary measures (B), and other test results (C).

7. **(B)**   Providing external rewards (such as tokens and prizes) for reading appeals to students who are extrinsically motivated. Intrinsically motivated students read for the pleasure and self-satisfaction of reading. Students who read below, at, and above grade level may be motivated extrinsically or intrinsically. Some students may be uninterested in earning tokens to acquire school supplies whether or not they are able to purchase their own supplies.

8. **(D)**   The teacher hopes to engage the students in critical thinking allowing them to express their opinions and realizing that students will have different interpretations of the statement. Answers (A), (B), and (C) are possible outcomes, but (D) is the best answer since it relates specifically to the teacher's aim.

9. **(C)**   There is sufficient evidence to suggest that the student is a victim of sexual abuse The situation is too serious to delay action (A) or to remain passive (B). In no case would it be appropriate to copy and distribute the poem to other teachers (D).

10. **(C)**   Teachers spend a great deal of their time asking questions, answering questions, and listening to questions. Questions are an important tool for teachers. Teachers use sentences, exclamations, and verbs (A, (B), D) in a variety of ways, but questions are essential to the learning process.

11. **(B)**   Simply asking a question about how a student feels is inadequate for determining the student's mental health (A); likewise, a simple query of this nature fails to constitute an invasion of privacy (C). There is no evidence that the teacher failed to deal with the problem (D); in fact, the teacher was effective in his approach.

12. **(C)**   According to Piaget, concrete ideas precede abstract ideas. By giving students a demonstration with fractions of a real object, the teacher helps the students to grasp the ideas of 1/2, 1/4, 1/8, and 1/16. Answers (A) and (B) may be factually true; however, they fail to serve as an instructional rationale. Answer (D) is based on Maslow's hierarchy of needs, not Piaget's theory of cognitive development.

13. **(B)**   Providing a review of previously studied material is a method of maximizing student recall. Some students might not feel very comfortable about singing a song (A), depending on their age, the subject matter and so forth. Without a review, students would not be expected to perform well on a quiz or test (C), and without a review or time to look over their homework, it is unlikely that they would have many questions to ask on their own (D).

14. **(B)**   This provides specific information to correct a student's mistake. Answer (A) is a response to a correct answer (not incorrect, as specified in the question). Answers (C) and (D) do not provide specific information.

15. **(C)**   Computerized tests can measure higher-order thinking skills. Research has supported that computers are motivational for many students (A), that students write longer papers when they use computers than when they write with pen and paper (B), and that, as wonderful as technology is, sometimes it fails, and teachers must have alternative plans (D).

16. **(A)**   This has to be the teacher's first consideration. The other options (B, C, D) are not viable if the students do not have access to technology at home. Although technology can be very helpful, many students have limited access to it.

17. **(B)**   With appropriate instruction, the student can usually develop the necessary accommodation strategies to succeed in reading, writing, math, and other subject areas. Answers (A), (C), and (D) are false statements.

18. **(D)**   Performance on subject-matter tests indicates a student's skills or knowledge at a particular point in time. They do not measure intelligence (A) or aptitude (B), nor do they predict how well a student will perform in the future.

19. **(B)**   In general, educators believe that corporal punishment should be avoided. Unfortunately, there are still those who practice forms of corporal punishment; hence, (A) is an incorrect answer. (C) is a false statement. Although corporal punishment might be effective with some students (D), it is not the approach to take with most students.

20. **(B)** The teacher is getting feedback to help her know what her students have learned and whether they have missed key points. This helps the teacher increase her teaching effectiveness. Answers (A) and (C) may be by-products of the teacher's classroom assessment technique; however, they are not the best answers. Answer (D) is incorrect; getting student feedback is not a waste of time.

21. **(A)** According to Bloom's taxonomy, evaluation is the most difficult or most advanced process; the other terms (B, C, D) are used to describe lower-level thinking and processing skills.

22. **(D)** An inspection of students' work is the most effective way to check their understanding. Asking questions (A, B, C) rarely provide the feedback the teacher needs to assess students' understanding.

23. **(B)** The example illustrates a deductive reasoning task. Inductive reasoning (A) would be giving the class some information and asking them to form a rule or generalization. Answers (C) and (D) are examples of inductive tasks.

24. **(B)** The examples given all require students to elaborate on previous responses. Correcting an answer (A) would be saying, "No, that is not the answer." Answers (C) and (D) mean the same thing; an example of accepting or affirming an answer would be saying, "Yes, good answer."

25. **(C)** When a child who is normally well-behaved exhibits uncharacteristic behaviors, it is usually a normal reaction to some immediate stimulus. Nothing in the scenario given indicates physical symptoms of illness (A), nor does anything in the description indicate a pervasive or lasting condition requiring professional intervention (B, D).

26. **(C)** The best response is to emphasize that occupations are open to both men and women and that most people make career choices based on their abilities and their preferences. Answers (A) and (B) fail to take advantage of the opportunity to teach the class about equal opportunity in career choices, and answer (D) implies that popular opinion determines career choices.

27. **(B)** This assignment asks students to gather information or explore long-term goals, goals many years in the future. Short-term goals (A, C)

are those which can be achieved in days, weeks, or maybe months. Answer (D), synthesize, is a more complicated process than merely gathering information.

28. **(D)** The outcome or product of an instructional activity is to help students improve their work. Answers (A), (B), and (C) may be true statements, but they describe a teacher's priorities or expectations, rather than an instructional goal.

29. **(C)** Teachers must take into consideration the values and norms of the school community and its special characteristics. The standards by which student behaviors are judged must be acceptable to the community. Although there may be value to the ideas offered in the other answers (A, B, D), they are not as good as answer (C).

30. **(D)** Learning is a partnership, with both teacher and students playing important parts; classroom control is dependent on both the teacher and the students. The other statements (A, B, C) are false.

31. **(C)** Now that the student has been diagnosed, it is important that she and her parents understand the educational implications and options available to them. Answer (A) is wrong as it fails to address the problem. Although Answers (B) and (D) might be possibilities, they are not the best answers to the question. After meeting with the student and her parents, the teacher will want to explore other ways to meet the student's educational needs (B) and continue to encourage her (D); however, the student may already be trying hard and doing the best she can.

32. **(B)** This is the best answer because it identifies two topics for students to have a choice if they prefer that the teacher provide the writing prompt and still it provides an opportunity for those students who like to choose their own topic. Answers (A) and (C) are limited in that they fail to provide an option for the student who wants to choose his/her own topic, and answer (D) fails to take into account those students who prefer to have a teacher suggest a topic for their writing. Answer (B) provides the best option for all learning styles and preferences.

33. **(D)** By allowing students to measure with a ruler, the teacher has provided applications of the law or rule that 12 inches equals one foot. By allowing them to make measurements, she has gone beyond teaching a stated principle or law (B). Since students have measured only with a

ruler, they have not learned cause-and-effect (A) or comparison and contrast (C).

34. **(C)** Drill and practice is a good way for students to acquire memory skills or attain knowledge. Analysis, divergent thinking, and critical thinking (A, B, D) require more complex skills than those addressed in drill and practice.

35. **(C)** The teacher is asking the student questions to allow the student to correct a spelling error. Spelling does not allow for divergent or creative thinking (A). Although the teacher reminds the student of a mnemonic, the teacher is not teaching the mnemonic (B); finally, applying spelling rules or guides to improve spelling would be an example of deductive reasoning, not inductive reasoning (D).

36. **(A)** Engaging students in weekly and monthly reviews will promote long-term retention. Giving students an outline helps them to anticipate and organize information, but it does not address the goal of long-term retention (B). Daily worksheets and homework help short-term memory, not long-term retention (C, D).

37. **(A)** Mastery teaching and testing allows students to rework and retake tests until they have achieved a specified standard of performance. Although attaining high scores on tests is an indicator of a high-achieving class, it does not necessarily mean mastery testing (B). When students use books and materials, the test is described as being an open-book test (C). Students with special needs may require testing accommodations, but that is not a characteristic of mastery testing (D).

38. **(D)** The teacher's grade book is confidential (B) and not open to the public. It is also a record of student performance and attendance (A) and a record of all graded items given throughout the school year (C).

39. **(B)** To meet the legal definition of "learning disability," measures on standardized tests are needed and there must be a discrepancy between the student's intellectual aptitude and his or her score on a standardized achievement test. The other factors (A, C, D) may affect a student's propensity to learn and achievement; however, they, in and of themselves, do not constitute a learning disability.

40. **(D)** This is the best answer because it contains information which is technically correct and which expresses a concern about the difference in the student's standardized test score and usual performance in math class. (A) is technically correct; however, it doesn't really provide as much complete information as answer (D). Answer (B) tends to provide the student with a false impression; while it is true that the student scored in the top half, as one of the best students in class, the student could have expected to have scored perhaps in the top ten percent or at least the top quartile. (C) is a false statement.

41. **(A)** This is clear and unequivocal feedback. The other responses (B, C, D) send unclear and/or mixed messages.

42. **(C)** Test reliability refers to the stability, dependability, and pre-dictability of a test. Content validity refers to whether the test measures what it is meant to measure (A), and construct validity refers to explaining the test in terms of psychological properties or other variables (B). Statistical variance is a term used to describe a statistical quality of the test (D).

43. **(C)** Essay-type tests often measure lower-order thinking, although they are adaptable for measuring higher-order thinking, as well. In general, essay tests are not more difficult or easier than objective-type tests although some students prefer one kind of test over another (B). Although essays are often described as subjective measures, teachers should identify the criteria upon which the essay will be graded so as to minimize subjectivity (A) even though all tests—to some extent—are graded subjectively. Finally, teachers do not favor essay tests because they take longer to grade than other kinds of tests (D).

44. **(B)** A letter grade system is an ordinal system where A is greater than B which is greater than C and so forth; the letters indicate rank order. A nominal scale, answer (A), is one where the label or designation has no quantitative meaning. An interval measurement, answer (C), is one where the distance between numbers is the same; when numerical grades are translated in letter grades, they lose this characteristic. For example, a student who earns a B may not be exactly 10 points below the student who earned an A or 10 points above the student who earned a C (e.g., a 97, 83, and 79 translated into A, B, C). A ratio measurement scale, answer (D), has an absolute or natural zero with empirical meaning in addition to having the characteristics of nominal, ordinal, and interval measurements.

45. **(C)** The best method is to provide affirmation and encouragement to students who answer correctly and encourage students to try again if they do not answer correctly. Answer (A) is demoralizing for students, since it is false praise when they have failed to answer the questions correctly. Answers (B) and (D) are irrelevant to the teacher's goals of promoting on task behaviors and student motivation.

46. **(B)** By asking her students to identify the period of the piece, the teacher is asking students to distinguish between two related periods. She is not asking students to judge the music against a set of criteria (A), nor is she asking them to describe or define the pieces (C). Appreciate (D) is a term used to describe an attitude not a behavior.

47. **(A)** Answer (A) is an application question, requiring students to look at examples and apply their knowledge in order to identify the type. Answers (B) and (C) are questions requiring simple memory skills.

48. **(B)** By telling her students about equivalent measurements, she has stated a principle or law. She has not taught cause-and-effect (A, C) or provided applications of the principle (D).

49. **(C)** A quiet classroom may be appropriate for some learning and inappropriate for others. It is not necessarily a good or bad learning environment (A, B), nor does it demonstrate that the teacher has appropriate control of the students (D)—e.g., the students might all be asleep.

50. **(A)** Research shows that one factor contributing to students' success in school is parental involvement in school-related activities. There is no evidence that parents who are involved are stricter (B), easier to get along with than parents who are not involved (C), or that they are more easily influenced by teachers (D). Simply stated, because they are involved in school activities, these parents probably communicate to their children the value they place on education.

51. **(C)** The best teachers should plan activities for students who finish their classroom work before their peers. Answers (A) and (D) are merely punitive measures which are not instructive regarding time management. Although answer (B) may imply a need for better time management, it does not provide the students with a remedy for staying out of trouble.

52. **(B)** Showing a video can help students who are not strong readers

to understand a written text as well as allow students to see a story and to become aware of the differences in text and film (A, C, D). However, a teacher does not use visual media to simply kill time or give students a "day off."

53. **(A)**   The teacher should give the student the information and let her make her own decision, just as the teacher should do for all her students. In open competition, there is no way for a teacher to know who will earn parts (B) or to assume that the student should ask for a job on the crew (C). The student may not know enough to ask about the play (D).

54. **(C)**   Although all four answers could be verified as correct upon further investigation, at this point the only thing the teacher can reasonably conclude is that a number of factors could be contributing to the student's lower score on the standardized test.

55. **(C)**   The teacher should allow the students to evaluate the list and add some names to show that they do recognize the diversity of individuals who have contributed to America's greatness. Answer (D) is sarcastic, and answer (A) is too harsh. Answer (B) does not allow the students to amend their list.

56. **(A)**   This is the best answer since it demonstrates that the teacher is making her classroom fully accessible for students with special needs. Spacing of the desks has nothing to do with providing students with individual attention (C). Having desks spaced three feet apart would not contribute to feelings of interdependence (B). Collaborative learning is an effective instructional technique, so the teacher would not want to discourage collaborative learning (D).

57. **(D)**   The teacher should approach the student directly and propose an intervention for him to get help. There is insufficient evidence for the teacher to conclude that the student is upset by sexual issues (A), and the other options (B, C) are too indirect to address the seriousness of the behaviors that the teacher observes.

58. **(A)**   A teacher has a responsibility to make immediate referrals when he or she suspects that a student is using drugs. Answers (B) and (C) are inadequate and inappropriate responses. If the teacher waits until he or she has conclusive evidence (D), it may be too late.

59. **(B)** In the example given, the listener is not reflecting on (A) or analyzing (D) the speaker's message or trying to program or influence the speaker (C). The listener is merely saying back what he or she heard the speaker say.

60. **(A)** This method allows the teacher to gather information about each student that can be used to tailor assignments to each individual's interest and experiences. Answers (C) and (D) describe motivational activities which may or may not have anything to do with the interests, feelings, or experiences of students. Answer (B) is a poor answer because it abdicates the teacher's responsibility for directing and guiding students.

61. **(C)** Teachers often teach through example or metaphor. The best metaphor is the telephone system (which sends and processes information), a person making a call (who sends information), and the telephone instrument itself (which receives the information and sends it through the system). Answers (A), (B), and (D) describe a system and two information receivers/senders.

62. **(A)** A positive statement of encouragement will boost the confidence of some students and will not undercut anyone's self-esteem. Answers (B), (C), and (D) are almost certain to generate anxiety that will interfere with test performance for some students.

63. **(B)** Having students do work every day is an example of distributed or spaced practice; mathematics is one subject where this kind of practice is particularly needed. An example of massed practice (B) would be assigning students 200 problems to complete the day before the test. Timed practice (C) would be asking students to complete an assignment in a specified amount of time. Concept mapping (D) refers to a way of taking notes or organizing information.

64. **(A)** The best time to study for memory retention is within 8 hours of information first being presented. Twenty-four hours later (B), the average learner will recall less than 50 percent of the information. If the material is not studied for over 24 hours, memory will deteriorate even further, diminishing to around 20-25 percent within 48 hours. Even if there is a short review before the test (C), memory will not be as strong as it is shortly after the material is first presented.

65. **(A)** Putting together or arranging elements to make a whole pattern or product is synthesis. Answers (B), (C), and (D) are examples of tasks requiring analysis, not synthesis.

66. **(D)** Answers (A) and (B) describe different cultural responses or customs; generally speaking, in the south, there is greater use of the terms "sir" and "ma'am," but a simple "Yes" or "No" does not indicate disrespect. Neither does calling students by a title ("Mr." or "Ms.") show disrespect (C). However, addressing one group of students by a title ("Mr.") and not using an equivalent title ("Ms.") with another group of students shows differential treatment, implying that one group (male) is due more respect than the other group (female).

67. **(B)** Learning cycle means that the process repeats itself, moving in an unending and continuous cycle, as the teacher and students interact with one another and the content. A process based on steps would be linear not cyclical (A); an approach based on developmental stages would also be a linear process (C). The teacher does facilitate the process (D), but clearly this answer is not as good as (B).

68. **(A)** Inductive reasoning involves making generalizations based on a particular fact or example. Deductive reasoning (B) would be used if students were to discuss the characteristics of romance and then compose a music piece encompassing those characteristics. Oral interpretation (C) is a type of dramatic speech, and evaluation (D) involves judging the quality or merits of a work or product.

69. **(C)** This is not a closed question, but an open question, requiring some thoughtful reflecting and speculation to answer. Answers (A), (B), and (D) are examples of closed questions, requiring a simple statement of recall to answer the question.

70. **(A)** The use of a teacher-made subject-specific or task-specific pre-test is a common and effective way to determine a student's understanding in a particular area. Neither what students may have studied in the past nor their past performance (B, C) are reliable indicators of present knowledge and skills, nor are general achievement tests (D).

71. **(B)** Answers (A), (C), and (D) would be premature, since the teacher has not suspected the student of cheating before or of requiring extra attention, but has always considered the student to be one of the best

in the class. It is also premature to assume that the student needs psychological intervention since, at this point, the teacher has not even talked to the student about his/her feelings when preparing for and taking a test.

72. **(A)** New technologies can be helpful to students in many ways. Answer (B) would stifle the student's creativity and result in less sophisticated writing. Answer (C) has not been proven effective as a technique to help students improve their spelling. Answer (D) means that the teacher would not be applying standards of good writing in evaluating the student's work.

73. **(C)** The teacher must intervene in the situation and attempt to help the two students resolve their differences by communicating with each other. Answer (A) resorts to physical coercion, and answer (B) escalates the situation into one involving the principal. Answer (D) is negligent, failing to take action and letting the situation deteriorate further.

74. **(B)** This answer addresses an appreciation of cultural and religious differences as indicated in the question. Answer (C) is a cliché or adage, not a statement of fact. Answers (A) and (D) are factual statements, but they do not address the question posed.

75. **(C)** Although the student should seek counseling (D) and will eventually need to tell her mother what happened (A), the teacher's legal responsibility is to report the assault to the appropriate authorities. It would not be appropriate for the teacher to call the student's mother (B).

76. **(A)** In order to communicate completely and explicitly what the rules and expectations are, the teacher would select answer (A). Answers (B), (C), and (D) would not accomplish what the teacher has identified as his aim.

77. **(D)** Making a student an object of ridicule is never an appropriate way of correcting misconduct (A), nor is it appropriate to make the student wait to discover the penalty for misconduct (C). The rules and the consequences for breaking the rules should be clear. As a rule, students should be treated the same for infractions; to do otherwise would be unfair and inconsistent (B).

78. **(A)** This is the most effective and efficient way to provide this student with the same testing opportunity that his or her classmates will have. The other methods suggested (B, C, D) have possible advantages and/or disadvantages.

79. **(C)** The best way to handle the situation is to involve parents in their children's reading activity. The research supports the importance of parents reading with their children. Children as young as second grade will not have sufficiently developed reading skills (and in many cases, computer skills) to successfully test themselves and each other, and there might be problems with students not doing their own work (A, B). Many children might not be able to come to school early or stay late (D).

80. **(A)** Using class time efficiently is an important part of successful teaching. Answers (B) and (D) are irrelevant to the situation described. The information provided is insufficient for concluding that the teacher is rigid or unreasonable (C).

81. **(C)** Content validity refers to whether or not the test measures what it was designed or meant to measure. For example, a test of writing should measure how well students write, not how well they understand current events. Answer (B) refers to the statistical characteristics of the test (A), but they have nothing to do with content validity, nor does answer (D), which refers to normative characteristics of a test.

82. **(A)** The question asks about additional information that the teacher should provide. Answer (C) does not really provide any additional information about the upcoming test and answer (B) could create debilitating anxiety for students. A teacher should describe a test in positive terms that will motivate and encourage students to do their best.

83. **(C)** If the top grade in the class was a C, then the student is still at the top of the class. The teacher cannot show the grade book without violating students' rights of confidentiality of grades (A). Going over the answer key with the student will merely show which answers were missed and will not allay his concerns over his ranking in the class (B); encouraging the student to work harder also fails to address his concerns (D).

84. **(C)** Reserved and quiet students also have contributions to make to the class discussion, although they may be somewhat reluctant to do so. It is not a good idea to pick on these students (A), as they may become more

withdrawn, nor is ignoring them a good idea (B), since that doesn't help them become more assertive. Just because they sit in the back of the room doesn't mean that they are troublemakers; teachers should be careful not to jump to too many conclusions (D).

85. **(B)** Holistic scoring refers to the overall effectiveness or success of the writing, not an analysis of its individual components, such as spelling, punctuation, grammar, and so forth. Answers (A), (C), and (D) describe holistic scoring.

86. **(A)** Short-range objectives are the products of the learning goals based on the skills, knowledge, and attitudes to be attained through the educational process. The other answers (B, C, D) may be useful follow-up techniques, but (A) is the starting point.

87. **(A)** Many students need time to reflect before they give an answer, and teachers often fail to allow enough time to lapse before they give an example or ask another question. Answer (D) would be appropriate if the teacher gave the student ample time and the student still did not answer. If, after the example, the student still did not answer, then the teacher could call on another student (C). Answer (B) is an inappropriate response.

88. **(C)** Web addresses are changing and sites the teacher may have found in planning the assignment may not still be at the same address by the time the students get the assignment. It is very unlikely that students will accidentally access inappropriate web sites since there are warnings about adult-content and most school districts use filtering software to restrict access to inappropriate sites (A). A teacher can easily access the history of a computer to see which sites a student using the computer has accessed (B), and with the incredible amount of information on the World Wide Web, it is highly unlikely that a student will not find enough information. In fact, on the Internet, the problem is deciding which information to use since there is so much data available (D).

89. **(C)** Criterion-referenced tests are scored according to how well a student's answers match the established criteria or set of knowledge and skills defined by the test. Tests that compare student performance with the performance of other students are norm-referenced tests (A, B). Percentage scores indicate the number of questions a student has answered correctly (D).

90. **(D)** The teacher gives the student appropriate feedback and still gives the student a chance to think about the correct answer without simply providing the correct answer. The other choices (A, B, C) are correct (at least, in part), but they are not the best answer.

91. **(C)** Web-filtering devices restrict access to certain web sites as specified by the individual who installs the filter. It will not safeguard First Amendment Rights, as it restricts certain information (A). Moreover, it will not ensure that students do not access information offensive to others (B) or that they will learn how to use the Internet for research (D).

92. **(D)** Many times, teachers fail to give students enough time to think about their answers especially if their first response is incorrect. Answers (A) and (C), while not technically incorrect, are not as good as (D) because they fail to provide the student with any feedback or chance to self-correct his/her answer. Answer (B) gives the student a false impression that he or she almost had the correct answer.

93. **(D)** At best, this procedure can be said to promote school safety. It cannot be assumed that the procedure is sufficient to accomplish the goal of school safety (B). Answers (A) and (C) are not desirable consequences.

94. **(C)** When students work with each other in groups, they are involved in collaboration. The other answers (A, B, D) refer to teacher-directed or teacher-centered learning activities

95. **(B)** This is clear and unequivocal feedback. Answers (A) and (D) are unclear as to whether they are correct or not. While answer (C) indicates acceptance of the answer, it is not as clear as (B).

96. **(D)** Grades are traditional and have widespread acceptance among students and parents. However, there are some arguments against traditional grading systems, including that grades encourage students to take easier classes (A), that easy and difficult courses carry the same weight in most school systems (when grades are weighted, the more difficult classes carry more weight, not the easier ones) (B), and that grades fail to accurately reflect student performance (C).

97. **(C)** Since the student exhibits the positive characteristics of punctuality, consistency, and politeness (among other strengths), it is unlikely that she is using drugs (A), that she lacks motivation to succeed (B), or

that she is yielding to peer pressure (D). In this case, it is most likely that the student has some academic deficiencies which impair her ability to perform well in class and on her assignments.

98. **(A)**   Based on the information provided, the only reasonable conclusion is that the student has some competition from his younger and older siblings at home. Without further investigation (and perhaps prying), the teacher cannot conclude that the student is jealous or has problems with his stepfather (B, C). Answer (D) would only be a reasonable conclusion if the student underwent psychological therapy or treatment and cannot be assumed as the result of a parent-teacher conference.

99. **(C)**   This answer requires students to perform an activity using the specified skill of determining the meaning of words in sentences. Dictionary skills (A) are important, but they are not the skill specified in the question. Using words in a sentence (B) is not the same as the specified skill of identifying the meaning of words and phrases in sentences. Answer (B) requires construction skill, whereas the task required by the skill is deconstruction. Answer (D) is irrelevant. A picture could depict a feeling, a concept, an image or impression, not necessarily the meaning of the words used in the passage.

100. **(A)**   The students have developed criteria against which they can decide or judge if someone is intelligent. The students were gathering characteristics, not examples (B), and the students have yet to test their criteria (C). Instead of creative thinking, in this activity students are engaged in critical thinking (D).

101. **(A)**   "Demonstrate" is a word used to show application or that the student has learned to apply knowledge to perform a task. The other questions deal with other aspects of Bloom's taxonomy—answers (B) and (C) with the knowledge and comprehension levels, respectively, and answer (D) with analysis.

102. **(A)**   The first thing a teacher must decide is what the students should be able to do to show their understanding; this requires examining the instructional and performance objectives. The teacher must also evaluate the level of understanding required. If the teacher is interested in knowledge, then matching terms with definitions would be suitable; if the teacher wants to measure students' analysis of concepts, then such a test would be inappropriate. Features of the test, how many points it will be

worth, how long it should be, and the format should be decided later (B, C, D).

103. **(D)**   All the strategies listed (A, B, C) are attempts to discourage cheating behaviors among students.

104. **(D)**   A combination of auditory, visual, and tactile-kinesthetic methods appears to be most effective. (D) is a combination of (A), (B), and (C).

105. **(A)**   According to general psychological principles regarding rewards and punishments (positive and negative reinforcements), rewards promote the occurrence of behavior. Answer (B) is false and answers (C) and (D) contain distinctions not addressed in the question.

106. **(D)**   Questions can engage the students' attention (A), evaluate students' knowledge (B), and invite students to learn (C). Questions can also be used to help students discover new information and to practice or rehearse information.

107. **(C)**   This is the best example of existing and easily available resources to teach about nutritional values of certain foods. The other options (A, B, C) might yield interesting information, but not the information requested in this question.

108. **(A)**   The question provides information about the teachers' attitudes and backgrounds with computers. Research shows that teacher experience is positively related to students' achievement using computers. The other answers (B, C, D) contain irrelevant information that in themselves would not affect student progress in a differential manner.

109. **(B)**   In teaching literature, different genres share basic characteristics regardless of the writer's nationality or culture (C, A). Writers from any culture may be easier or more difficult to understand, depending on the writing style and features of the individual writer (D).

110. **(B)**   Loud noise (such as that from a mower) can severely distract some students, so the teacher should postpone or delay the test. The teacher should not administer the test (A, C). The teacher could complain (D), but that would not have any immediate impact for his students.

111. **(C)**   Authentic assessments are projects or collections that represent student work over time and can show student progress versus student

performance at one point in time, such as pen and paper tests (A) and essay tests (D). Although recent research confirms that cheating is widespread among students, teachers should always stress the importance of doing one's own work whether on tests or other assignments (B).

112. **(A)** Although the teacher may prefer a quiet class, keeping the class quiet is not necessarily an instructional benefit. (Some experts say that "Students who talk are students who learn.") Answers (B), (C), and (D) are instructional benefits. A review of previously learned material (B) is beneficial for learning new material (D), and having direction gives students a purpose to focus their attention (C).

113. **(A)** Reciting the Pledge of Allegiance is an example of reinforcing retention through recitation. Students often recite the Pledge without understanding the meaning of the words (B). Because students are reciting the same words, this is not an example of language development (D). Behavior modification (C) refers to attempts to change undesirable behaviors and is irrelevant to the situation described.

114. **(C)** A full and complete answer is required to allay the student's worries and help him/her prepare for the test. Answer (D) is inadequate. Answers (A) and (B) are not really answers to the question; they are, instead, attempts to evade answering the question.

115. **(D)** By allowing students to take each other's blood pressure, the teacher is providing a hands-on experience (A) which is tactile-kinesthetic (C), and giving his students the chance to apply their learning (B).

116. **(A)** When the teacher demonstrates two ways of solving a problem, he is giving students two examples or strategies to compare and contrast. This is one of the ways of organizing information or analyzing information. The teacher did not provide a definition (A) or show cause and effect (D). Answer (C) is a contradiction in terms; an application is concrete, not abstract.

117. **(D)** Different students require different approaches. In various situations, any of the options (A, B, C) might be effective, but answer (D) is the best general practice.

118. **(A)** A long-range goal covers a longer period of time and deals with broader, more global concepts, such as language usage. Although the goals provided in answers (B), (C), and (D) might be worthy goals, they are limited in time length and scope of achievement. The outcomes specified in answers (B), (C), and (D) are more specific than the outcome in answer (A).

119. **(C)** Students are more likely to be able to identify with a former student who shares many characteristics with them and to listen to his or her experience than to learn from a motion picture (A), a dated video (B), or by writing a research paper (D).

120. **(B)** Although it is important for students to learn the actual procedures of the drill (D), that is not the first thing. Before students practice for the weather drill, they must know that their teacher will take care of them. Answers (A) and (C) are irrelevant to the teacher's goal of helping students to stay calm and to feel safe and secure.

121. **(C)** The technical information about second grade, third month of instruction as the meaning of the 2.3 grade equivalency score is correct in answers (C) and (D); however, (D) is not as good a choice as (C) because (D) does not explain the meaning of the score. Answer (A) is false. Answer (B) could be considered a correct or truthful answer; however, it does not suggest a remedy or imply that the student needs to improve to be on grade level. Answer (C) is the best answer because it contains factual information, and it explains that the student's parents and the teacher need to work together to help the student improve his/her reading.

122. **(A)** A percentile score ranks a student in comparison to others taking the test. Percentile scores have nothing to do with the percentage of questions a student answers either correctly or incorrectly (B, D). A raw score standardized by using a statistical formula is a standard score (C).

123. **(C)** A biased test is one that discriminates against individuals on the basis of cultural, ethnic, or other factors. For example, a test that asks rural children about city activities would be biased against the rural children. Children from the city would be expected to know more about skyscrapers than children from the farm, and vice versa. An intelligence test or aptitude test is designed to discriminate between those who are smart

and those not as smart (A) which has nothing to do with test bias. The general purpose of any test is to discriminate between those who understand and who prepare versus those who do not (B, D).

124. **(C)** Different students respond differently to different kinds of stimuli. (A) and (B) are basically the same answer, just worded differently. (D) is a poor choice because even when teachers plan an activity that is different than the norm, there should be an instructional principle or rationale behind the activity.

125. **(D)** This question requires an analysis of the situation or problem in order to answer. Answer (A) requires application, the level below analysis; Answer (C) requires comprehension, the level below application, and answer (B) requires knowledge, the lowest level, according to Bloom's taxonomy.

126. **(B)** Since the teacher is engaging the class in conversation, they might as well discuss the question in Spanish. Answer (A) is demeaning to the student, and although answer (D) is accurate, it fails to take advantage of the opportunity to teach the student something about which he or she is interested. Resorting to English (C) in a Spanish class is not as effective as continuing the discussion in Spanish.

127. **(D)** By summarizing significant points of discussion before moving to new material, the teacher can provide the class with a review. Telling students what they will study next or asking them to form hypotheses (A, C) helps them to anticipate new information, but does not necessarily connect with what was previously learned. Homework might provide a review, but not necessarily; homework could be based on just one aspect of the lesson or could be the material to study next (B).

128. **(A)** A line graph showing the grades of a student is a system of recording the progress of individual students. The others given (B, C, D), the pie chart, the scatter chart, and the bar graph, would show the progress of students as a whole.

129. **(D)** Walking to the back of the room is the least intrusive way to interrupt the students' disruptive behavior. The other methods listed (A, B, C) may get results, but they are much more disruptive to the regular classroom activity.

130. **(A)** The purpose of the test is the first consideration in test selection. A good test will measure what the teacher needs to measure. After the purpose of the test is determined, then the other factors (B, C, D) must be evaluated.

131. **(D)** Students' threats of suicide must be taken seriously and teachers must refer to trained professionals to take action in face of such threats. Answers (A), (B), and (C) are inadequate responses to threats of suicide.

132. **(A)** If teachers want to be consistent in enforcing classroom rules, they should avoid making rules that they do not want to enforce. The other answers (B, C, D) are not inconsistent with demonstrating that decisions and actions have consequences.

133. **(A)** A teacher may show a video to a class as long is there is no charge to the student. Teachers may not sell copies of taped television programs (B); time limits apply to the use of videos of television programs used in the classroom (C), and trademarked and copyrighted images on the Internet (D) have the same protections as those in other media.

134. **(D)** Standing with arms crossed or behind furniture conveys fear or distrust, signifying a distant and aloof individual. Warm and caring individuals (A), physical individuals (B), and open individuals (C) tend to stand with their arms in open, wide gestures or with arms relaxed at their sides.

135. **(B)** Asking students to imagine is a creative act or task. Critical thinking would require analysis and evaluation (A). Convergent thinking would require synthesis or a bringing together of elements (C). Cause-and-effect thinking requires sequential analysis of a process or processes (D).

136. **(C)** Not all children are ready to read in first grade. If the student is performing well in other areas, he may not yet be ready to read. Taking extreme action (A, B, D) at this point in time may cause more trouble than benefit relative to the student's reading readiness.

137. **(A)** This lets the student know what she has done correctly. The other answers (B, C, D) are affirming, but vague.

138. **(D)** This answer is an example of using a "real world" problem, determining the price of items on sale. Answers (A) and (B) are not "real

world" examples. Answer (C), likewise, might have little to do with the real world today, and a matching test measures recognition or memory, not understanding.

139. **(B)**   Students who are social individuals who avoid conflicts and try to placate others are especially susceptible to peer pressure. The teacher is justified in being concerned. Answers (A), (C), and (D) are unsupported by the scenario described.

140. **(D)**   A teacher cannot take information from the student's permanent record. If a parent and/or student conference is required, the teacher might request that a school administrator or counselor be present to discuss information from the permanent record (A, C), but the teacher may not take that information from the permanent record; likewise, the teacher may not make photocopies of documents in the student's permanent file (B).

FTCE

Florida Teacher Certification Exam—
Professional Education Test

Answer Sheets

FTCE
Practice Test 1
ANSWER SHEET

1. Ⓐ Ⓑ Ⓒ Ⓓ	29. Ⓐ Ⓑ Ⓒ Ⓓ	57. Ⓐ Ⓑ Ⓒ Ⓓ
2. Ⓐ Ⓑ Ⓒ Ⓓ	30. Ⓐ Ⓑ Ⓒ Ⓓ	58. Ⓐ Ⓑ Ⓒ Ⓓ
3. Ⓐ Ⓑ Ⓒ Ⓓ	31. Ⓐ Ⓑ Ⓒ Ⓓ	59. Ⓐ Ⓑ Ⓒ Ⓓ
4. Ⓐ Ⓑ Ⓒ Ⓓ	32. Ⓐ Ⓑ Ⓒ Ⓓ	60. Ⓐ Ⓑ Ⓒ Ⓓ
5. Ⓐ Ⓑ Ⓒ Ⓓ	33. Ⓐ Ⓑ Ⓒ Ⓓ	61. Ⓐ Ⓑ Ⓒ Ⓓ
6. Ⓐ Ⓑ Ⓒ Ⓓ	34. Ⓐ Ⓑ Ⓒ Ⓓ	62. Ⓐ Ⓑ Ⓒ Ⓓ
7. Ⓐ Ⓑ Ⓒ Ⓓ	35. Ⓐ Ⓑ Ⓒ Ⓓ	63. Ⓐ Ⓑ Ⓒ Ⓓ
8. Ⓐ Ⓑ Ⓒ Ⓓ	36. Ⓐ Ⓑ Ⓒ Ⓓ	64. Ⓐ Ⓑ Ⓒ Ⓓ
9. Ⓐ Ⓑ Ⓒ Ⓓ	37. Ⓐ Ⓑ Ⓒ Ⓓ	65. Ⓐ Ⓑ Ⓒ Ⓓ
10. Ⓐ Ⓑ Ⓒ Ⓓ	38. Ⓐ Ⓑ Ⓒ Ⓓ	66. Ⓐ Ⓑ Ⓒ Ⓓ
11. Ⓐ Ⓑ Ⓒ Ⓓ	39. Ⓐ Ⓑ Ⓒ Ⓓ	67. Ⓐ Ⓑ Ⓒ Ⓓ
12. Ⓐ Ⓑ Ⓒ Ⓓ	40. Ⓐ Ⓑ Ⓒ Ⓓ	68. Ⓐ Ⓑ Ⓒ Ⓓ
13. Ⓐ Ⓑ Ⓒ Ⓓ	41. Ⓐ Ⓑ Ⓒ Ⓓ	69. Ⓐ Ⓑ Ⓒ Ⓓ
14. Ⓐ Ⓑ Ⓒ Ⓓ	42. Ⓐ Ⓑ Ⓒ Ⓓ	70. Ⓐ Ⓑ Ⓒ Ⓓ
15. Ⓐ Ⓑ Ⓒ Ⓓ	43. Ⓐ Ⓑ Ⓒ Ⓓ	71. Ⓐ Ⓑ Ⓒ Ⓓ
16. Ⓐ Ⓑ Ⓒ Ⓓ	44. Ⓐ Ⓑ Ⓒ Ⓓ	72. Ⓐ Ⓑ Ⓒ Ⓓ
17. Ⓐ Ⓑ Ⓒ Ⓓ	45. Ⓐ Ⓑ Ⓒ Ⓓ	73. Ⓐ Ⓑ Ⓒ Ⓓ
18. Ⓐ Ⓑ Ⓒ Ⓓ	46. Ⓐ Ⓑ Ⓒ Ⓓ	74. Ⓐ Ⓑ Ⓒ Ⓓ
19. Ⓐ Ⓑ Ⓒ Ⓓ	47. Ⓐ Ⓑ Ⓒ Ⓓ	75. Ⓐ Ⓑ Ⓒ Ⓓ
20. Ⓐ Ⓑ Ⓒ Ⓓ	48. Ⓐ Ⓑ Ⓒ Ⓓ	76. Ⓐ Ⓑ Ⓒ Ⓓ
21. Ⓐ Ⓑ Ⓒ Ⓓ	49. Ⓐ Ⓑ Ⓒ Ⓓ	77. Ⓐ Ⓑ Ⓒ Ⓓ
22. Ⓐ Ⓑ Ⓒ Ⓓ	50. Ⓐ Ⓑ Ⓒ Ⓓ	78. Ⓐ Ⓑ Ⓒ Ⓓ
23. Ⓐ Ⓑ Ⓒ Ⓓ	51. Ⓐ Ⓑ Ⓒ Ⓓ	79. Ⓐ Ⓑ Ⓒ Ⓓ
24. Ⓐ Ⓑ Ⓒ Ⓓ	52. Ⓐ Ⓑ Ⓒ Ⓓ	80. Ⓐ Ⓑ Ⓒ Ⓓ
25. Ⓐ Ⓑ Ⓒ Ⓓ	53. Ⓐ Ⓑ Ⓒ Ⓓ	81. Ⓐ Ⓑ Ⓒ Ⓓ
26. Ⓐ Ⓑ Ⓒ Ⓓ	54. Ⓐ Ⓑ Ⓒ Ⓓ	82. Ⓐ Ⓑ Ⓒ Ⓓ
27. Ⓐ Ⓑ Ⓒ Ⓓ	55. Ⓐ Ⓑ Ⓒ Ⓓ	83. Ⓐ Ⓑ Ⓒ Ⓓ
28. Ⓐ Ⓑ Ⓒ Ⓓ	56. Ⓐ Ⓑ Ⓒ Ⓓ	84. Ⓐ Ⓑ Ⓒ Ⓓ

85. Ⓐ Ⓑ Ⓒ Ⓓ
86. Ⓐ Ⓑ Ⓒ Ⓓ
87. Ⓐ Ⓑ Ⓒ Ⓓ
88. Ⓐ Ⓑ Ⓒ Ⓓ
89. Ⓐ Ⓑ Ⓒ Ⓓ
90. Ⓐ Ⓑ Ⓒ Ⓓ
91. Ⓐ Ⓑ Ⓒ Ⓓ
92. Ⓐ Ⓑ Ⓒ Ⓓ
93. Ⓐ Ⓑ Ⓒ Ⓓ
94. Ⓐ Ⓑ Ⓒ Ⓓ
95. Ⓐ Ⓑ Ⓒ Ⓓ
96. Ⓐ Ⓑ Ⓒ Ⓓ
97. Ⓐ Ⓑ Ⓒ Ⓓ
98. Ⓐ Ⓑ Ⓒ Ⓓ
99. Ⓐ Ⓑ Ⓒ Ⓓ
100. Ⓐ Ⓑ Ⓒ Ⓓ
101. Ⓐ Ⓑ Ⓒ Ⓓ
102. Ⓐ Ⓑ Ⓒ Ⓓ
103. Ⓐ Ⓑ Ⓒ Ⓓ
104. Ⓐ Ⓑ Ⓒ Ⓓ
105. Ⓐ Ⓑ Ⓒ Ⓓ
106. Ⓐ Ⓑ Ⓒ Ⓓ
107. Ⓐ Ⓑ Ⓒ Ⓓ
108. Ⓐ Ⓑ Ⓒ Ⓓ
109. Ⓐ Ⓑ Ⓒ Ⓓ
110. Ⓐ Ⓑ Ⓒ Ⓓ
111. Ⓐ Ⓑ Ⓒ Ⓓ
112. Ⓐ Ⓑ Ⓒ Ⓓ

113 Ⓐ Ⓑ Ⓒ Ⓓ
114. Ⓐ Ⓑ Ⓒ Ⓓ
115. Ⓐ Ⓑ Ⓒ Ⓓ
116. Ⓐ Ⓑ Ⓒ Ⓓ
117. Ⓐ Ⓑ Ⓒ Ⓓ
118. Ⓐ Ⓑ Ⓒ Ⓓ
119. Ⓐ Ⓑ Ⓒ Ⓓ
120. Ⓐ Ⓑ Ⓒ Ⓓ
121. Ⓐ Ⓑ Ⓒ Ⓓ
122. Ⓐ Ⓑ Ⓒ Ⓓ
123. Ⓐ Ⓑ Ⓒ Ⓓ
124. Ⓐ Ⓑ Ⓒ Ⓓ
125. Ⓐ Ⓑ Ⓒ Ⓓ
126. Ⓐ Ⓑ Ⓒ Ⓓ
127. Ⓐ Ⓑ Ⓒ Ⓓ
128. Ⓐ Ⓑ Ⓒ Ⓓ
129. Ⓐ Ⓑ Ⓒ Ⓓ
130. Ⓐ Ⓑ Ⓒ Ⓓ
131. Ⓐ Ⓑ Ⓒ Ⓓ
132. Ⓐ Ⓑ Ⓒ Ⓓ
133. Ⓐ Ⓑ Ⓒ Ⓓ
134. Ⓐ Ⓑ Ⓒ Ⓓ
135. Ⓐ Ⓑ Ⓒ Ⓓ
136. Ⓐ Ⓑ Ⓒ Ⓓ
137. Ⓐ Ⓑ Ⓒ Ⓓ
138. Ⓐ Ⓑ Ⓒ Ⓓ
139. Ⓐ Ⓑ Ⓒ Ⓓ
140. Ⓐ Ⓑ Ⓒ Ⓓ

FTCE
Practice Test 2
ANSWER SHEET

1. Ⓐ Ⓑ Ⓒ Ⓓ	29. Ⓐ Ⓑ Ⓒ Ⓓ	57. Ⓐ Ⓑ Ⓒ Ⓓ
2. Ⓐ Ⓑ Ⓒ Ⓓ	30. Ⓐ Ⓑ Ⓒ Ⓓ	58. Ⓐ Ⓑ Ⓒ Ⓓ
3. Ⓐ Ⓑ Ⓒ Ⓓ	31. Ⓐ Ⓑ Ⓒ Ⓓ	59. Ⓐ Ⓑ Ⓒ Ⓓ
4. Ⓐ Ⓑ Ⓒ Ⓓ	32. Ⓐ Ⓑ Ⓒ Ⓓ	60. Ⓐ Ⓑ Ⓒ Ⓓ
5. Ⓐ Ⓑ Ⓒ Ⓓ	33. Ⓐ Ⓑ Ⓒ Ⓓ	61. Ⓐ Ⓑ Ⓒ Ⓓ
6. Ⓐ Ⓑ Ⓒ Ⓓ	34. Ⓐ Ⓑ Ⓒ Ⓓ	62. Ⓐ Ⓑ Ⓒ Ⓓ
7. Ⓐ Ⓑ Ⓒ Ⓓ	35. Ⓐ Ⓑ Ⓒ Ⓓ	63. Ⓐ Ⓑ Ⓒ Ⓓ
8. Ⓐ Ⓑ Ⓒ Ⓓ	36. Ⓐ Ⓑ Ⓒ Ⓓ	64. Ⓐ Ⓑ Ⓒ Ⓓ
9. Ⓐ Ⓑ Ⓒ Ⓓ	37. Ⓐ Ⓑ Ⓒ Ⓓ	65. Ⓐ Ⓑ Ⓒ Ⓓ
10. Ⓐ Ⓑ Ⓒ Ⓓ	38. Ⓐ Ⓑ Ⓒ Ⓓ	66. Ⓐ Ⓑ Ⓒ Ⓓ
11. Ⓐ Ⓑ Ⓒ Ⓓ	39. Ⓐ Ⓑ Ⓒ Ⓓ	67. Ⓐ Ⓑ Ⓒ Ⓓ
12. Ⓐ Ⓑ Ⓒ Ⓓ	40. Ⓐ Ⓑ Ⓒ Ⓓ	68. Ⓐ Ⓑ Ⓒ Ⓓ
13. Ⓐ Ⓑ Ⓒ Ⓓ	41. Ⓐ Ⓑ Ⓒ Ⓓ	69. Ⓐ Ⓑ Ⓒ Ⓓ
14. Ⓐ Ⓑ Ⓒ Ⓓ	42. Ⓐ Ⓑ Ⓒ Ⓓ	70. Ⓐ Ⓑ Ⓒ Ⓓ
15. Ⓐ Ⓑ Ⓒ Ⓓ	43. Ⓐ Ⓑ Ⓒ Ⓓ	71. Ⓐ Ⓑ Ⓒ Ⓓ
16. Ⓐ Ⓑ Ⓒ Ⓓ	44. Ⓐ Ⓑ Ⓒ Ⓓ	72. Ⓐ Ⓑ Ⓒ Ⓓ
17. Ⓐ Ⓑ Ⓒ Ⓓ	45. Ⓐ Ⓑ Ⓒ Ⓓ	73. Ⓐ Ⓑ Ⓒ Ⓓ
18. Ⓐ Ⓑ Ⓒ Ⓓ	46. Ⓐ Ⓑ Ⓒ Ⓓ	74. Ⓐ Ⓑ Ⓒ Ⓓ
19. Ⓐ Ⓑ Ⓒ Ⓓ	47. Ⓐ Ⓑ Ⓒ Ⓓ	75. Ⓐ Ⓑ Ⓒ Ⓓ
20. Ⓐ Ⓑ Ⓒ Ⓓ	48. Ⓐ Ⓑ Ⓒ Ⓓ	76. Ⓐ Ⓑ Ⓒ Ⓓ
21. Ⓐ Ⓑ Ⓒ Ⓓ	49. Ⓐ Ⓑ Ⓒ Ⓓ	77. Ⓐ Ⓑ Ⓒ Ⓓ
22. Ⓐ Ⓑ Ⓒ Ⓓ	50. Ⓐ Ⓑ Ⓒ Ⓓ	78. Ⓐ Ⓑ Ⓒ Ⓓ
23. Ⓐ Ⓑ Ⓒ Ⓓ	51. Ⓐ Ⓑ Ⓒ Ⓓ	79. Ⓐ Ⓑ Ⓒ Ⓓ
24. Ⓐ Ⓑ Ⓒ Ⓓ	52. Ⓐ Ⓑ Ⓒ Ⓓ	80. Ⓐ Ⓑ Ⓒ Ⓓ
25. Ⓐ Ⓑ Ⓒ Ⓓ	53. Ⓐ Ⓑ Ⓒ Ⓓ	81. Ⓐ Ⓑ Ⓒ Ⓓ
26. Ⓐ Ⓑ Ⓒ Ⓓ	54. Ⓐ Ⓑ Ⓒ Ⓓ	82. Ⓐ Ⓑ Ⓒ Ⓓ
27. Ⓐ Ⓑ Ⓒ Ⓓ	55. Ⓐ Ⓑ Ⓒ Ⓓ	83. Ⓐ Ⓑ Ⓒ Ⓓ
28. Ⓐ Ⓑ Ⓒ Ⓓ	56. Ⓐ Ⓑ Ⓒ Ⓓ	84. Ⓐ Ⓑ Ⓒ Ⓓ

85.	Ⓐ Ⓑ Ⓒ Ⓓ				113	Ⓐ Ⓑ Ⓒ Ⓓ		
86.	Ⓐ Ⓑ Ⓒ Ⓓ				114.	Ⓐ Ⓑ Ⓒ Ⓓ		
87.	Ⓐ Ⓑ Ⓒ Ⓓ				115.	Ⓐ Ⓑ Ⓒ Ⓓ		
88.	Ⓐ Ⓑ Ⓒ Ⓓ				116.	Ⓐ Ⓑ Ⓒ Ⓓ		
89.	Ⓐ Ⓑ Ⓒ Ⓓ				117.	Ⓐ Ⓑ Ⓒ Ⓓ		
90.	Ⓐ Ⓑ Ⓒ Ⓓ				118.	Ⓐ Ⓑ Ⓒ Ⓓ		
91.	Ⓐ Ⓑ Ⓒ Ⓓ				119.	Ⓐ Ⓑ Ⓒ Ⓓ		
92.	Ⓐ Ⓑ Ⓒ Ⓓ				120.	Ⓐ Ⓑ Ⓒ Ⓓ		
93.	Ⓐ Ⓑ Ⓒ Ⓓ				121.	Ⓐ Ⓑ Ⓒ Ⓓ		
94.	Ⓐ Ⓑ Ⓒ Ⓓ				122.	Ⓐ Ⓑ Ⓒ Ⓓ		
95.	Ⓐ Ⓑ Ⓒ Ⓓ				123.	Ⓐ Ⓑ Ⓒ Ⓓ		
96.	Ⓐ Ⓑ Ⓒ Ⓓ				124.	Ⓐ Ⓑ Ⓒ Ⓓ		
97.	Ⓐ Ⓑ Ⓒ Ⓓ				125.	Ⓐ Ⓑ Ⓒ Ⓓ		
98.	Ⓐ Ⓑ Ⓒ Ⓓ				126.	Ⓐ Ⓑ Ⓒ Ⓓ		
99.	Ⓐ Ⓑ Ⓒ Ⓓ				127.	Ⓐ Ⓑ Ⓒ Ⓓ		
100.	Ⓐ Ⓑ Ⓒ Ⓓ				128.	Ⓐ Ⓑ Ⓒ Ⓓ		
101.	Ⓐ Ⓑ Ⓒ Ⓓ				129.	Ⓐ Ⓑ Ⓒ Ⓓ		
102.	Ⓐ Ⓑ Ⓒ Ⓓ				130.	Ⓐ Ⓑ Ⓒ Ⓓ		
103.	Ⓐ Ⓑ Ⓒ Ⓓ				131.	Ⓐ Ⓑ Ⓒ Ⓓ		
104.	Ⓐ Ⓑ Ⓒ Ⓓ				132.	Ⓐ Ⓑ Ⓒ Ⓓ		
105.	Ⓐ Ⓑ Ⓒ Ⓓ				133.	Ⓐ Ⓑ Ⓒ Ⓓ		
106.	Ⓐ Ⓑ Ⓒ Ⓓ				134.	Ⓐ Ⓑ Ⓒ Ⓓ		
107.	Ⓐ Ⓑ Ⓒ Ⓓ				135.	Ⓐ Ⓑ Ⓒ Ⓓ		
108.	Ⓐ Ⓑ Ⓒ Ⓓ				136.	Ⓐ Ⓑ Ⓒ Ⓓ		
109.	Ⓐ Ⓑ Ⓒ Ⓓ				137.	Ⓐ Ⓑ Ⓒ Ⓓ		
110.	Ⓐ Ⓑ Ⓒ Ⓓ				138.	Ⓐ Ⓑ Ⓒ Ⓓ		
111.	Ⓐ Ⓑ Ⓒ Ⓓ				139.	Ⓐ Ⓑ Ⓒ Ⓓ		
112.	Ⓐ Ⓑ Ⓒ Ⓓ				140.	Ⓐ Ⓑ Ⓒ Ⓓ		

FTCE

ANSWER SHEET

1. Ⓐ Ⓑ Ⓒ Ⓓ	29. Ⓐ Ⓑ Ⓒ Ⓓ	57. Ⓐ Ⓑ Ⓒ Ⓓ
2. Ⓐ Ⓑ Ⓒ Ⓓ	30. Ⓐ Ⓑ Ⓒ Ⓓ	58. Ⓐ Ⓑ Ⓒ Ⓓ
3. Ⓐ Ⓑ Ⓒ Ⓓ	31. Ⓐ Ⓑ Ⓒ Ⓓ	59. Ⓐ Ⓑ Ⓒ Ⓓ
4. Ⓐ Ⓑ Ⓒ Ⓓ	32. Ⓐ Ⓑ Ⓒ Ⓓ	60. Ⓐ Ⓑ Ⓒ Ⓓ
5. Ⓐ Ⓑ Ⓒ Ⓓ	33. Ⓐ Ⓑ Ⓒ Ⓓ	61. Ⓐ Ⓑ Ⓒ Ⓓ
6. Ⓐ Ⓑ Ⓒ Ⓓ	34. Ⓐ Ⓑ Ⓒ Ⓓ	62. Ⓐ Ⓑ Ⓒ Ⓓ
7. Ⓐ Ⓑ Ⓒ Ⓓ	35. Ⓐ Ⓑ Ⓒ Ⓓ	63. Ⓐ Ⓑ Ⓒ Ⓓ
8. Ⓐ Ⓑ Ⓒ Ⓓ	36. Ⓐ Ⓑ Ⓒ Ⓓ	64. Ⓐ Ⓑ Ⓒ Ⓓ
9. Ⓐ Ⓑ Ⓒ Ⓓ	37. Ⓐ Ⓑ Ⓒ Ⓓ	65. Ⓐ Ⓑ Ⓒ Ⓓ
10. Ⓐ Ⓑ Ⓒ Ⓓ	38. Ⓐ Ⓑ Ⓒ Ⓓ	66. Ⓐ Ⓑ Ⓒ Ⓓ
11. Ⓐ Ⓑ Ⓒ Ⓓ	39. Ⓐ Ⓑ Ⓒ Ⓓ	67. Ⓐ Ⓑ Ⓒ Ⓓ
12. Ⓐ Ⓑ Ⓒ Ⓓ	40. Ⓐ Ⓑ Ⓒ Ⓓ	68. Ⓐ Ⓑ Ⓒ Ⓓ
13. Ⓐ Ⓑ Ⓒ Ⓓ	41. Ⓐ Ⓑ Ⓒ Ⓓ	69. Ⓐ Ⓑ Ⓒ Ⓓ
14. Ⓐ Ⓑ Ⓒ Ⓓ	42. Ⓐ Ⓑ Ⓒ Ⓓ	70. Ⓐ Ⓑ Ⓒ Ⓓ
15. Ⓐ Ⓑ Ⓒ Ⓓ	43. Ⓐ Ⓑ Ⓒ Ⓓ	71. Ⓐ Ⓑ Ⓒ Ⓓ
16. Ⓐ Ⓑ Ⓒ Ⓓ	44. Ⓐ Ⓑ Ⓒ Ⓓ	72. Ⓐ Ⓑ Ⓒ Ⓓ
17. Ⓐ Ⓑ Ⓒ Ⓓ	45. Ⓐ Ⓑ Ⓒ Ⓓ	73. Ⓐ Ⓑ Ⓒ Ⓓ
18. Ⓐ Ⓑ Ⓒ Ⓓ	46. Ⓐ Ⓑ Ⓒ Ⓓ	74. Ⓐ Ⓑ Ⓒ Ⓓ
19. Ⓐ Ⓑ Ⓒ Ⓓ	47. Ⓐ Ⓑ Ⓒ Ⓓ	75. Ⓐ Ⓑ Ⓒ Ⓓ
20. Ⓐ Ⓑ Ⓒ Ⓓ	48. Ⓐ Ⓑ Ⓒ Ⓓ	76. Ⓐ Ⓑ Ⓒ Ⓓ
21. Ⓐ Ⓑ Ⓒ Ⓓ	49. Ⓐ Ⓑ Ⓒ Ⓓ	77. Ⓐ Ⓑ Ⓒ Ⓓ
22. Ⓐ Ⓑ Ⓒ Ⓓ	50. Ⓐ Ⓑ Ⓒ Ⓓ	78. Ⓐ Ⓑ Ⓒ Ⓓ
23. Ⓐ Ⓑ Ⓒ Ⓓ	51. Ⓐ Ⓑ Ⓒ Ⓓ	79. Ⓐ Ⓑ Ⓒ Ⓓ
24. Ⓐ Ⓑ Ⓒ Ⓓ	52. Ⓐ Ⓑ Ⓒ Ⓓ	80. Ⓐ Ⓑ Ⓒ Ⓓ
25. Ⓐ Ⓑ Ⓒ Ⓓ	53. Ⓐ Ⓑ Ⓒ Ⓓ	81. Ⓐ Ⓑ Ⓒ Ⓓ
26. Ⓐ Ⓑ Ⓒ Ⓓ	54. Ⓐ Ⓑ Ⓒ Ⓓ	82. Ⓐ Ⓑ Ⓒ Ⓓ
27. Ⓐ Ⓑ Ⓒ Ⓓ	55. Ⓐ Ⓑ Ⓒ Ⓓ	83. Ⓐ Ⓑ Ⓒ Ⓓ
28. Ⓐ Ⓑ Ⓒ Ⓓ	56. Ⓐ Ⓑ Ⓒ Ⓓ	84. Ⓐ Ⓑ Ⓒ Ⓓ

85. Ⓐ Ⓑ Ⓒ Ⓓ
86. Ⓐ Ⓑ Ⓒ Ⓓ
87. Ⓐ Ⓑ Ⓒ Ⓓ
88. Ⓐ Ⓑ Ⓒ Ⓓ
89. Ⓐ Ⓑ Ⓒ Ⓓ
90. Ⓐ Ⓑ Ⓒ Ⓓ
91. Ⓐ Ⓑ Ⓒ Ⓓ
92. Ⓐ Ⓑ Ⓒ Ⓓ
93. Ⓐ Ⓑ Ⓒ Ⓓ
94. Ⓐ Ⓑ Ⓒ Ⓓ
95. Ⓐ Ⓑ Ⓒ Ⓓ
96. Ⓐ Ⓑ Ⓒ Ⓓ
97. Ⓐ Ⓑ Ⓒ Ⓓ
98. Ⓐ Ⓑ Ⓒ Ⓓ
99. Ⓐ Ⓑ Ⓒ Ⓓ
100. Ⓐ Ⓑ Ⓒ Ⓓ
101. Ⓐ Ⓑ Ⓒ Ⓓ
102. Ⓐ Ⓑ Ⓒ Ⓓ
103. Ⓐ Ⓑ Ⓒ Ⓓ
104. Ⓐ Ⓑ Ⓒ Ⓓ
105. Ⓐ Ⓑ Ⓒ Ⓓ
106. Ⓐ Ⓑ Ⓒ Ⓓ
107. Ⓐ Ⓑ Ⓒ Ⓓ
108. Ⓐ Ⓑ Ⓒ Ⓓ
109. Ⓐ Ⓑ Ⓒ Ⓓ
110. Ⓐ Ⓑ Ⓒ Ⓓ
111. Ⓐ Ⓑ Ⓒ Ⓓ
112. Ⓐ Ⓑ Ⓒ Ⓓ

113. Ⓐ Ⓑ Ⓒ Ⓓ
114. Ⓐ Ⓑ Ⓒ Ⓓ
115. Ⓐ Ⓑ Ⓒ Ⓓ
116. Ⓐ Ⓑ Ⓒ Ⓓ
117. Ⓐ Ⓑ Ⓒ Ⓓ
118. Ⓐ Ⓑ Ⓒ Ⓓ
119. Ⓐ Ⓑ Ⓒ Ⓓ
120. Ⓐ Ⓑ Ⓒ Ⓓ
121. Ⓐ Ⓑ Ⓒ Ⓓ
122. Ⓐ Ⓑ Ⓒ Ⓓ
123. Ⓐ Ⓑ Ⓒ Ⓓ
124. Ⓐ Ⓑ Ⓒ Ⓓ
125. Ⓐ Ⓑ Ⓒ Ⓓ
126. Ⓐ Ⓑ Ⓒ Ⓓ
127. Ⓐ Ⓑ Ⓒ Ⓓ
128. Ⓐ Ⓑ Ⓒ Ⓓ
129. Ⓐ Ⓑ Ⓒ Ⓓ
130. Ⓐ Ⓑ Ⓒ Ⓓ
131. Ⓐ Ⓑ Ⓒ Ⓓ
132. Ⓐ Ⓑ Ⓒ Ⓓ
133. Ⓐ Ⓑ Ⓒ Ⓓ
134. Ⓐ Ⓑ Ⓒ Ⓓ
135. Ⓐ Ⓑ Ⓒ Ⓓ
136. Ⓐ Ⓑ Ⓒ Ⓓ
137. Ⓐ Ⓑ Ⓒ Ⓓ
138. Ⓐ Ⓑ Ⓒ Ⓓ
139. Ⓐ Ⓑ Ⓒ Ⓓ
140. Ⓐ Ⓑ Ⓒ Ⓓ

FTCE

ANSWER SHEET

1. Ⓐ Ⓑ Ⓒ Ⓓ	29. Ⓐ Ⓑ Ⓒ Ⓓ	57. Ⓐ Ⓑ Ⓒ Ⓓ
2. Ⓐ Ⓑ Ⓒ Ⓓ	30. Ⓐ Ⓑ Ⓒ Ⓓ	58. Ⓐ Ⓑ Ⓒ Ⓓ
3. Ⓐ Ⓑ Ⓒ Ⓓ	31. Ⓐ Ⓑ Ⓒ Ⓓ	59. Ⓐ Ⓑ Ⓒ Ⓓ
4. Ⓐ Ⓑ Ⓒ Ⓓ	32. Ⓐ Ⓑ Ⓒ Ⓓ	60. Ⓐ Ⓑ Ⓒ Ⓓ
5. Ⓐ Ⓑ Ⓒ Ⓓ	33. Ⓐ Ⓑ Ⓒ Ⓓ	61. Ⓐ Ⓑ Ⓒ Ⓓ
6. Ⓐ Ⓑ Ⓒ Ⓓ	34. Ⓐ Ⓑ Ⓒ Ⓓ	62. Ⓐ Ⓑ Ⓒ Ⓓ
7. Ⓐ Ⓑ Ⓒ Ⓓ	35. Ⓐ Ⓑ Ⓒ Ⓓ	63. Ⓐ Ⓑ Ⓒ Ⓓ
8. Ⓐ Ⓑ Ⓒ Ⓓ	36. Ⓐ Ⓑ Ⓒ Ⓓ	64. Ⓐ Ⓑ Ⓒ Ⓓ
9. Ⓐ Ⓑ Ⓒ Ⓓ	37. Ⓐ Ⓑ Ⓒ Ⓓ	65. Ⓐ Ⓑ Ⓒ Ⓓ
10. Ⓐ Ⓑ Ⓒ Ⓓ	38. Ⓐ Ⓑ Ⓒ Ⓓ	66. Ⓐ Ⓑ Ⓒ Ⓓ
11. Ⓐ Ⓑ Ⓒ Ⓓ	39. Ⓐ Ⓑ Ⓒ Ⓓ	67. Ⓐ Ⓑ Ⓒ Ⓓ
12. Ⓐ Ⓑ Ⓒ Ⓓ	40. Ⓐ Ⓑ Ⓒ Ⓓ	68. Ⓐ Ⓑ Ⓒ Ⓓ
13. Ⓐ Ⓑ Ⓒ Ⓓ	41. Ⓐ Ⓑ Ⓒ Ⓓ	69. Ⓐ Ⓑ Ⓒ Ⓓ
14. Ⓐ Ⓑ Ⓒ Ⓓ	42. Ⓐ Ⓑ Ⓒ Ⓓ	70. Ⓐ Ⓑ Ⓒ Ⓓ
15. Ⓐ Ⓑ Ⓒ Ⓓ	43. Ⓐ Ⓑ Ⓒ Ⓓ	71. Ⓐ Ⓑ Ⓒ Ⓓ
16. Ⓐ Ⓑ Ⓒ Ⓓ	44. Ⓐ Ⓑ Ⓒ Ⓓ	72. Ⓐ Ⓑ Ⓒ Ⓓ
17. Ⓐ Ⓑ Ⓒ Ⓓ	45. Ⓐ Ⓑ Ⓒ Ⓓ	73. Ⓐ Ⓑ Ⓒ Ⓓ
18. Ⓐ Ⓑ Ⓒ Ⓓ	46. Ⓐ Ⓑ Ⓒ Ⓓ	74. Ⓐ Ⓑ Ⓒ Ⓓ
19. Ⓐ Ⓑ Ⓒ Ⓓ	47. Ⓐ Ⓑ Ⓒ Ⓓ	75. Ⓐ Ⓑ Ⓒ Ⓓ
20. Ⓐ Ⓑ Ⓒ Ⓓ	48. Ⓐ Ⓑ Ⓒ Ⓓ	76. Ⓐ Ⓑ Ⓒ Ⓓ
21. Ⓐ Ⓑ Ⓒ Ⓓ	49. Ⓐ Ⓑ Ⓒ Ⓓ	77. Ⓐ Ⓑ Ⓒ Ⓓ
22. Ⓐ Ⓑ Ⓒ Ⓓ	50. Ⓐ Ⓑ Ⓒ Ⓓ	78. Ⓐ Ⓑ Ⓒ Ⓓ
23. Ⓐ Ⓑ Ⓒ Ⓓ	51. Ⓐ Ⓑ Ⓒ Ⓓ	79. Ⓐ Ⓑ Ⓒ Ⓓ
24. Ⓐ Ⓑ Ⓒ Ⓓ	52. Ⓐ Ⓑ Ⓒ Ⓓ	80. Ⓐ Ⓑ Ⓒ Ⓓ
25. Ⓐ Ⓑ Ⓒ Ⓓ	53. Ⓐ Ⓑ Ⓒ Ⓓ	81. Ⓐ Ⓑ Ⓒ Ⓓ
26. Ⓐ Ⓑ Ⓒ Ⓓ	54. Ⓐ Ⓑ Ⓒ Ⓓ	82. Ⓐ Ⓑ Ⓒ Ⓓ
27. Ⓐ Ⓑ Ⓒ Ⓓ	55. Ⓐ Ⓑ Ⓒ Ⓓ	83. Ⓐ Ⓑ Ⓒ Ⓓ
28. Ⓐ Ⓑ Ⓒ Ⓓ	56. Ⓐ Ⓑ Ⓒ Ⓓ	84. Ⓐ Ⓑ Ⓒ Ⓓ

85. Ⓐ Ⓑ Ⓒ Ⓓ
86. Ⓐ Ⓑ Ⓒ Ⓓ
87. Ⓐ Ⓑ Ⓒ Ⓓ
88. Ⓐ Ⓑ Ⓒ Ⓓ
89. Ⓐ Ⓑ Ⓒ Ⓓ
90. Ⓐ Ⓑ Ⓒ Ⓓ
91. Ⓐ Ⓑ Ⓒ Ⓓ
92. Ⓐ Ⓑ Ⓒ Ⓓ
93. Ⓐ Ⓑ Ⓒ Ⓓ
94. Ⓐ Ⓑ Ⓒ Ⓓ
95. Ⓐ Ⓑ Ⓒ Ⓓ
96. Ⓐ Ⓑ Ⓒ Ⓓ
97. Ⓐ Ⓑ Ⓒ Ⓓ
98. Ⓐ Ⓑ Ⓒ Ⓓ
99. Ⓐ Ⓑ Ⓒ Ⓓ
100. Ⓐ Ⓑ Ⓒ Ⓓ
101. Ⓐ Ⓑ Ⓒ Ⓓ
102. Ⓐ Ⓑ Ⓒ Ⓓ
103. Ⓐ Ⓑ Ⓒ Ⓓ
104. Ⓐ Ⓑ Ⓒ Ⓓ
105. Ⓐ Ⓑ Ⓒ Ⓓ
106. Ⓐ Ⓑ Ⓒ Ⓓ
107. Ⓐ Ⓑ Ⓒ Ⓓ
108. Ⓐ Ⓑ Ⓒ Ⓓ
109. Ⓐ Ⓑ Ⓒ Ⓓ
110. Ⓐ Ⓑ Ⓒ Ⓓ
111. Ⓐ Ⓑ Ⓒ Ⓓ
112. Ⓐ Ⓑ Ⓒ Ⓓ

113 Ⓐ Ⓑ Ⓒ Ⓓ
114. Ⓐ Ⓑ Ⓒ Ⓓ
115. Ⓐ Ⓑ Ⓒ Ⓓ
116. Ⓐ Ⓑ Ⓒ Ⓓ
117. Ⓐ Ⓑ Ⓒ Ⓓ
118. Ⓐ Ⓑ Ⓒ Ⓓ
119. Ⓐ Ⓑ Ⓒ Ⓓ
120. Ⓐ Ⓑ Ⓒ Ⓓ
121. Ⓐ Ⓑ Ⓒ Ⓓ
122. Ⓐ Ⓑ Ⓒ Ⓓ
123. Ⓐ Ⓑ Ⓒ Ⓓ
124. Ⓐ Ⓑ Ⓒ Ⓓ
125. Ⓐ Ⓑ Ⓒ Ⓓ
126. Ⓐ Ⓑ Ⓒ Ⓓ
127. Ⓐ Ⓑ Ⓒ Ⓓ
128. Ⓐ Ⓑ Ⓒ Ⓓ
129. Ⓐ Ⓑ Ⓒ Ⓓ
130. Ⓐ Ⓑ Ⓒ Ⓓ
131. Ⓐ Ⓑ Ⓒ Ⓓ
132. Ⓐ Ⓑ Ⓒ Ⓓ
133. Ⓐ Ⓑ Ⓒ Ⓓ
134. Ⓐ Ⓑ Ⓒ Ⓓ
135. Ⓐ Ⓑ Ⓒ Ⓓ
136. Ⓐ Ⓑ Ⓒ Ⓓ
137. Ⓐ Ⓑ Ⓒ Ⓓ
138. Ⓐ Ⓑ Ⓒ Ⓓ
139. Ⓐ Ⓑ Ⓒ Ⓓ
140. Ⓐ Ⓑ Ⓒ Ⓓ

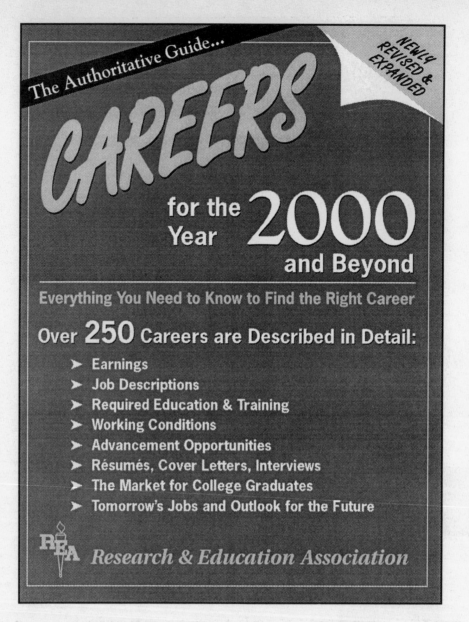

MAXnotes®
REA's Literature Study Guides

MAXnotes® are student-friendly. They offer a fresh look at masterpieces of literature, presented in a lively and interesting fashion. **MAXnotes®** offer the essentials of what you should know about the work, including outlines, explanations and discussions of the plot, character lists, analyses, and historical context. **MAXnotes®** are designed to help you think independently about literary works by raising various issues and thought-provoking ideas and questions. Written by literary experts who currently teach the subject, **MAXnotes®** enhance your understanding and enjoyment of the work.

Available **MAXnotes®** include the following:

Absalom, Absalom!
The Aeneid of Virgil
Animal Farm
Antony and Cleopatra
As I Lay Dying
As You Like It
The Autobiography of
    Malcolm X
The Awakening
Beloved
Beowulf
Billy Budd
The Bluest Eye, A Novel
Brave New World
The Canterbury Tales
The Catcher in the Rye
The Color Purple
The Crucible
Death in Venice
Death of a Salesman
The Divine Comedy I: Inferno
Dubliners
The Edible Woman
Emma
Euripides' Medea & Electra
Frankenstein
Gone with the Wind
The Grapes of Wrath
Great Expectations
The Great Gatsby
Gulliver's Travels
Handmaid's Tale
Hamlet
Hard Times
Heart of Darkness

Henry IV, Part I
Henry V
The House on Mango Street
Huckleberry Finn
I Know Why the Caged
    Bird Sings
The Iliad
Invisible Man
Jane Eyre
Jazz
The Joy Luck Club
Jude the Obscure
Julius Caesar
King Lear
Leaves of Grass
Les Misérables
Lord of the Flies
Macbeth
The Merchant of Venice
Metamorphoses of Ovid
Metamorphosis
Middlemarch
A Midsummer Night's Dream
Moby-Dick
Moll Flanders
Mrs. Dalloway
Much Ado About Nothing
Mules and Men
My Antonia
Native Son
1984
The Odyssey
Oedipus Trilogy
Of Mice and Men
On the Road

Othello
Paradise
Paradise Lost
A Passage to India
Plato's Republic
Portrait of a Lady
A Portrait of the Artist
    as a Young Man
Pride and Prejudice
A Raisin in the Sun
Richard II
Romeo and Juliet
The Scarlet Letter
Sir Gawain and the
    Green Knight
Slaughterhouse-Five
Song of Solomon
The Sound and the Fury
The Stranger
Sula
The Sun Also Rises
A Tale of Two Cities
The Taming of the Shrew
Tar Baby
The Tempest
Tess of the D'Urbervilles
Their Eyes Were Watching God
Things Fall Apart
To Kill a Mockingbird
To the Lighthouse
Twelfth Night
Uncle Tom's Cabin
Waiting for Godot
Wuthering Heights
Guide to Literary Terms

RESEARCH & EDUCATION ASSOCIATION
61 Ethel Road W. • Piscataway, New Jersey 08854
Phone: (732) 819-8880   **website: www.rea.com**

Please send me more information about MAXnotes®.

Name _____

Address _____

City _____ State _____ Zip _____

"The ESSENTIALS"
of Math & Science

Each book in the ESSENTIALS series offers all essential information of the field it covers. It summarizes what every textbook in the particular field must include, and is designed to help students in preparing for exams and doing homework. The ESSENTIALS are excellent supplements to any class text.

The ESSENTIALS are complete and concise with quick access to needed information. They serve as a handy reference source at all times. The ESSENTIALS are prepared with REA's customary concern for high professional quality and student needs.

Available in the following titles:

Advanced Calculus I & II
Algebra & Trigonometry I & II
Anatomy & Physiology
Anthropology
Astronomy
Automatic Control Systems /
    Robotics I & II
Biology I & II
Boolean Algebra
Calculus I, II, & III
Chemistry
Complex Variables I & II
Computer Science I & II
Data Structures I & II
Differential Equations I & II
Electric Circuits I & II
Electromagnetics I & II

Electronics I & II
Electronic Communications I & II
Fluid Mechanics /
    Dynamics I & II
Fourier Analysis
Geometry I & II
Group Theory I & II
Heat Transfer I & II
LaPlace Transforms
Linear Algebra
Math for Computer Applications
Math for Engineers I & II
Math Made Nice-n-Easy Series
Mechanics I, II, & III
Microbiology
Modern Algebra
Molecular Structures of Life

Numerical Analysis I & II
Organic Chemistry I & II
Physical Chemistry I & II
Physics I & II
Pre-Calculus
Probability
Psychology I & II
Real Variables
Set Theory
Sociology
Statistics I & II
Strength of Materials &
    Mechanics of Solids I & II
Thermodynamics I & II
Topology
Transport Phenomena I & II
Vector Analysis

*If you would like more information about any of these books,
complete the coupon below and return it to us or visit your local bookstore.*

RESEARCH & EDUCATION ASSOCIATION
61 Ethel Road W. • Piscataway, New Jersey 08854
Phone: (732) 819-8880   **website: www.rea.com**

Please send me more information about your Math & Science Essentials books

Name _____

Address _____

City _____ State _____ Zip _____

REA's **Problem Solvers**

The "PROBLEM SOLVERS" are comprehensive supplemental text-books designed to save time in finding solutions to problems. Each "PROBLEM SOLVER" is the first of its kind ever produced in its field. It is the product of a massive effort to illustrate almost any imaginable problem in exceptional depth, detail, and clarity. Each problem is worked out in detail with a step-by-step solution, and the problems are arranged in order of complexity from elementary to advanced. Each book is fully indexed for locating problems rapidly.

ACCOUNTING
ADVANCED CALCULUS
ALGEBRA & TRIGONOMETRY
AUTOMATIC CONTROL
   SYSTEMS/ROBOTICS
BIOLOGY
BUSINESS, ACCOUNTING, & FINANCE
CALCULUS
CHEMISTRY
COMPLEX VARIABLES
DIFFERENTIAL EQUATIONS
ECONOMICS
ELECTRICAL MACHINES
ELECTRIC CIRCUITS
ELECTROMAGNETICS
ELECTRONIC COMMUNICATIONS
ELECTRONICS
FINITE & DISCRETE MATH
FLUID MECHANICS/DYNAMICS
GENETICS
GEOMETRY
HEAT TRANSFER

LINEAR ALGEBRA
MACHINE DESIGN
MATHEMATICS for ENGINEERS
MECHANICS
NUMERICAL ANALYSIS
OPERATIONS RESEARCH
OPTICS
ORGANIC CHEMISTRY
PHYSICAL CHEMISTRY
PHYSICS
PRE-CALCULUS
PROBABILITY
PSYCHOLOGY
STATISTICS
STRENGTH OF MATERIALS &
   MECHANICS OF SOLIDS
TECHNICAL DESIGN GRAPHICS
THERMODYNAMICS
TOPOLOGY
TRANSPORT PHENOMENA
VECTOR ANALYSIS

If you would like more information about any of these books,
complete the coupon below and return it to us or visit your local bookstore.

REA's Test Preps
The Best in Test Preparation

- REA "Test Preps" are **far more** comprehensive than any other test preparation series
- Each book contains up to **eight** full-length practice tests based on the most recent exams
- **Every** type of question likely to be given on the exams is included
- Answers are accompanied by **full** and **detailed** explanations

REA has published over 60 Test Preparation volumes in several series. They include:

Advanced Placement Exams (APs)
Biology
Calculus AB & Calculus BC
Chemistry
Computer Science
English Language & Composition
English Literature & Composition
European History
Government & Politics
Physics
Psychology
Statistics
Spanish Language
United States History

**College-Level Examination
   Program (CLEP)**
Analyzing and Interpreting Literature
College Algebra
Freshman College Composition
General Examinations
General Examinations Review
History of the United States I
Human Growth and Development
Introductory Sociology
Principles of Marketing
Spanish

SAT II: Subject Tests
American History
Biology E/M
Chemistry
English Language Proficiency Test
French
German

SAT II: Subject Tests (cont'd)
Literature
Mathematics Level IC, IIC
Physics
Spanish
Writing

Graduate Record Exams (GREs)
Biology
Chemistry
Computer Science
Economics
Engineering
General
History
Literature in English
Mathematics
Physics
Psychology
Sociology

ACT - ACT Assessment

ASVAB - Armed Services Vocational
   Aptitude Battery

CBEST - California Basic Educational
   Skills Test

CDL - Commercial Driver License Exam

CLAST - College-Level Academic Skills Test

ELM - Entry Level Mathematics

ExCET - Exam for the Certification of
   Educators in Texas

FE (EIT) - Fundamentals of
   Engineering Exam

FE Review - Fundamentals of
   Engineering Review

GED - High School Equivalency
   Diploma Exam (U.S. & Canadian
   editions)

GMAT - Graduate Management
   Admission Test

LSAT - Law School Admission Test

MAT - Miller Analogies Test

MCAT - Medical College Admission
   Test

MSAT - Multiple Subjects
   Assessment for Teachers

NJ HSPT- New Jersey High School
   Proficiency Test

PPST - Pre-Professional Skills Tests

PRAXIS II/NTE - Core Battery

PSAT - Preliminary Scholastic
   Assessment Test

SAT I - Reasoning Test

SAT I - Quick Study & Review

TASP - Texas Academic Skills
   Program

TOEFL - Test of English as a
   Foreign Language

TOEIC - Test of English for
   International Communication

REA's Test Prep Books Are The Best!

(a sample of the <u>hundreds of letters</u> REA receives each year)

" I am writing to congratulate you on preparing an exceptional study guide. In five years of teaching this course I have never encountered a more thorough, comprehensive, concise and realistic preparation for this examination. "

Teacher, Davie, FL

" I have found your publications, *The Best Test Preparation...*, to be exactly that. "

Teacher, Aptos, CA

" I used your *CLEP Introductory Sociology* book and rank it 99% – thank you! "

Student, Jerusalem, Israel

" Your GMAT book greatly helped me on the test. Thank you. "

Student, Oxford, OH

" I recently got the French SAT II Exam book from REA. I congratulate you on first-rate French practice tests."

Instructor, Los Angeles, CA

" Your AP English Literature and Composition book is most impressive."

Student, Montgomery, AL

" The REA LSAT Test Preparation guide is a winner! "

Instructor, Spartanburg, SC

(more on front page)